Praise for Chri:

"As one who spent some four decades studying and documenting its diversity, growth, and challenges, Roger E. Hedlund is eminently suited to tell the story of Christianity in India, spanning over two thousand years. It is no easy task to carry out this historic survey in just about three hundred pages. This scholarly work is a mini companion to the *Oxford Encyclopaedia of South Asian Christianity*, of which Hedlund was the chief editor. This book not only addresses the contribution of the mainline Protestant and Catholic missions in India but also discusses how the indigenous churches and new Christian movements transformed the face of contemporary Christianity. A distinct feature of this book is its examination of how the Christian missionaries engaged with the Hindu community in diverse times and contexts, which resulted in mutual edification and enrichment. This book is meant not just for the Christian community of scholars, pastors, and seminarians but to every right-thinking individual who would like to explore and appreciate the rightful place of Christianity in the story of India over two millennia!"

Joshua Kalapati, Madras Christian College

"Scholars of contemporary Indian missiology and church history owe a debt of gratitude to Roger E. Hedlund, in his several avatars as a researcher, a guru, an editor and, foremost, I would say, a writer. His two-volume *Oxford Encyclopaedia of Asian Christianity* is a monumental work, unique for the range of its contents. Just the number of experts, from about all denominations in South Asia, that he could persuade to write for the encyclopedia gives it a permanent place on the reference shelf of every seminary, Bible college, and contemporary cultural studies and history department. India is an extremely dynamic subcontinent—in the fluidity of its politics and the impact that political processes of the last hundred years have had on issues of religion, especially of the Christian faith. The freedom movement of the early 1900s, the partition of the subcontinent in 1947 with its terrible bloodshed and the forced but incomplete exchange of populations, and the economic migrations of the last decades of the twentieth century have seen deep, and still not fully explored, changes in the religious topography. Hedlund, with his long stay and continuing refresher visits to India, has kept abreast of these developments, adding his scholarship and inquiry and often encouraging others to map the changes. The many scholars, especially in the southern states, he has in his long career identified, and guided, ensure his lasting impress in this area that is so important to the church, and critical for those engaged in ensuring freedom of faith in the country."

John Dayal, member of the National Integration Council of India

"Roger E. Hedlund has spent a lifetime in India. This volume represents decades of his wrestling with the realities, grappling with the questions, and thinking through implications of a 'Christianity made in India.' Only scholar-practitioners of his caliber can synthesize so brilliantly at a thirty-thousand-foot level and also highlight minutiae on the ground across two thousand years of South Asian Christian history. Welcome to indigenous expressions of faith most of us Westerners never knew!"

Amos Yong, Fuller Theological Seminary

"Masses of Indians worship Jesus apart from historic churches. In this nation, the second largest in the world, Christianity has been present for two thousand years. Today, large 'Jesus movements' pulsate. This 'Fourth Branch Christianity' grows alongside Protestant, Catholic, and Orthodox sectors. Particularly in communities where food and water are scarce, security is shaky, statuses are marginal, religious pluralism is complex, spiritual forces threaten, and dignity remains a distant dream, the gospel and the Spirit empower in unexpected ways. This clearly written book, cross-referenced to indigenous movements across continents, is an invaluable resource. If you care about Christianity tomorrow, you should read it."

Miriam Adeney, Seattle Pacific University

"This book, reflecting a culmination of decades devoted to understanding India, is of compelling importance. First, it challenges claims that Christianity in India is, or ever has been, an alien transplant imposed by colonialism. Second, it delves into intricacies of cultural hybridity that not only defines 'Indianness' itself but also various manifestations of Christianity in India. In fascinating encounters between the Christian message and local communities within ancient multireligious contexts, we learn that there never was a transformative movement that was not inspired by indigenous leadership. While Western missionaries may have provided infrastructural and technological assistance, such as schools, printing presses, and medical facilities, they were never primary agents of change. Colonial Christianity, wherever attempted, failed. No foreign influence ever generated a mass movement in India. This volume, in short, is a work of outstanding empathetic insight and historical understanding."

Robert Eric Frykenberg, professor emeritus, University of Wisconsin Madison

"Roger E. Hedlund's *Christianity Made in India* is a stimulating compilation of essays on the array of indigenous expressions of the church that have emerged in India. It also provides glimpses of prominent prime movers. Among the thematic accents of the volume are the following: (1) Christianity's existence in localized formats in India long before its introduction to most of the West, (2) the church in India as an exuberant illustration of the translatability of the Christian faith into many discrete cultural representations, and (3) the medley of local (indigenous) expressions of Christianity in India as showcases of unity in diversity rather than isolated autonomisms. This highly readable collection on ecclesial origins and variety in the cultural kaleidoscope that is India should be of great service to the church on its errand to the world."

Arthur G. McPhee, Asbury Theological Seminary (retired)

"The book opens a window on two thousand years of indigenous Christianity in India. Hedlund creates a vivid and sweeping overview by drawing on his years of research and writing on many different aspects of Christianity in that country. For the reader who knows nothing of the Christian heritage in India, this book is an excellent place to start. Those with an understanding of Christianity in that country will find the perspective and interpretation of the individuals and movements insightful and an incentive for further study. The footnotes and bibliographies provide a great source for further exploration on what God has been doing in India for the last two millennia."

Martin Shaw, vice president of International Ministries, WorldVenture

Christianity Made in India

Christianity Made in India

From Apostle Thomas to Mother Teresa

ROGER E. HEDLUND

FORTRESS PRESS
MINNEAPOLIS

CHRISTIANITY MADE IN INDIA
From Apostle Thomas to Mother Teresa

Copyright © 2017 Roger E. Hedlund. All rights reserved. Except for brief quotations in critical articles or reviews, no part of this book may be reproduced in any manner without prior written permission from the publisher.
Email copyright@1517.media or write to Permissions, Fortress Press, Box 1209, Minneapolis, MN 55440-1209.

Cover design: Rob Dewey

Print ISBN: 978-1-5064-3032-4
eBook ISBN: 978-1-5064-3033-1

The paper used in this publication meets the minimum requirements of American National Standard for Information Sciences — Permanence of Paper for Printed Library Materials, ANSI Z329.48-1984.

Manufactured in the U.S.A.

Contents

	Acknowledgments	xi
	List of Abbreviations	xiii
1.	Introduction "Beginning from Jerusalem"	1
2.	Foundations Thomas and the First Christians	11
3.	A Thousand Years of Silence? The Forgotten Golden Age of the Church	21
4.	Ziegenbalg The Beginnings of Protestant Christianity in India	31
5.	Carey and the Evangelical Experiment at Serampore	43
6.	Ramabai Dongre Medhavi Change Agent in Modern Indian History	53
7.	Evangelical Christians and Social Transformation	67
8.	Indigenous Churches of South Asia and Beyond	81

9.	Why Study New Movements? The Importance of India's New Christian Movements	95
10.	Religious Plurality and Christian Concerns Insights from India	117
11.	Poverty, Evangelisation, and Christian Identity	135
12.	Creative Ministries of New Christian Movements	145
13.	Living Water and the Holy Spirit	163
14.	Fourth Branch Christianity and the Historiography of New Christian Movements	177
15.	Christian Identity in a Pluralistic World	197
16.	Hindus and Christians Together for Two Thousand Years	211
17.	Conclusion "To the Ends of the Earth"	227
	Glossary of Indian Terms	235
	Index of Subjects	243
	Index of Authors	269
	Index of Biblical References	279

Acknowledgments

The chapters of this compilation represent an edited rendition of several essays and papers presented in whole or in part on several occasions over the years at conferences and other venues mainly in India and South Asia. To all who kindly granted permission for use of these materials in a new format, my thanks and appreciation.

This means that there must be a huge number of persons to be acknowledged and appreciated for their input. Alas! Many are forgotten and must be left un-named.

Among these are the facilities and staff of the David Allen Hubbard Library at Fuller Theological Seminary in Pasadena, California, for their kind assistance and the use of resources which helped to make revision possible. Dr. David Bundy, then Associate Provost for Library and Associate Professor of History at Fuller was of great help and encouragement. Also at Fuller, Professor Wilbert Shenk, Professor of Mission History and Contemporary Christianity, was particularly helpful in pointing me toward valuable Anabaptist and Pietist sources.

A special word of thanks and appreciation is due my friend and colleague, Prof. Jesudas M. Athyal, who initiated contact with Fortress Press with a view to possible publication of this manuscript in their new South Asian Theology Series. Thanks, Jesudas, for introducing me to Mr. Will Bergkamp and other colleagues at Fortress Press, and also connecting with my colleagues Prof. M. Gabriel and Dr. Joshua Kalapati at the Mylapore Institute in Chennai, India. We look forward to further collaboration.

Finally, last but not least, special thanks and appreciation to my long-suffering wife Thea June Hedlund for help and encouragement along the way and expertise in preparation of the final manuscript. Without your help it is not likely that *Christianity Made in India: From Apostle Thomas to Mother Teresa* would ever have made it through to its completion and intended destination.

List of Abbreviations

AIC	African Instituted Churches (African Independent Churches)
AOG	Assemblies of God
BCA	Baptist Christian Association
BCE	Before the Common Era
BJP	Bharatiya Janata Party
BMS	Baptist Missionary Society
CCC	Campus Crusade for Christ [Cru]
CE	Common Era
CHAI	Church History Association of India
CIO	Churches of Indigenous Origin research project
CMS	Church Missionary Society
CNI	Church of North India
COTR	Church on the Rock
CPM	Ceylon Pentecostal Mission
CSCA	Centre for the Study of Christianity in Asia
CSI	Church of South India
EFI	Evangelical Fellowship of India
EFICOR	EFI Commission on Relief
EIC	East India Company
FGC	First Generation Christian

FMC	Free Methodist Church
FMPB	Friends Missionary Prayer Band
GEMS	Gospel Echoing Missionary Society
IEM	Indian Evangelical Mission
IET	Indian Evangelical Team
IIC	Indian Instituted Church
IMA	India Missions Association
IMS	Indian Missionary Society
INC	Indian National Congress
IPC	Indian Pentecostal Church of God
ISPCK	Indian Society for the Promotion of Christian Knowledge
LDS	Latter Day Saints (Mormons: Church of Jesus Christ of Latter Day Saints)
LEF	Laymen's Evangelical Fellowship
LMS	London Missionary Society
MDMM	Mumbai Diocese Missionary Movement
MVM	Maharashtra Village Ministries
MOU	Memorandum of Understanding
MCI	Methodist Church in India
MTC	Mar Thoma Church
MTSEA	Mar Thoma Syrian Evangelistic Association
MTVEA	Mar Thoma Voluntary Evangelists Association
NMS	National Missionary Society of India
NRM	New Religious Movement
NTCI	New Testament Church of India
OBC	Other Backward Castes—lower Hindu castes (Shudras)
OESAC	*Oxford Encyclopaedia of South Asian Christianity*
OTI	Outreach Training Institute
RSS	Rastriya Swayamsevak Sangh (Hindu religious nationalists)
SAIACS	South Asia Institute for Advanced Christian Studies

SALTDC	South-East Asia Leadership Training & Development Centre
SPCK	Society for the Promotion of Christian Knowledge
SPG	Society for the Propagation of the Gospel
TPM	The Pentecostal Mission (formerly CPM)
UBS	Union Biblical Seminary
UTC	United Theological College
VHP	Vishva Hindu Parishad
WCC	World Council of Churches
WCO	World Cassette Outreach
WEA	World Evangelical Alliance (World Evangelical Fellowship)
YCLT	Yavatmal College for Leadership Training
YWAM	Youth With A Mission
ZBM	Zoram Baptist Mission

1.

Introduction

"Beginning from Jerusalem"

> Then they returned to Jerusalem from the mount called Olivet, which is near Jerusalem, a sabbath day's journey away. When they had entered the city, they went to the room upstairs where they were staying, Peter, and John, and James, and Andrew, Philip and Thomas, Bartholomew and Matthew, James son of Alphaeus, and Simon the Zealot, and Judas son of James. All these were constantly devoting themselves to prayer, together with certain women, including Mary the mother of Jesus, as well as his brothers. (Acts 1:12–14)

This familiar biblical text serves as an appropriate starting place for our study.[1] All very familiar: Jerusalem, the Sabbath, upper room, Peter, John, James, Mother Mary, and Jesus's brothers. All very Jewish. Jerusalem-centric. The people we meet at the beginning of the Apostolic Era in Acts 1 are all Jews. Jesus was a Jew. The original disciples were all Jews. The Christian Church began at Jerusalem as "a congregation of Jews who believed that Jesus was their Messiah," as New Testament scholar William LaSor observes.[2]

Indigenous Christianity is as old as Christianity itself. The earliest

---

1. This introduction was presented in part at the start of a week of lectures at Ashland Seminary, Ashland University, in Ashland, Ohio, USA, January 28–February 3, 2008, on "The Indigenous Church from a South Asian Perspective," with extracts from the author's book, *Quest for Identity: India's Churches of Indigenous Origin: The "Little Tradition" in Indian Christianity* (Delhi: ISPCK, 2000); and from a paper on "Nationalism" prepared for the Church History Association of India (CHAI) Triennial Conference, Aluva, Kerala, November 1–4, 2002.

2. William Sanford LaSor, *Church Alive,* Layman's Bible Commentary: Acts (Glendale, CA: Regal Books, 1972), 4.

indigenous church was at Jerusalem.[3] As Biblical scholar Lucien Legrand states it, "The Christian faith was strictly indigenous only to Palestine!"[4]

BIBLICAL-HISTORICAL PERSPECTIVE

The Jerusalem church consisted of thousands of believing Jews gathered by the Twelve into a Messianic community.[5] Centered in the Temple and under the leadership of James, this initial "Jerusalemite Judeo-Christianity" community remained "solidly ensconced in Jerusalem."[6] Biblical scholars discern as well a "Palestinian Judeo-Christianity" under the direction of Peter which was similar but less insular venturing in witness beyond Jerusalem.

However it was "Hellenistic Judeo-Christianity" which most actively engaged in mission to the Diaspora. This was "the Christianity of Philip and Stephen, Barnabas and Paul."[7] The church at Antioch, where the community was given a distinct and separate identity as "Christian," is the product of Hellenistic Judeo-Christian mission.[8] The church at Antioch, quite different in outlook from Jerusalem, was a mixed community of Hellenized Jews and Greek Gentiles.[9]

But there were other churches equally indigenous to their context. The Book of Acts records the emergence of a church in Samaria through the ministry of Philip to a marginalized population.[10] We read of a church at Damascus, but know nothing of its origins.[11] Peter's Cornelius visitation resulted in an Italian Gentile household of faith.[12] Diversity of expression according to culture and circumstances is characteristic of the churches of the New Testament era.

---

3. Acts 1:12–14.
4. Quoted by J. Samuel Escobar, "A Missiological Approach to Latin American Protestantism," *International Review of Mission LXXXVII*, no. 345 (April 1998): 161–73, at 165.
5. Lucien Legrand, *Unity and Plurality: Mission in the Bible* (Maryknoll, NY: Orbis, 1990), 100.
6. Ibid., 94, 95.
7. Ibid., 94.
8. Acts 11:19–26.
9. Raymond E. Brown, Joseph A. Fitzmyer, and Roland E. Murphy, eds., *The Jerome Biblical Commentary*, 2 vols. (Englewood Cliffs, NJ: Prentice-Hall, 1968), 2:190.
10. Acts 8:5–25. In the eyes of Palestinian Jews of that time, the Samaritan were a despised "outcaste" community, and followers of a deviant cult.
11. Acts 9:1.
12. Acts 10:1–48.

The Christian mission "to the ends of the earth" commenced from Antioch.

Jerusalem, however, questioned the resulting diversification with its apparent disregard for Jewish rites and tradition. Consequently a major consultation on mission was convened at Jerusalem to settle the issue.[13] Various options were considered. The decision to accept the Gentiles as equal members, without proselytising cultural conversion, validated the continuity of diverse human cultures and established a principle of multi-cultural liberty which would serve the formation of believing communities in any human society.

The Twelve chosen by Jesus are reminiscent of the twelve patriarchs and the twelve tribes, an obvious link with Old Testament Israel. "And yet the Twelve chosen by Jesus are obviously no longer the ancestors or even the ethnic representatives of these tribes. They are the prototypes of a Messianic Israel in which the criterion of membership is no longer carnal lineage but conversion and faith."[14] Not ethnicity but faith is the criterion for membership in the new Messianic community.

Whatever their background, all believers were invested with royal and priestly dignity, "a chosen race, a royal priesthood, a holy nation, God's own people. . . . Once you were no people but now you are God's people."[15] Such, according to the New Testament, is the *ekklesia*, called from above by God, summoned from below into community.[16] According to Küng, the Old Testament people of God were legitimately succeeded by the new called-forth people of the Covenant assembled around Jesus Christ. The *ekklesia* is to be understood both as the whole New Covenant community and also as the local household community expressions of it.[17]

The New Testament Church exhibited a diversity of structures and worship patterns. There seems to have been considerable flexibility, for example, in offices and leadership functions. It is not surprising that throughout history the Church has known a variety of forms. What Küng relates concerning ecclesiastical offices[18] applies to the

---

13. Acts 15:1–35.
14. Legrand, *Unity and Plurality*, 99.
15. 1 Peter 1:9–10.
16. Hans Küng, *Structures of the Church* (New York: Thomas Nelson, 1964), 12.
17. Ibid., 11.
18. Ibid., 207.

different cultural identities of the churches: they were truly local, i.e. indigenous, communities.

Cultural plurality is both acceptable and reasonable. A concern for unity is equally correct and compelling—a concern sometimes lacking among present-day Independent Churches. Multiple New Testament missions ought not be misconstrued as irresponsible duplication. Rather, here was an overflowing spiritual vitality "permeated by a basic concern for unity. This multiple mission was not content to express itself in anarchical abundance. The various tendencies sometimes collided in tumultuous confrontation, but the encounter was always accompanied by a quest for communion."[19] Underneath is an indelible unity, the bond of a common faith and purpose.

Contemporary indigenous Christian movements are legitimate heirs of this Biblical drive for unity in diversity.

INDIGENEITY AND TRANSLATABILITY IN GLOBAL PERSPECTIVE

The exceptional growth of the Church in the Non-Western world during the twentieth century has been characterised by a diversity of localized cultural expressions. As Paul Hiebert states, "The emergence of independent churches around the world expressing indigenous forms of Christianity is undermining the equation of Christianity with Western culture."[20] The centre of Christian influence numerically and theologically is shifting Southward to Africa, Latin America, and Asia.[21] Increasingly it is found in non-traditional (non-Catholic, non-Protestant, non-Syrian) Churches of Indigenous-Independent

---

19. Legrand, *Unity and Plurality*, 94.

20. Paul G. Hiebert, "Missiological Education for a Global Era," in *Missiological Education for the 21st Century*, ed. J. Dudley Woodberry, Charles Van Engen and Edgar J. Elliston (Maryknoll, NY: Orbis, 1996), 36.

21. The point has been well-documented by David Barrett, W. Bühlmann, W. Hollenweger, John Pobee, and others. See David Barrett, ed., *World Christian Encyclopedia* (Nairobi: Oxford University Press, 1982); W. Bühlmann, *The Coming of the Third Church* (Maryknoll, NY: Orbis, 1978); W. Hollenweger, *Pentecostalism: Origins and Developments Worldwide* (Peabody, MA: Hendrickson Publishers, 1997); John Pobee and Gabriel Ositelu II, *African Initiatives in Christianity* (Geneva: WCC Publications, 1998); Omer Degrijse, *Going Forth: Missionary Consciousness in Third World Catholic Churches* (Maryknoll, NY: Orbis, 1984); Sebastian Karotemprel, ed., *Heralds of the Gospel in Asia* Shillong, India: FABC Office of Evangelization, 1998); Mark A. Noll, *The New Shape of World Christianity: How American Experience Reflects Global Faith* (Downers Grove, IL: InterVarsity, 2009); Mark A. Noll, *From Every Tribe and Nation: A Historian's Discovery of the Global Christian Story* (Grand Rapids: Baker Academic, 2014).

variety, frequently Charismatic, not necessarily Pentecostal, but of substantial evangelical and cultural diversity. Predominantly it is a Church of the Poor.

Wherever the Gospel goes it takes root in the local culture. Indigenous movements are demonstrations of what Lamin Sanneh calls the "translatability" of the Gospel.[22] Africa leads the way, but new "grassroots" variations of the Christian faith are part of an essential ongoing process everywhere including India where, for the most part, little is known about such movements. Yet many exist, and they represent a significant expression of vibrant Christian faith in South Asia today as was documented by the Churches of Indigenous Origins (CIO) research project.[23]

THE INDIGENOUS CHRISTIANITY OF INDIA

Christianity has existed in India from the early beginnings of the Christian era, centuries before the arrival of the Christian faith in much of Europe. Christianity is an ancient religion of India and an important part of the Indian heritage. This early Christianity, associated with the Thomas tradition, has come down to us in an amalgamated version following the arrival of persecuted Syrian Christians in the fourth century and their integration with the existing Indian Christian community in Kerala. Our knowledge of the earliest Indian Christianity is scant. Moreover, with the arrival of the Portuguese, traces of this earliest indigenous tradition appear to have disappeared. As Metropolitan Chrysostom observes, the earliest cultural and liturgical expressions must have been Malayalam, but following the Portuguese only the Syriac remained.

> Syriac was not our original language for worship. When St. Thomas came, it must have been Malayalam here. Clearly, no group of people came with him. In any case, we have no clear idea about the worship forms during the early centuries; . . . the Portuguese, when they came, destroyed whatever there was. Syriac came in with our Persian rela-

---

22. Lamin Sanneh, *Translating the Message: The Missionary Impact on Culture* (Maryknoll, NY: Orbis, 1991).
23. This was a team project supported by the Pew Charitable Trusts administered through the Overseas Ministries Study Centre, New Haven, CT, USA, under the direction of Roger E. Hedlund in South India, and Prof. O. L. Snaitang in North East India, resulting in publication of several books and a spate of academic papers and articles.

tionship. Their bishops didn't learn Malayalam, and they imposed Syriac on us.[24]

Foundations for an indigenous Indian Christianity were laid by Roberto de Nobili, Bartolomeo Ziegenbalg and William Carey, each of whom presented a challenge to colonialism.

De Nobili[25] at Madurai immersed himself in the local Tamil culture, making radical adaptions inculturating and Tamilising the Christian faith. Ziegenbalg at Tranquebar[26] laid the foundations of an indigenous Church by introducing a four-fold Pietist model of mission consisting of Bible translation, schools, a simple expression of a local church, and a seminary for pastoral training.

Carey[27] and the Serampore Mission pioneered vernacular education, agricultural improvement, projects for the economic recovery of the poor and agitated for radical social reforms along with engaging in Bible translation and production of Bengali literature and preaching of the gospel—activities contributing to a Bengali cultural renewal and eventually to an Indian national movement. Carey's work was "an important influence in facilitating the Indian Renaissance."[28]

24. Jesudas M. Athyal and John J. Thatamanil, eds., *Metropolitan Chrysostom on Mission in the Market Place* (Tiruvalla, India; Christava Sahitya Samithy, 2002), 55.

25. See recent studies on de Nobili, viz. S. Rajamanickam, *Roberto de Nobili on Indian Customs*, ed. S. Rajamanickam (Palayamkottai, India: De Nobili Research Institute, St. Zavier's College, 1989); A. Sauliére, *His Star in the East,* revised and ed. S. Rajamnickam (Anand, India: Gujarat Sahitya Prakash, 1995); Thomas Anchukandam, *Roberto de Nobili's Responsio (1610): A Vindication of Inculturation and Adaptation* (Bangalore: Kristu Jyoti Publications, 1996); Anand Amaladass, SJ, and Francix X. Clooney, SJ, ed., *Preaching Wisdom to the Wise: Three Treatises by Roberto de Nobili, S.J., Missionary and Scholar in 17th Century India* (St. Louis: Institute of Jesuit Sources, 2000).

26. Hugald Grafé, *The History of Christianity in Tamilnadu*, vol. 4 of History of Christianity in India, part 2 (Bangalore: Church History Association of India, 1982), 188. Also see Daniel Jeyaraj, "Early Tamil Bible Translation in Tranquebar," *Dharma Deepika* (June 1997): 67–77; and Daniel Jeyaraj, "Dual Identity of Christians in Tranquebar," *Dharma Deepika* (December 1997): 9–18.

27. See various essays in the compendium, J. T. K. Daniel and R. E. Hedlund, eds., *Carey's Obligation and India's Renaissance* (Serampore, India: Council of Serampore College, 1993): N. R. Ray, "William Carey: A Linguist with a Difference," 153–56; S. K. Chatterjee, "William Carey and the Linguistic Renaissance in India," 157–75; Christopher Arangaden, "Carey's Legacy of Bible Translation," 176–86; Binoy Bhusan Roy, "William Carey and the Asiatic Society," 246–55; A. K. Ghosh, "William Carey: The Botanist," 259–63; Ashish Kumar Massey and June Hedlund, "William Carey and the Emergence of Modern India," 299–308; Evangeline Rajkumar, "William Carey's Mission of Compassion and Justice," 323–33; Ruth Mangalwadi, "William Carey and the Emancipation of Women," 334–45; M. M. Thomas, "William Carey's Vision of the Gospel: Its Relevance in India Today," 346–53.

28. Malay Dewanji, *William Carey and the Indian Renaissance* (Delhi: ISPCK, 1996), 43.

Missionary initiatives on behalf of the poor and opposing the rapacious deeds of the East India Company thus presented a critique of colonialism. Through Bible translation, the simple plan of a local Church, and the training of local believers, Carey as well as Ziegenbalg aimed for an Indian Church indigenous to the local cultures and not a replication of European Christianity.

That the outcome was something less was due to successors of a lesser sensitivity and different vision. The impulse for an indigenous Church was lost in the next generations. But a degree of recovery of the indigenous intent is found in emerging new Christian movements of the late nineteenth and early twentieth centuries. It continues today.

CONCLUSION

As Burrows states, "Christianity today is a global movement marked by numerous cultural differences and internal plurality. It is polycentric, largely non-Western. It is multicultural."[29] It began from Jerusalem. It continues today in multiplied new movements. It is this reality which we explore in the chapters which follow.

SOURCES FOR FURTHER REFERENCE

Amaladass, Anand, SJ, and Francis X. Clooney, SJ. *Preaching Wisdom to the Wise: Three Treatises by Roberto de Nobili, S.J., Missionary and Scholar in 17th Century India*. St. Louis: Institute of Jesuit Sources, 2000.

Anchukandam, Thomas. *Roberto de Nobili's Responsio (1610): A Vindication of Inculturation and Adaptation*. Bangalore: Kristu Jyoti Publications, 1996.

Athyal, Jesudas M., and John J. Thatamanil, eds. *Metropolitan Chrysostom on Mission in the Market Place*. Tiruvalla, India: Christava Sahitya Samithy, 2002.

---

29. William R. Burrows, "Reconciling All in Christ: An Old New Paradigm for Mission," *Mission Studies* XV–1, no. 29 (1998): 79–98.

Barrett, David, ed. *World Christian Encyclopedia.* Nairobi: Oxford University Press, 1982.

Bühlmann, W. *The Coming of the Third Church.* Maryknoll, NY: Orbis, 1978.

Burrows, William R. "Reconciling All in Christ: An Old New Paradigm for Mission." *Mission Studies* XV–1, no. 29 (1998): 79–98.

Daniel, J. T. K., and R. E. Hedlund, eds. *Carey's Obligation and India's Renaissance.* Serampore, India: Council of Serampore College, 1993.

Degrijse, Omer. *Going Forth: Missionary Consciousness in Third World Catholic Churches.* Maryknoll, NY: Orbis, 1984.

Dewanji, Malay. *William Carey and the Indian Renaissance.* Delhi, ISPCK: 1996.

Escobar, J. Samuel. "A Missiological Approach to Latin American Protestantism." *International Review of Mission* LXXXVII, no. 345 (April 1998): 165.

Grafé, Hugald. *The History of Christianity in Tamilnadu.* History of Christianity in India, volume 4, part 2. Bangalore: Church History Association of India, 1982.

Hedlund, Roger E. *Quest for Identity: India's Churches of Indigenous Origin; The "Little Tradition" in Indian Christianity.* Delhi: ISPCK, 2000.

Hiebert, Paul G. "Missiological Education for a Global Era." In *Missiological Education for the 21st Century,* ed. J. Dudley Woodberry, Charles Van Engen and Edgar J. Elliston. Maryknoll, NY: Orbis, 1996.

Hollenweger, W. *Pentecostalism, Origins and Developments Worldwide.* Peabody, MA: Hendrickson Publishers, 1997.

Jeyaraj, Daniel. "Dual Identity of Christians in Tranquebar." *Dharma Deepika: A South Asian Journal of Missiological Research* (December 1997): 9–18.

———. "Early Tamil Bible Translation in Tranquebar." *Dharma Deepika: A South Asian Journal of Missiological Research* (June 1997): 67–77.

Karotemprel, Sebastian, ed. *Heralds of the Gospel in Asia.* Shillong, India: India: FABC Office of Evangelization, 1998.

Küng, Hans. *Structures of the Church.* New York: Thomas Nelson, 1964.

LaSor, William Sanford. *Church Alive*. Layman's Bible Commentary: Acts. Glendale, CA: Regal Books, 1972.

Legrand, Lucien. *Unity and Plurality: Mission in the Bible*. Maryknoll, NY: Orbis, 1990.

Noll, Mark A. *The New Shape of World Christianity: How American Experience Reflects Global Faith*. Downers Grove, IL: InterVarsity, 2009.

Pobee, John, and Gabriel Ositelu II. *African Initiatives in Christianity*. Geneva: World Council of Churches Publications, 1998.

Rajamanickam, S. *Roberto de Nobili on Indian Customs*. Palayamkottai, India: De Nobili Research Institute, St. Xavier's College, 1989.

Sanneh, Lamin. *Translating the Message: The Missionary Impact on Culture*. Maryknoll, NY: Orbis, 1991.

Sauliére, A. *His Star in the East*. Revised and edited by Fr. S. Rajamnickam. Anand, India: Gujarat Sahitya Prakash, 1995.

2.

Foundations

Thomas and the First Christians

The story of Indian Christianity begins in the first century CE with the arrival of the Apostle Thomas.[1] In the town of Parur, in the South Indian state of Kerala, the old Church of Kottakkavu is said to be the site at which Thomas founded the first Christian Church in India.[2] According to tradition Thomas arrived in 52 CE, preached the gospel and established churches in Kerala, then traveled to the East coast where he was martyred (at a place now known as St. Thomas Mount). His body was brought to Mylapore and laid to rest in a tomb which is maintained and accessible at the San Thome Cathedral.

THOMAS TRADITION

The story of Thomas Christianity is of great significance for the history of Christianity in India. As historian Stephen Neill states, despite a lack of absolute certainty, there is a high degree of probability that by the sixth century there were well-established churches in South India and that this community had been strengthened by a Christian immigration in the fourth century. It is also probable that at least a section of the indigenous Indian Church originated in the Tamil region. The Christian community in Kerala appears to have

---

1. Originally a draft chapter for the author's book manuscript *Introducing Christianity In India* intended for publication in India.
2. Andrew Todhunter, "In the Footsteps of the Apostles," *National Geographic* (March 2012), 47.

been prosperous and enjoying the favour of local rulers.[3] These and other factors suggest the strongest possibility that the Apostle Thomas could have come to India and that the church in Kerala dates back to him. "Kerala's Thomas Christians—like Christians elsewhere in Asia and in Africa and Latin America—have made the faith uniquely their own, incorporating traditional art, architecture, and natural symbolism."[4] The very "Indianness" of Thomas Christianity in itself supports the hypothesis of its apostolic origin.

The ancient Christian community of India together with similar communities in other parts of Asia comprise an extensive "Eastern Christianity" of Syria, Armenia, Iraq, Iran and India in contrast to the "Western Christianity" of the Greek and Latin world of Europe. Many of the Christian communities of Asia disappeared with the rise of Islam, although some continued to exist in weakened form. But not so in India "where Christian life has remained vigorous" for the past twenty centuries.[5]

APOSTOLIC CHRISTIANITY

Kerala is recognized as the birthplace of Christianity in India. Christianity is one of the ancient religions of India, as India's first Prime Minister, Pundit Jawaharlal Nehru, pointed out. The story has been told and retold in multiplied publications. The Church History Association of India (CHAI) devotes more than 100 pages in the first volume of its History of Christianity in India series to the Thomas tradition and questions concerning the origins and history of the earliest Christians in India. According to the best received traditions, Christianity has existed here from Apostolic (first century) times. Historically Christianity has been a respected presence in India. The vibrant Thomas Christian community itself is custodian of countless oral traditions preserving the Thomas saga in story and song. Kerala's Christianity is not only an ancient religion of India, it is one of the earliest Churches in the world. The presence of Apostolic Christianity in India from the very beginning refutes the notion that Christianity is a foreign religion imported by missionaries and colonialists.

---

3. Stephen Neill, *A History of Christianity in India: The Beginnings to AD 1707* (New York: Cambridge University Press, 1984), 48–49.
4. Todhunter, "In the Footsteps of the Apostles," 47.
5. Leonard Fernando and G. Gispert-Sauch, eds., *Christianity in India: Two Thousand Years of Faith* (New Delhi: Viking Penguin, 2004), 57.

History tells otherwise. Christianity was firmly planted in Indian soil long before it arrived in Northern Europe. Belief in their Apostolic origin is a deep-rooted tradition among the Thomas Christians and helped them preserve their Christian identity and faith.[6]

The existence of oral traditions as well as palm-leaf manuscripts, copper-plates, stone inscriptions, and other artifacts preserved by leading families attest the antiquity and authenticity of the Thomas Christian community. "Many Thomas Christian families of Kerala still trace the original conversion of their community to the time of the Apostle, or to any of a number of migrations which occurred during the many centuries prior to the arrival of the Portuguese in 1498."[7]

Who were these original Indian Christians? Tradition has it that among Thomas's converts were several Brahmans. If so, this helps to explain the caste-like status accorded the early Christian community whose customs and practices were similar to those of the surrounding Hindus. Also not to be overlooked is a significant Jewish element. A Diaspora Jewish colony, dating from the Old Testament period, was located in Cranganore and engaged in trade with the Mediteranean world. Exact date of the first Jewish settlement is not definite, and there are several conflicting theories. In any event the Jews found in Cranganore a haven of refuge and a centre for trade, and evidence indicates such a settlement existed during the first century of the Christian era.[8] According to one tradition, the Apostle Thomas arrived in a trading vessel from Alexandria. If so, it is entirely possible that the Apostle found ready converts among the Jewish settlers. These early Jewish Christian converts believed in Jesus as the Christ, but also retained Jewish traditions and called themselves *Nazrani* as Jewish disciples of Jesus of Nazareth whom they accepted as the promised Messiah.[9]

Conflicting theories notwithstanding, the Thomas Christians maintained a distinct identity with lifestyle, customs, traditions and

---

6. Francis Thonippara, "St. Thomas Christians: The First Indigenous Church of India," in *Christianity Is Indian: The Emergence of an Indigenous Community*, ed. Roger E. Hedlund, rev. ed. (Delhi: ISPCK, 2004), 61.

7. Robert Eric Frykenberg, *Christianity in India: From Beginnings to the Present* (New York: Oxford University Press, 2008), 101.

8. S. S. Koder, "Kerala and Her Jews," (a short history), Cochin Synagogue, Mattancheri, Kerala, n.d., 1, 3.

9. New World Encyclopedia, "Saint Thomas Christians," *New World Encyclopedia,* at http://tinyurl.com/ycnodo5q.

a respectable social status borrowed from the Hindu environment. The Thomas Christians were no threat to their Hindu neighbours. The Christians were a small minority who learned to live at peace with the larger community. The *Nazrani* apparently did not seek conversions from other castes—and this enabled them to survive.[10] Rightly or wrongly, Hinduism often is perceived as accommodating and tolerant. Certainly throughout India's long history at various times different religious groups learned to live side by side. Not so much tolerance, perhaps, as "an inclusivistic tendency that accommodates other religious groups by absorbing their basic beliefs as one's own."[11] This being so, the survival and Christian identity of the ancient Thomas community is amazing. Among the many explanatory factors one must consider the "Syrianization" of the Thomas Christians.

SYRIAN CONNECTION

Migrating "Syrian" Christians from Persia arriving in Malabar, India, in the fourth century (345 CE), came into direct contact with the Indian Christian community with whom they interacted and amalgamated thus reinvigorating the Indian Christian community. Indian Christianity, however, pre-dated the arrival of Christians from Persia. The Indian Church already existed and had a long and independent history of its own. "Indian Christianity is as old as Christianity itself."[12]

The Christian migrants from Persia were not so much Persian as "Syrian" with connections going back to Antioch of Syria[13] and the use of "Syriac" as their language of worship. The origins of Christianity in Persia, shrouded in legend, include a Thomas tradition. One immigrant group associated with Thomas of Cana, a Syrian merchant, in the fourth century brought spiritual resurgence—and prosperity—to the declining Thomas Christian community in India. Welcomed by the Thomas Christians, the Syrians nevertheless

---

10. Anand Amaladass, "Dialogue between Hindus and the St. Thomas Christians," in *Hindu-Christian Dialogue: Perspectives and Encounters*, ed. Harold Coward (Delhi: Motilal Banarsidass Publishers, 1993), 16, 17.
11. Ibid., 18.
12. Thonippara, "St. Thomas Christians," 62.
13. See biblical references to "Antioch of Syria" in the Acts of the Apostles 11:19, 26; 13:1, 14; 14:19, 26; 15:35; and 18:22; the Letter of Paul to the Galatians 2:11; and the Second Letter of Paul to Timothy 3:11.

retained a distinct identity. Subsequently emerged two streams of Malabar Christians: The "Northists" descending from Christians of St. Thomas, and the "Southists" from Thomas of Cana.[14]

The connection between the Church in India and Syrian-Persian Christianity began in the third or fourth century. Gradually everything ecclesiastical in India became essentially East-Syrian. This preserved a strong Christian tradition, but at the cost of preventing the Indian Church from developing a distinctly Indian Christian culture.[15] By the fifth century "the ecclesiastical ties between Persia and the Christians of India were regularized and strengthened" resulting in use of Syriac as their ecclesiastical language as well as hierarchical dependency on the Persian Church.[16] The reinforcements brought fresh vigour, but gradually the original Indian Christianity was eclipsed, absorbed and Syrianized. This early modification has continued to the present time. Nevertheless this ancient Syrian Christianity which amalgamated with the earlier Indian Christian community is of great historic importance as the locus of pre-Portuguese Christianity in India.[17]

Indian Christianity comprises an ancient community as well as a present entity which is making an important cultural contribution as a moral and spiritual force in contemporary society. Today at least six Syrian Christian denominations accept the Thomas apostolic tradition as to the origins of Christianity in India. These include the Orthodox Syrian Church (in two sections), the Independent Syrian Church of Malabar (Kunnamkulam Diocese), the (Reformed) Mar Thoma Church, the Malankara (Syrian Rite) Catholic Church, the (Chaldean) Church of the East, and the St. Thomas Evangelical Church as well as a section of the Church of South India.[18] The institutions and personnel of India's ancient Christian community are an integral part of modern democratic India in which they continue to play a vital role. Syrian Christians were active in India's Indepen-

---

14. A. M. Mundadan, *From the Beginning up to the Middle of the Sixteenth Century*, History of Christianity in India, vol. 1 (Bangalore: Church History Association of India, 1989), 64; also see Leslie Brown, *The Indian Christians of St. Thomas* (New York: Cambridge University Press, 1982).

15. Mundadan, *From the Beginning*, 115.

16. Samuel H. Moffett, *A History of Christianity in Asia*, vol. 1 (Maryknoll, NY: Orbis Books, 1998), 267–68.

17. Mar Aprem, *The Chaldean Syrian Church of the East* (Delhi: ISPCK, 1983).

18. See Brown, *Indian Christians of St. Thomas* for further information about the Thomas Christians including the story of their divisions.

dence movement, and continue to contribute to nation-building in diverse fields such as the arts, science and technology, linguistics, literature, education, social and political involvement.[19]

PLURALITY AND ORALITY

From the beginning the Syrian Christians of Kerala shared a common world with the majority "Hindu" population. The plural society of Kerala "allowed for the interpenetration of Hindu, Christian and Syrian codes," states Visvanathan.[20] The Syrian Christians were seen as part of the Hindu caste system with accompanying notions of hierarchy, status and pollution. Their traditional occupation as traders, as well as landowners, gave the Syrian Christians a high caste status. Rituals and practices pertaining to occupation, food, marriage, birth, and death likewise gave them a caste-like identity.[21]

Oral traditions are of particular interest in light of the absence of documentary evidence from the earliest era. Historian D. Arthur Jeyakumar feels that the Western tradition (of Thomas travelling by overland trade routes and arriving in North India) is not sufficiently supported, but prefers the Indian Malabar tradition of Thomas in India which is an oral tradition passed down by word of mouth from generation to generation in story and song still today. The earliest documents that connect Thomas to India are from outside of India, but from these sources we learn that it was commonly understood that Thomas had evangelized India where he also suffered martyrdom:

- *Doctrine of the Apostles*, written in Edessa ca. 250 CE, points to India as Thomas's field of activity;
- St. Ephraim, a hymn writer of Syria (d. 373 CE), mentions the tradition of Thomas's mission in India in his hymn "On Thomas the Apostle";

---

19. Leonardo Fernando, "Christian Contribution to Nation-Building," in *The Oxford Encyclopaedia of South Asian Christianity*, ed. R. E. Hedlund, J. M. Athyal, J. Kalapati, and Jessica Richard (New Delhi: Oxford University Press, 2011).

20. Susan Visvanathan, *The Christians of Kerala: History, Belief and Ritual among the Yakoba* (New Delhi: Oxford University Press, 1993), 1.

21. Ibid., 3.

- St. Gregory of Nazianzen in the 4th century associates Thomas with India;
- St. Ambrose of Milan (333–397 CE), based on accounts of travellers as well as Greek and Latin classics, identified Thomas with India;
- Bishop Gregory of Tours (538–593 CE) in his book *In Gloria Martyrdom* mentions that Thomas was killed in India (and his remains brought to Edessa and buried there).[22]

DOCUMENTATION

But there is more. The India/Malabar tradition includes testimonials by outside visitors who encountered the Thomas Christians in Malabar or visited Thomas's tomb in Mylapore. These include Mar Solomon, a Nestorian Bishop who gives an account of the Thomas tradition in his Book of the Bee (1222); Marco Polo, the famous traveller from Venice, who gives an account of his visit to the site of Thomas's tomb (1292); John of Monte Corvino, a Franciscan monk who spent some time in India on his way to China, and mentions a "Church of St. Thomas the Apostle" in a letter from Peking (January 8, 1305); Odoric of Pordenone who, in an account of his travels in India (ca. 1324), mentions the presence of Christians in a region where pepper grows and where the body of "Blessed Thomas the Apostle" was laid to rest; John de Marignoli gave an account of his travels (1349 CE) through the province of India where the Church of St. Thomas was found and the Thomas Christians owned pepper gardens; one Nicolo de Conti who visited the Tomb of St. Thomas in a large and beautiful church of "Nestorian heretics" numbering a thousand.[23] Despite contradictions and inconclusive opinions, the tradition can be neither proven nor dis-proven, but it is entirely possible that St Thomas could be the founder of Christianity in India.[24]

---

22. D. Arthur Jeyakumar, *History of Christianity in India: Selected Themes*, rev. ed. (Arasaradi, Madurai: Tamilnadu Theological Seminary, 2007), 7.
23. Ibid., 9–10.
24. Ibid., 17.

CONTINUITY

The essential point is that early in the era someone brought the gospel to India, and that Christianity has continuously existed in India since the earliest time. That Christianity is an ancient religion of India is proven historical fact. The reports given by visitors are of particular importance providing rare glimpses of the continuity of the Thomas Christians as a peaceful and prosperous community in South India during the thirteenth and fourteenth centuries. Indian Christianity today is an essential component of World Christianity.

SOURCES FOR FURTHER REFERENCE

Amaladass, Anand. "Dialogue between Hindus and the St. Thomas Christians." In *Hindu-Christian Dialogue: Perspectives and Encounters*, edited by Harold Coward. Delhi: Motilal Banarsidass Publishers, 1993.

Aprem, Mar. *The Chaldean Syrian Church of the East*. Delhi: ISPCK, 1983.

Brown, Leslie. *The Indian Christians of St. Thomas*. New York: Cambridge University Press, 1982. [An Indian reprint is available at the St. Thomas Service and Community Centre, Greams Road, Chennai, for sale in India only, not for export.]

Fernando, Leonardo. "Christian Contribution to Nation-Building." In *The Oxford Encyclopaedia of South Asian Christianity*, edited by R. E. Hedlund, J. M. Athyal, J. Kalapati, and Jessica Richard. New Delhi: Oxford University Press, 2012.

Fernando, Leonard, and G. Gispert-Sauchs, eds. *Christianity in India: Two Thousand Years of Faith*. New Delhi: Viking Penguin, 2004.

Frykenberg, Robert Eric. *Christianity in India: From Beginnings to the Present*. New York: Oxford University Press, 2008.

Jeyakumar, Arthur D. *History of Christianity in India: Selected Themes*, rev. ed. Arasaradi, Madurai: Tamilnadu Theological Seminary, 2007.

Moffett, Samuel H. *A History of Christianity in Asia*. Vol. 1. Maryknoll, NY: Orbis Books, 1998.

Mundadan, A. M. *From the Beginning up to the Middle of the Sixteenth Century*. History of Christianity in India, volume 1. Bangalore: Church History Association of India, 1989.

Neill, Stephen. *A History of Christianity in India: The Beginnings to AD 1707*. New York: Cambridge University Press, 1984.

Thonippara, Francis. "St. Thomas Christians: The First Indigenous Church of India." In *Christianity Is Indian: The Emergence of an Indigenous Community*, edited by Roger E. Hedlund. Rev. ed. Delhi: ISPCK, 2004 (2000).

Todhunter, Andrew. "In the Footsteps of the Apostles." *National Geographic*. March 2012.

Visvanathan, Susan. *The Christians of Kerala: History, Belief and Ritual among the Yakoba*. New Delhi: Oxford University Press, 1993.

3.

A Thousand Years of Silence?

The Forgotten Golden Age of the Church

Christianity originated in the Near East, and during the first few centuries it had its greatest centers, its most prestigious churches and monasteries, in Syria, Palestine and Mesopotamia. Early Eastern Christians wrote and thought in Syriac, a language closely related to the Aramaic of Jesus and his apostles.[1]

CHURCH OF THE EAST

As we have seen, Christianity arrived in India at a very early time, brought to India by the Apostle Thomas who is believed to have preached the gospel and founded the first churches in Kerala, then, according to well-received tradition, to have travelled to the East coast of South India where he was martyred and his body laid to rest in Mylapore. That, seemingly, might have been the end of the story of these Nasrani (Nazarenes: Christians, disciples of Jesus of Nazareth), but for the Portuguese. The existence of the Malabar Christians has been known to the West since the time of Marco Polo of Venice (ca. 1254–1324)[2] and other visitors. South Indian Christian congregations belonging to the Nestorian "Church of the East"

---

1. Philip Jenkins, *The Lost History of Christianity: The Thousand-Year Golden Age of the Church in the Middle East, Africa, and Asia—and How It Died* (New York: HarperOne, 2008), ix. I acknowledge with gratitude the input of Jenkins's book through much of this chapter.

2. Leslie Brown, *The Indian Christians of St Thomas* (Cambridge: Cambridge University Press, 1956), 1. (An Indian edition is available for sale in India only, not for export, at St Thomas Service & Community Centre, 122 Greams Road, Chennai, and at B. I. Publications, 150 Mount Road, Chennai.)

network were known in the seventh century,[3] and fifteenth century visitors to the tomb of St. Thomas and the monastery of Thomas the Apostle at Mylapore report some thirty thousand Christian families there.[4]

Silent years? Not entirely. Nestorians and Jacobites, Orthodox and Monophysites, these were some of the ancient varieties of Christianities found in Mesopotamia, Syria, Iraq and Iran, Egypt and Ethiopia. "We must never think of these churches as fringe sects," Philip Jenkins points out, but as the Christian mainstream in much of the world.[5] Monophysite Churches still exist today in Syria, Egypt, Ethiopia and Armenia.[6] Constantinople, Damascus and Baghdad were the dominant cultural and political centres of the early medieval world during which Christianity's leading edge remained in the East.[7]

EASTERN CHRISTIAN CENTRES

The seven so-called ecumenical councils held between 325 and 787 CE, defining basic doctrines of Christianity, were convened in important Eastern Christian centres of Nicaea, Constantinople, Ephesus, and Chalcedon. Decisions reached continue to be normative for the Eastern Orthodox Churches and the Roman Catholic Church as well as for many Protestants.[8] Hardly "silent" years. Christianity for much of its early history was tricontinental with strong representation in Europe, Africa, and Asia. "Christianity became predominantly European not because this continent had any obvious affinity for that faith, but by default."[9] Europe is the only continent where Christianity was not destroyed. "As late as the eleventh century, Asia was still home to at least a third of the world's Christians, and perhaps a tenth of all Christians still lived in Africa."[10] Mesopotamia (Iraq) remained a

---

3. Klaus Koschorke, Frieder Ludwig, and Mariano Delgado, eds., *A History of Christianity in Asia, Africa, and Latin America, 1450–1990: A Documentary Sourcebook* (Grand Rapids: Eerdmans, 2007), 3.
4. Ibid., 4.
5. Jenkins, *Lost History of Christianity*, xi.
6. Linda Woodhead, *An Introduction to Christianity* (Cambridge: Cambridge University Press, 2008), 73.
7. Ibid., 62, 63.
8. Risto Saarinen, "Ecumenical Councils," in *Global Dictionary of Theology*, ed. William A. Dyrness and Veli-Matti Kärkkäinen (Downers Grove, IL: InterVarsity Press, 2008), 262–63.
9. Jenkins, *Lost History of Christianity*, 3.
10. Ibid., 4.

Christian spiritual centre equal to that of France, Germany or Ireland in terms of "the number and splendour of its churches and monasteries, its vast scholarship and dazzling spirituality."[11] History records persecutions and mass defections during the later Middle Ages across Asia and the Middle East that "uprooted what were then some of the world's most numerous Christian communities, churches that possessed a vibrant lineal and cultural connection to the earliest Jesus movement of Syria and Palestine."[12] Remnants of Eastern Christianity still are found in the Middle East, but are decimated by so-called jihadist wars in Iran, Iraq and Syria.

KERALA PLURALISM

Meanwhile in India the peaceable Thomas Christians, augmented by immigrant Syrian Christians from Persia (Iran), shared a common world with the Malabar Hindus.

Pluralist Kerala society allowed for an interpenetration of Hindu, Christian and Syrian cultural codes.[13] This is visible in domestic and ecclesiastic architecture but also in regard to food, occupation, marriage, birth and death, and related rituals. Jewish practices also are found, especially concerning timing of events and purification from pollution[14]—an indicator of the Jewish roots of some of the early converts.

Genealogies were charted and maintained, every individual Christian an agent of history and part of the historical process. Genealogies serve as expressions of social memory.[15] Genealogies are utilitarian memory devices. Oral genealogies are considered valid for three generations. However, a written genealogy is required for a family to claim status as an "old family" of eight or more generations.[16] Knowledge of family history is important to answer the subjective "Who am I?" question. Narrative history is useful for explaining the origin of priesthood in a particular family and important for establishing links between the Mesopotamian Church and the Indian Church.[17]

11. Ibid., 6.
12. Ibid., 2.
13. Susan Visvanathan, *The Christians of Kerala: History, Belief and Ritual among the Yakoba* (New Delhi: Oxford University Press, 2003 [1993]), 1, 3, 9.
14. Ibid., 4, 123.
15. Ibid., 41, 77.
16. Ibid., 79.
17. Ibid., 83.

ENTER THE PORTUGUESE

Advent of the Portuguese in India brought new challenges to the Thomas Christians. Initial cordiality between the native Kerala Christians and the arriving Portuguese gradually dimmed. Manipulations by the Roman Catholic Archbishop at Goa to bring the ancient Indian Church into union with Rome created ongoing tension.

The Portuguese were dissatisfied with the Syrian Christians' interpretation of Christianity, and demanded a totally Latin mode of worship.[18] The Syrians resisted this imposition, having "no desire to transfer their allegiance from the Patriarch of the Eastern Church and receive patronage from Rome."[19] The Latinizing of the Indian Church reached its peak at the 1599 Synod of Diamper—"the most controversial and most important single event in all the century and a half of the Portuguese period of Indian church history (roughly 1498 to 1653)."[20] Its goal of a permanent union of Syrian and Roman Christianity in India failed, and "the fateful Synod of Diamper led instead to such division in the Indian churches that they still remain torn asunder to this day."[21] The intended Latinization sparked an open rebellion, the Koonen Cross Revolt on January 3, 1653, and a dramatic assembly marking the restoration of Indian autonomy to the St. Thomas Christians of Kerala. A few months later they consecrated a Metropolitan and ordained twelve priests of their own, and "the revolt spread like wildfire."[22]

ANGLICAN EVANGELICALS

Advent of British rule brought ecclesiastical contact with India's Syrian Christians and an offer to provide Malayalam translations of the Bible—an offer which was gratefully accepted.[23] Missionaries of the Church Missionary Society were entrusted with the translation task. The original intention was "to sustain and support a unique and

---

18. Ibid., 15.
19. Ibid.
20. Samuel Hugh Moffett, *A History of Christianity in Asia*, vol. 2, *1500 to 1900* (Maryknoll, NY: Orbis Books, 2005), 14.
21. Ibid., 15.
22. Ibid., 18.
23. Visvanathan, *The Christians of Kerala*, 18.

ancient Church rather than to bring about change."[24] Change however was inevitable. Translation of the Bible and the Anglican Prayer Book "into the Malayalam vernacular instead of Syriac . . . had paved the way for schism."[25] Under the leadership of Abraham Malpan (1796–1846), a scholar-priest at the Syrian College (seminary), the Bible, sermons and hymns assumed greater importance, and reformers proposed vernacularization of liturgy and prayers, and "repudiated the mediatory powers of the saints and Mary."[26] The result was a prolonged struggle of reformers against traditionalists:

> Indian reform versus Antiochene authority that led to final schism in 1888–1889, when a pivotal court case awarded church property and ecclesiastical authority to Antioch. The Mar Thoma reformists lost their church buildings and seminary, the Syrian Orthodox traditionalists (Jacobites as they were known) kept the property but lost the most actively evangelistic wing of their church.[27]

Rivalry in the Orthodox hierarchy for the title of Metropolitan caused further dissension. Meanwhile a series of revivals nourished the growth of the reformed Mar Thoma Church. "The high point of the year for the Mar Thoma Church is still today the Maramon Convention of the Evangelistic Association" with attendance of forty thousand (40,000) to eighty thousand (80,000), considered "the largest regular annual gathering of Christians anywhere in the world."[28]

ANIMATED FOR MISSION

Much of today's Islamic world was previously Christian, as Philip Jenkins reminds us.[29] Rather than Dark Ages, these should be seen as the Golden Age of the Church. "The culture and learning of the ancient world had never been lost; nor . . . had the connection with the primitive church."[30] The Nestorian Church of the East was animated for mission with more than nineteen Metropolitans and eighty-five bishops, with new Metropolitan sees near Tehran, in

24. Ibid., 20.
25. Moffett, *A History of Christianity in Asia,* 417.
26. Visvanathan, *The Christians of Kerala,* 21.
27. Moffett, *A History of Christianity in Asia,* 418.
28. Ibid.
29. Jenkins, *Lost History of Christianity,* 4.
30. Ibid., 7.

Syria, Turkestan, Armenia, Arabia, and Yemen. Monks were commissioned to carry the faith to central Asia and China. Multiple languages in which the Church functioned included Syriac, Persian, Turkish, Soghdian, and Chinese, but not Latin which scarcely mattered.[31] It seems likely that the Nestorian monks engaged in dialogue with Buddhist missionaries. Around the year 780, a "Nestorian community erected a monument that recounted the Christian message in Buddhist and Taoist terms."[32] The world in which the Nestorians lived and worked increasingly was "culturally and spiritually Christian, but politically Muslim."[33] No Christendom here. Millions of Christians lived under potentially hostile Persian, Muslim, Hindu, or Chinese rule "as a minority faith operating far from centres of power, usually suffering official discrimination, and facing the recurrent danger of persecution."[34]

HOW IT DIED

Yet this older Christian world came to an end, destroyed, forgotten to all but a few academic scholars. "Church hierarchies were destroyed, priests and monks were killed, enslaved, or expelled, and monasteries and cathedrals fell silent." Christian populations shrank, "the result of persecution or ethnic and religious cleansing."[35] This "brutal purge of Christianity," states Jenkins, left European Christianity cut off from its roots.[36]

Silence. The myth of Islamic tolerance. But still a remnant remains. The Coptic Church of Egypt. Ethiopian Christianity. Hidden Christians of Japan. Crypto-Christians. Secret believers. "The Christian impact on Islam was profound, and can be traced at the deepest roots of that faith."[37] This is important for Christians. "Only by understanding the lost Eastern Christianities can we understand where Islam comes from, and how very close it is to Christianity."[38] This is most evident in Sufism "whose practices so often recall the bygone

---

31. Ibid., 11.
32. Ibid., 15.
33. Ibid., 16.
34. Ibid., 20.
35. Ibid., 23.
36. Ibid., 25.
37. Ibid., 37.
38. Ibid., 38.

world of the Christian monks."[39] Sufism, "the mystical segment of Islam that emphasizes the personal experience of God as opposed to religious dogmatism and ritual," is said to be illuminated by the Spirit of Christ and his teachings.[40]

SILK ROAD MISSION

The missionaries of the ancient Church of the East travelled the route of the Silk Road merchants in quest for the unreached peoples of their world. The early Nestorian "Business as Mission" ventures took place in dusty bazaars, and the missionaries' mode of travel was by camelback. Not surprisingly "the word for merchant became a code word for missionary along the ancient Silk Road."[41] Despite some limitations, the Nestorians became established in areas along the Silk Road having the best trading contacts with the outside world.[42] The Christian faith survived and spread along the Silk Road. It seems likely that Christian and Mahayana Buddhist missionaries sometimes collaborated. Discovery of a collection of "Jesus Sutras" reveal a generous utilization of the local language and Buddhist format for presenting a distinctively Christian message. "Christians presented their faith in the form of sutras, on the lines already made familiar by Buddhist missionaries and teachers."[43]

Gradually, however, religious hostility increased. Christian populations were systematically targeted for persecution and massacre.[44] As persecution intensified, it became difficult to practice either Jewish or Christian faiths.[45] Under warlord Amir Timur[46] (1336–1405) urban

---

39. Ibid., 38. For further information on the receptivity of the Gospel among Sufi Muslims, consider the work of the Syrian Muslim novelist and Christ-follower Mazhar Mallouhi whose writings are highly attractive among Muslim seekers in the Arab world, e.g., his commentary *A Sufi Reading of the Gospel of John* (2004) distributed by a Muslim Sufi publisher in Asia, also *An Eastern Reading of the Gospel of Luke* (1998) published in Beirut, as well as *Genesis: The Origin of the World and Humanity* (2001) in which Mazhar presents the spiritual roots of Islam, Christianity and Judaism and focuses on Christ as the fulfillment of God's covenant with Abraham (Paul-Gordon Chandler, *Pilgrims of Christ on the Muslim Road: Exploring a New Path between Two Faiths* [Lanham, MD: Rowman & Littlefield Publishers, 2007], 148).

40. Chandler, *Pilgrims of Christ*, 148–49.

41. Gene Daniels, "The Silk Road." Issachar Initiative available at http://tinyurl.com/y9mhyycy.

42. Jenkins, *Lost History of Christianity*, 66.

43. Ibid., 92.

44. Ibid., 119.

45. Ibid., 137–38.

46. Further information on Timur (or Tamerline) is available at http://tinyurl.com/ybjjsykt.

society came to an end, and the Silk Road ceased to function.[47] Asian churches survived only in name. Since then Islam has been dominant in the Middle East.

TO JERUSALEM?

Meanwhile in modern China a contemporary "Back to Jerusalem" movement aims to restore the ancient Silk Road as a highway for sending one hundred thousand (100,000) missionaries across Central Asia and the Middle East to preach the gospel and plant Churches in Muslim, Buddhist and Hindu communities all the way from China to Jerusalem.[48] This recent "Back to Jerusalem" movement appears to have some invisible roots in earlier Chinese Evangelical developments in the era prior to Mao.

Parallels may be found in India where conversion movements to Christ have contributed to cultural change and social transformation and a renewed self-image among various tribes and peoples, sometimes over an extended period. An example is seen in the Garo community of Meghalaya in Northeast India. Christian presence in the Garo Hills dates to the mid-nineteenth century. "Baptist missionaries organized the first schools (1878) and hospitals (1908) in the Garo Hills."[49] The Catholics followed. Today some 90 percent of the Garos are Christians, mainly Baptist and Catholic. Since the 1990s new Charismatic churches attract dissatisfied Baptists and Catholics. A minority of traditional Garo religion persists. By many this minority is expected soon to cease to exist, which for others is cause for regret. It is said that "in a variety of ways, Garo Christianity remains connected to the earlier pre-Christian religious orientation."[50]

A recent study concludes that among the Garo conversion to Christianity did not eradicate all of the traditional divinities or demons, some of which continue to inflict illness.[51] If so, this would

---

47. Jenkins, *Lost History of Christianity*, 138.
48. Ibid., 255. Also see David Aikman, *Jesus in Beijing* (Washington, DC: Regnery Publishing, 2003), 192, 195, 201, 203. Also Miriam Adeney, *Kingdom without Borders: The Untold Story of Global Christianity* (Downers Grove, IL: InterVarsity Press, 2009), 55–57.
49. Erik de Maaker, "Have the *Mitdes* Gone Silent? Conversion, Rhetoric, and the Continuing Importance of the Lower Deities in Northeast India," in *Asia in the Making of Christianity: Conversion, Agency, and Indigeneity, 1600s to the Present*, ed. Richard Fox Young and Jonathan A. Seitz (Boston: Brill, 2013), 141.
50. Ibid., 136.
51. Ibid., 140.

imply that conversion did not provide protection against all of the traditional divinities or demons, that they might have become silent but continue to harass people.[52] Alas, if so.

Not surprisingly, "many Christians feel that the mainline Baptist and Catholic churches are unable to protect their followers from these sorts of malice."[53] Hence, perhaps, there is an open venue for the newer Charismatic Churches—much despised by the Garo Baptists—whose theology and practice have a place for exorcism and Holy Spirit empowerment and protection.[54]

SOURCES FOR FURTHER REFERENCE

Adeney, Miriam. *Kingdom without Borders: The Untold Story of Global Christianity*. Downers Grove, IL: InterVarsity Press, 2009.

Aikman, David. *Jesus in Beijing*. Washington, DC: Regnery Publishing, 2003.

Brown, Leslie. *The Indian Christians of St Thomas*. Cambridge: Cambridge University Press, 1956.

Chandler, Paul-Gordon. *Pilgrims of Christ on the Muslim Road: Exploring a New Path between Two Faiths*. Lanham, MD: Rowman & Littlefield Publishers, 2007.

Downs, Frederick. *North East India in the Nineteenth and Twentieth Centuries*. History of Christianity in India, volume 5, part 5. Bangalore: Church History Association of India, 1992.

Jenkins, Philip. *The Lost History of Christianity: The Thousand-Year Golden Age of the Church in the Middle East, Africa, and Asia—and How It Died*. New York: HarperOne, 2008.

---

52. Ibid., 159.
53. Ibid., 156.
54. See O. L. Snaitang, ed., *Churches of Indigenous Origins in Northeast India* (Delhi:ISPCK, 2000). Several Charismatic type Churches originating in Northeast India include the Nagaland Christian Revival Church, the Assembly Church of Jesus Christ (Full Gospel) India based in Shillong, as well as others.

Koschorke, Klaus, Frieder Ludwig, and Mariano Delgado, eds. *A History of Christianity in Asia, Africa, and Latin America, 1450–1990: A Documentary Sourcebook*. Grand Rapids: Eerdmans, 2007.

Maaker, Erik de. "Have the *Mitdes* Gone Silent? Conversion, Rhetoric, and the Continuing Importance of the Lower Deities in Northeast India." In *Asia in the Making of Christianity: Conversion, Agency, and Indigeneity, 1600s to the Present*, edited by Richard Young and Jonathan A. Seitz, 135–59. Boston: Brill Publishing, 2013.

Moffett, Samuel Hugh. *A History of Christianity in Asia*. Volume 2, *1500 to 1900*. Maryknoll, NY: Orbis Books, 2005.

Saarinen, Risto. "Ecumenical Councils." In *Global Dictionary of Theology*, edited by William A. Dyrness and Veli-Matti Kärkkäinen. Downers Grove, IL: InterVarsity Press, 2008.

Visvanathan, Susan. *The Christians of Kerala: History, Belief and Ritual among the Yakoba*. New Delhi: Oxford University Press, 2003 (1993).

Woodhead, Linda. *An Introduction to Christianity*. Cambridge: Cambridge University Press, 2008.

4.

Ziegenbalg

The Beginnings of Protestant Christianity in India

In the year 2006, Lutherans and others celebrated the tercentennial of the arrival in India of Bartholomäus Ziegenbalg and Heinrich Plütschau and the founding of the Tranquebar Mission. Lutherans in India lay special claim to Ziegenbalg who was a Lutheran Pietist from Germany who came to India through the agency of the Danish-Halle Mission. In a real sense Ziegenbalg's mission marks the genesis of Protestant Christianity in India. Not only Lutherans but also Anglicans rightly claim Ziegenbalg through links with the Society for the Promotion of Christian Knowledge (SPCK) and the Society for the Propagation of the Gospel (SPG).

PIETISM

But there is more stemming from Ziegenbalg and the Danish-Halle Mission's identification with Pietism. Ziegenbalg's mission was a prototype of missionary scholarship, Bible translation, schools for educating the common people, for a believers' church and for training of local preachers and pastors. Pietism was characterized by warm-hearted faith with an "experience" of Jesus[1] nurtured by the Bible in the hands of the laity with the church as a fellowship of believers—ingredients reflected in the Pietist model of mission.

Historically Pietism was a spiritual movement within post-Refor-

---

1. Experiential religion is a hallmark of modern Pentecostalism which finds precedents in Pietism as well as in Evangelicalism and the Wesleyan Holiness Movement.

mation European Protestantism. Essentially a devotional movement, nourished by Bible studies in the home and in edification meetings, Pietism contributed to the Protestant missionary awakening and movement.[2] Pietism is seen in the hymns of Paul Gerhardt and the music of Heinrich Schütz and J. S. Bach. Johann Arndt's theology moved beyond orthodox doctrine and external ceremonies to a vibrant, living faith expressed in daily practice. Philip Jakob Spener built upon the theology of Johan Arndt. It is said that "Spener continued Luther's Reformation."[3] "Spener believed that reborn people would be heavenly minded, live godly lives, and have the new nature permeate their beings."[4]

Spener was succeeded by A. H. Francke who developed Halle Pietism, making Lutheran Pietism the dominant cultural force in eighteenth century Germany and Prussia.[5] Francke's theology was based in his conversion, a direct religious experience, emotional and life-transforming, grounded in the biblical Word of God. From this rebirth comes hermeneutical certainty. Repentance leads to conversion, and is at the centre of theological study. In Francke's Halle, theology had to do with the care of souls.[6] The Moravian Church and Mission also were an expression of Pietism, but the centre of it was Halle University (associated with the names of Spener and Francke) from which sprang the Danish-Halle Mission of the seventeeth to eighteenth centuries.

IMPACT ON CULTURE

Agents and impulses of Francke's radical ideals reached Tranquebar (Tarangambadi) in 1706; spreading to Thanjavur by the 1730s, Tirunelveli by the 1770s, Travancore (Tiruvanthapuram) and Serampore (Srírampur) by the 1800s, and other parts of India thereafter.[7]

The earliest Protestant missionaries at Tranquebar and Serampore

---

2. See Carter Lindberg, ed., *The Pietist Theologians: An Introduction to Theology in the Seventeenth & Eighteenth Centuries* (Malden, MA: Blackwell Publishing, 2005).
3. K. James Stein, "Philipp Jakob Spener (1635–1705)," in Lindberg, *Pietist Theologians*, 96.
4. Ibid., 91.
5. Lindberg, *The Pietist Theologians*, 1–20.
6. Markus Matthias, "August Hermann Francke (1663–1727)," in Lindberg, *Pietist Theologians*, 100–114.
7. Robert Eric Frykenberg, *Christianity in India: From Beginnings to the Present*, Oxford History of the Christian Church (New York: Oxford University Press, 2008), 145.

increased the spread of diverse forms of Christianity, and had a profound impact on culture (especially education, through schools). Entire villages and communities converted. Social institutions emerged for care of the poor, the sick, widows and orphans. "Tirunelveli Evangelicals transformed the entire area, bringing about a profound change in local culture and society."[8] At the same time ancient literature and literary gifts were preserved, and cultural values enhanced. Local informants, Hindu as well as Christian, exercised considerable influence upon the missionaries as language informants and culture brokers.[9]

Caste was a complicating factor. Missionary opposition to caste received modification in actual practice which required concessions to caste. Compromise? Possibly so. In actuality caste contributed to the identification of Christians as Indian. "As 'caste' Christians, they would return to their native villages and retain contact with relatives who remained Hindus."[10] In this and other ways the local Christians made Christianity visible (and acceptable) to the local population. The mission workers especially were "visible" to the larger community.

NATIVE AGENCY

Grammars, dictionaries and studies of culture and religion published by missionaries were essentially the work of local correspondents (informants) who generally are overlooked in research on missionaries in India. Ziegenbalg, for example, used a Tamil poet as well as an accountant/writer to help him.[11] The role of informants was enormous: "native agents influenced the knowledge that the missionaries acquired about Indian society and the Hindu religion."[12]

Movements toward Christian faith likewise were not generally through the efforts of foreign missionaries. Most often "the gospel message was brought by local Indian believers, brought in their own native (mother) tongue, and introduced as the language of faith to

---

8. Robert Eric Frykenberg, "Christians in India," in *Christians and Missionaries in India: Cross-Cultural Communication since 1500*, ed. R. E. Frykenberg (Grand Rapids: Eerdmans, 2003), 52.

9. Heike Liebau, "Country Priests, Catechists, and Schoolmasters as Cultural, Religious, and Social Middlemen in the Context of the Tranquebar Mission," in Frykenberg, *Christians and Missionaries in India*, 72.

10. Ibid., 83.
11. Ibid., 89.
12. Ibid., 92.

non-Christians by local people who had become converts somewhere else and had then brought it home with them."[13] As research continues to demonstrate, "the primary agency in recent movements of Christianization has not been the missionaries but the new converts themselves."[14]

In Tirunelveli, the local Indian Christians continued to control and develop their own institutions. Thus,

> the Gospel was interpreted in new ways and extended to new peoples, reaching ever lower stratas of society, seeking out peoples in ever more remote jungle areas, and touching more women and children. Help for peoples in want—people hitherto neglected, impaired, diseased, or relegated to exclusion and oppression—entered increasingly into Christian consciousness.[15]

Support structures were generated by the Tirunelveli congregations themselves. "From the very beginning, following the Halle pattern, a system of universal education was instituted within each congregation."[16]

EVANGELICALISM

Evangelicalism has roots in Pietism. "The Continental pietist movements played a significant role in the beginning of evangelical movements in Britain, and the main themes of pietism anticipated the main themes of evangelicalism."[17] Lutheran Pietism is one of the important strands which, combined with others in the formation of the movement of Evangelical Christianity associated with John and Charles Wesley, found diverse expressions including that of William Carey and the Baptists of Serampore. The Tranquebar Mission provided a model for Carey at Serampore. Pietism had a profound influence on the Wesleys leading to the birth of Methodism and the Evangelical Awakening in England and America. From this Jonathan Edwards's

---

13. Robert E. Frykenberg, "Historical Introduction," in *Tirunelveli's Evangelical Christians: Two Centuries of Family* Vamsavazhi *Traditions*, ed. David Packiamuthu and Sarojini Packiamuthu (Bangalore: SAIACS Press, 2003), xxii.

14. Mark A. Noll, *The New Shape of World Christianity: How American Experience Reflects Global Faith* (Downers Grove, IL: InterVarsity Press, 2009), 106.

15. Frykenberg, "Historical Introduction," xxvii.

16. Ibid., xxxiii.

17. Mark A. Noll, *The Rise of Evangelicalism: The Age of Edwards, Whitefield and the Wesleys* (Downers Grove, IL: InterVarsity Press, 2003), 18.

impact upon Baptists in England would eventuate in William Carey's *An Enquiry into the Obligation of Christians to Use Means for the Conversion of the Heathens*[18] and formation of the Baptist Missionary Society and the coming of the Baptists to Bengal. The Basel Mission, the Berlin Mission, the Gossner Mission and other evangelical agencies which soon followed had Pietist roots.

Not much noticed is a significant influence of High-Church spirituality on the budding Evangelical movement. The Society for the Promotion of Christian Knowledge (SPCK) and the Society for the Propagation of the Gospel (SPG) "represented an extension of High-Church activism already well developed in the local religious societies. Both provided early evangelicals, especially John and Charles Wesley, with multiplied opportunities for Christian service."[19] Moreover, "Samuel and Susannah Wesley, the parents of John and Charles, were both diligent advocates of this High-Church apostolic primitivism." True, later forms of evangelicalism would turn to the Book of Acts as their model for primitive Christianity, "but the primitivist urge remained a very important High-Church bequest to nascent evangelicalism."[20]

Then in 1735 John Wesley decided to accept an SPCK call to Georgia to serve the English settlers and preach to the Native Americans. The Moravians with whom John and Charles Wesley traveled to Georgia held "definite views on the question of Christian assurance" as a normal aspect of Christian experience. Under this influence Wesley was moving "from a straightforward High-Church concentration on moral duties as responses to divine revelation toward an experiential reliance on divine grace as both God's free gift and God's enablement for service."[21] Later, having returned to London, at Aldersgate, hearing a reading from Luther's preface to Romans, John Wesley felt himself touched by God's grace: "I felt my heart strangely warmed. I felt I did trust in Christ, Christ alone for salvation, and an assurance was given me that he had taken away *my* sins, even *mine*, and saved *me* from the law of sin and death."[22] Despite doubts which

---

18. William Carey, *An Enquiry into the Obligation of Christians to Use Means for the Conversion of the Heathens* (Leicester, UK: Ann Ireland, and other Booksellers, 1792).

19. Noll, *The Rise of Evangelicalism*, 67.

20. Ibid., 66.

21. Ibid., 85.

22. Ibid., 97. The highlighted words—*my, mine, me*—are italicized in the original quotation of Wesley's own words dated May 24, 1738, and the emphasis should be retained in Noll's quotation from Wesley's published *Works*.

followed and persisted, John's experience at Aldersgate was decisive, as also that of Charles Wesley a week prior, and normative:

> The Wesleys had learned a new way of talking about God's redeeming grace, and then they had experienced that grace themselves. This experience unleashed preaching, hymn writing and society organizing of tremendous energy. Because of that activity, in turn, the Wesleys' experiences of May 1738 became emblematic for the whole evangelical movement.[23]

THE BAPTISTS

The origin of evangelicalism among English Baptists involved an internal theological evolution as well as participation in the new religious currents of the era. Historian Noll reports that in 1770 there was a small-scale revival among Arminian Baptists that led to the founding of the New Connexion of General Baptists. This evangelical movement was soon eclipsed by an evangelical turn among the Particular Baptists. The latter had remained doctrinally orthodox, but often in an extreme Calvinist form that discouraged active evangelism and that "placed more stress on correct doctrinal formulas than on active piety." Several were drawn toward evangelicalism by contacts with other moderates and through the works of Jonathan Edwards.[24] A widening circle of British Baptists began to feel "an increasing burden to take the gospel message to unbelievers wherever they might be found."[25] Among them was William Carey, whose *Enquiry* was one among many publications favouring the cause of mission, but Carey's was "the most influential."[26]

TRANQUEBAR

Carey was ever mindful of his Moravian and Pietist forerunners, Ziegenbalg and the Tranquebar Mission. Today, we too should remember with gratitude the accomplishments of these early pioneers. An important title by Professor Daniel Jeyaraj bears witness to

---

23. Ibid., 98.
24. Ibid., 163.
25. Ibid., 208.
26. Ibid., 208–9.

the careful scholarship of the Halle Pietists,[27] appropriately set in the context of mission and Ziegenbalg's study of Indian culture. "Heathenism," an offensive term today, must be understood in terms of its usage three hundred years ago, as in contrast to "Christendom" (itself a problematic concept), not as a pejorative expression. The book is the work of an international scholar, a Tamil Christian and product of Pietism, a leading authority on the Tranquebar Mission.

Following the sixteenth century Protestant Reformation, Europe in the seventeenth century "appeared to be Christian only on the surface."[28] Prof. Daniel Jeyaraj establishes that but for Pietism, Protestant Europe might not at all have engaged in cross-cultural mission activity in the eighteenth century. Pietism emphasized a heart-felt religion based on study of the Bible, and "Pietists were willing to share their Christian faith and material resources with those who did not have them."[29]

South India in the eighteenth century was an area of conflict between the English East India Company (EIC) and the French East India Company in Pondicherry, and accompanying bribery, corruption, nepotism and violence were rampant.[30] With the death of Mughal Emperor Aurangazeb in 1707, his viceroys became powerful. "The Nawabs of Arcot requested the soldiers of the English East India Company to help them collect revenues and suppress any revolt."[31] The EIC officers, having come to India in order to become rich, were greedy and charged huge sums of money for this service. If the Nawabs lacked cash, they paid in lands, often entire feudal kingdoms handed over to the EIC. "Ultimately it was the ordinary people who suffered greatly—at the hands of the cruel revenue officers."[32]

Such was the context in which Bartholomäus Ziegenbalg and Henry Plütschau reached the Danish colony (1619–1845) of Tran-

---

27. One scholar remarked that persons who had flunked the Halle University exams were sent to Tranquebar! This should not be misconstrued. Ziegenbalg's achievements provide sufficient rebuttal to which Professor Daniel Jeyaraj's "Malabarian Heathenism" bears witness. Vide Daniel Jeyaraj, *A German Exploration of Indian Society: Ziegenbalg's "Malabarian Heathenism"* (Delhi: ISPCK, 2006).

28. Daniel Jeyaraj, "The History of Christianity in India: An Overview from a Protestant Perspective" in *Missiology for the Twenty-first Century: South Asian Perspectives*, ed. Roger E. Hedlund and Paul Joshua Bhakiaraj (Delhi: ISPCK, 2004), 199.

29. Ibid.

30. This account of the Tranquebar Mission is drawn from Prof. Daniel Jeyaraj's description in his essay, ibid., 199–201.

31. Ibid., 199.

32. Ibid., 200.

quebar (Tarangkampadi, "village on the sea shore"), in 1706. The trade treaty signed in 1619 stipulated that the Danes in Tranquebar should have full freedom to practice their Lutheran faith—but that did not permit them to have missionaries in their colonies. The influence of Philip Jakob Spener (at Halle) through his friend Franz Julius Luetkens, a chaplain to the Royal Court of Denmark, was instrumental "in convincing King Frederick IV to send missionaries to Tranquebar."[33] Ziegenbalg and Plütschau were identified as suitable candidates, and were persuaded to go to Copenhagen. There the Danish Bishop Bornemann, after much difficulty, ordained them as Danish missionaries who were expected to adhere to the Danish Church Order and teachings. Neither the King nor the Danish clergy consulted the Directors of the Danish East India Company. The latter were enraged, and sent secret directives to Governor Hassius in Tranquebar "to suppress the work of the missionaries from the very beginning."[34] This was to be done in the name of "neutrality and non-interference."

Tranquebar was a plural society of Shaivites, Vaishnavites and devotees of popular religious sects (fifty-one temples), Muslims (two mosques), and a negligible minority of Roman Catholic Indians and European Protestants. Ziegenbalg founded Jerusalem, the first Lutheran Church meant for Indians, in 1707. In 1718, a second, more spacious church building, New Jerusalem, was dedicated for Christian worship. Ziegenbalg was a devoted scholar who mastered the Tamil language, translated the New Testament and part of the Old into Tamil, wrote other books, produced a Tamil-German dictionary and other tools which initiated the production of Tamil Christian literature. Ziegenbalg and the early German missionaries adapted their Pietist Halle educational tradition to the formation of Christian faith and character in Tamilnadu.[35]

His biographer records Ziegenbalg's Tamil language achievement and facility by which he effectively communicated the Christian message.[36] He also compiled several volumes on Tamil *bhakti* piety.[37]

---

33. Ibid.
34. Ibid.
35. Hugu Grafe, *The History of Christianity in Tamilnadu*, History of Christianity in India, vol. 4, part 2 (Bangalore: Church History Association of India, 1982), 188.
36. Erich Beyreuther, *Bartholomaeus Ziegenbalg* (Madras, India: Christian Literature Service, 1955), 26.
37. James A. Scherer, "Bartholomew Ziegenbalg," *Missiology* (October 1999): 493.

He was a pioneer in the Western study of South Indian culture.[38] What Ziegenbalg began has been carried on by succeeding generations of scholars. The translation project was always a joint effort

> of missionaries with knowledge of Greek and Hebrew, and Tamils with sound knowledge of their own mother tongue and of some European languages. In this translation three cultures meet: the Biblical culture met the Tamil culture through that of the European missionaries. In this joint venture the Tamil people could hear the Hebrew prophets, Jesus Christ and the Apostles speak in Tamil. As Ziegenbalg called it, this translation has been the strong foundation of an indigenous Church in India.[39]

Ziegenbalg prepared the ground for an indigenous Tamil Christianity, distinct from the Danish colonial Church. "From the beginning, Ziegenbalg appears to have grasped the principle of inculturation, developing an indigenous church with Indian characteristics in architecture, music, caste, and customs."[40] Christian Friedrich Schwartz was to build upon the work of Ziegenbalg in laying the foundation for "what was to become the largest and strongest evangelical Christian community in India."[41]

SEMINARY

In 1716, the Danish-Halle missionaries at Tranquebar founded a seminary, and Aaron, one of its students, was ordained in December 1733 as the first Protestant pastor.[42] Soon the Christians of the Tranquebar Mission moved to different parts of India, and missionaries established other churches. German missionary Benjamin Schultze became founder of the Lutheran church in the city of Madras (1726). Rajanaikkan, a soldier in the service of the King of Tanjore, founded the first Lutheran church in Tanjore (1727/28). The Swede, John

---

38. Hans-Werner Gensichen, "Ziegenbalg, Bartholomäus," in *Biographical Dictionary of Christian Missions,* ed. Gerald H. Anderson (New York: Simon & Schuster Macmillan, 1997), 761–62.
39. Daniel Jeyaraj, "Early Tamil Bible Translation in Tranquebar," *Dharma Deepika* (June 1997): 75.
40. Scherer, "Bartholomew Ziegenbalg," 493.
41. Robert Eric Frykenberg, "The Legacy of Christian Friedrich Schwartz," *International Bulletin of Missionary Research* (July 1999): 132.
42. Daniel Jeyaraj, ed., *Ordination of the First Protestant Indian Pastor Aaron* (Chennai, India: Lutheran Heritage Archives, 1998).

Zecharias Kiernander, founded the Old Mission Church (1770) in Calcutta. Missionary Christian Frederick Schwartz was instrumental in establishing Lutheran churches in Tiruchirapalli (1762). One of his women converts, Clarinda, founded a church in Palayamkottai (1785). Throughout the eighteenth century, fifty-four Tranquebar missionaries, some fourteen ordained Indian pastors, many Indian catechists, and numerous lay women and men established the Protestant Church in India despite persistant anti-Christian sentiments.[43]

The Word of God translated into Tamil was the major instrument in sustaining the mission of the churches that resulted from the Tranquebar Mission.[44] From Ziegenbalg at Tranquebar we move to Bengal some ninety years later and the arrival of William Carey, whose arrival marked a new phase in mission and initiated a spate of literary, spiritual, and social uplift at Serampore.

SOURCES FOR FURTHER REFERENCE

Durnbaugh, Donald F. *The Believers' Church: The History and Character of Radical Protestantism.* New York: Macmillian, 1968. Especially chapter 5, "Free Church Pietists."

Frykenberg, Robert Eric. *Christianity in India: From Beginnings to the Present.* Oxford History of the Christian Church. New York: Oxford University Press, 2008.

———, ed. *Christians and Missionaries in India: Cross-Cultural Communication since 1500.* Grand Rapids: Eerdmans, 2003.

Geldback, Erich. "'Evangelisch,' 'Evangelikal' & Pietism: Some Remarks on Early Evangelicalism & Globalization from a German Perspective." In *A Global Faith: Essays on Evangelicalism and Globalization*, edited by M. Hutchinson and O. Kalu. Sydney: Centre for the Study of Australian Christianity, 1998.

Hedlund, Roger E., Jesudas M. Athyal, Joshua Kalapati, and Jessica Richard, eds. *The Oxford Encyclopaedia of South Asian Christianity.* 2 vols. New Delhi: Oxford University Press, 2012.

---

43. Jeyaraj, "History of Christianity in India," 201.
44. D. Dennis Hudson, *Protestant Origins in India: Tamil Evangelical Christians 1706–1835* (Grand Rapids: Eerdmans, 2000).

Jeyaraj, Daniel. *A German Exploration of Indian Society: Ziegenbalg's "Malabarian Heathenism."* Delhi: ISPCK, 2006.

———. "The History of Christianity in India: An Overview from a Protestant Perspective." In *Missiology for the 21st Century: South Asian Perspectives*, edited by Roger E. Hedlund and Paul Joshua Bhakiaraj. Delhi: ISPCK, 2004.

———, ed. *Ordination of the First Protestant Indian Pastor Aaron*. Chennai, India: Lutheran Heritage Archives, 1998.

Lindberg, Carter, ed. *The Pietist Theologians: An Introduction to Theology in the Seventeenth & Eighteenth Centuries*. Malden, MA: Blackwell Publishing, 2005.

McGrath, Alister. *Evangelicalism & the Future of Christianity*. Downers Grove, IL: InterVarsity Press, 1995.

Moffett, Samuel Hugh. *A History of Christianity in Asia*. Vol. 2, *1500–1900*. Maryknoll, NY: Orbis Books, 2005.

Packiamuthu, David, and Sarojini Packiamuthu, eds. *Tirunelveli's Evangelical Christians: Two Centuries of Family Vamsavazhi Traditions*. Bangalore: SAIACS Press, 2003.

Spener, Philip Jacob. *Pia Desideria*. Translated, edited, and with an introduction by Theodore G. Tappert. Philadelphia: Fortress Press, 1967 (1964).

Ward, W. R. "Evangelical Identity in the Eighteenth Century." In *Christianity Reborn: The Global Expansion of Evangelicalism in the Twentieth Century*, edited by Donald M. Lewis. Grand Rapids: Eerdmans, 2004.

5.

Carey and the Evangelical Experiment at Serampore

The pioneer missionaries at Serampore arrived in India at a time of social and cultural degradation.[1] The decline of the Mogul rule saw the ascendency of the Europeans of which the British East India Company was one. That the East India Company was least interested in social and cultural reform is clearly evident. Carey's egalitarian and humanitarian principles did not find friendly reception among the rapacious officers of the Company. An examination of available documents is revealing.

DIFFERING MOTIVES

Antipathy of the East India Company toward the missionaries stemmed from their differing motives and objectives—one capitalistic, and the other, humanitarian. The objective of the Company was entirely one of profit, the enrichment of the investors. The motive of the missionaries was humanitarian—the economic, intellectual, moral, political, social, and spiritual liberation and upliftment of the

---

1. An excerpt from my essay "Evangelical Christians and Social Transformation," in *Integral Mission, The Way Forward: Essays in Honour of Dr. Saphir P. Athyal*, ed. C. V. Mathew (Tiruvalla, India: CSS, 2008). Also see Roger E. Hedlund, "William Carey's American Connections: Implications for the Serampore Mission, Indigenous Christianity and India's Renaissance" (PhD thesis, University of Madras, Chennai, January 2003).

people of Bengal. The officers of the Company had reason to distrust these altruistic motives. Forces were set in motion leading ultimately to Independence and new India's birth as a modern democracy. Carey and Serampore were important catalysts for that process in Bengal.

The missionaries did not engage the political system directly—although they did not hesitate to utilise the offices of their evangelical colleagues in positions of power to expose and combat evil. Theirs was more a role of service, education, and example, as is personified in Carey. The missionaries' social impact was considerable: the first Bengali newspaper, Bengali literary activity, agitation against female infanticide, against voluntary drowning, against widow-burning (suttee), against child sacrifice, Jagannath worship at Puri, Ghat murders, the hook-swinging festival, leper burning, and slavery. All of these social evils were publicised in London by Wilberforce[2] in the House of Commons.

Charity would not remove poverty and suffering. Therefore various plans were introduced to improve economic conditions including the first savings bank in India.[3] Although the savings bank attempt apparently failed after four years, at that point the Government took up the idea. Through this means the missionaries hoped to promote habits of frugality and industry, especially in the rising Christian community, states John Clark Marshman.[4]

WHY HORTICULTURE?

Carey's interest in horticulture was part of his grand design for the upliftment of the poor and suffering. Correspondence from Fuller (head of the Baptist Missionary Society) in England reveals that he on occasion sent packets of seeds for Carey's use. Foundation of an agricultural society, and Carey's botanical garden, were for the "increase of material wealth and individual prosperity" of the people of Bengal.[5]

---

2. For a "solid historical account" of the life and contributions of Wilberforce, see Stephen Tomkins, *William Wilberforce: A Biography* (Grand Rapids: Eerdmans, 2007).

3. S. K. Chatterjee, "William Carey and Serampore," Serampore College, revised 1990 (1988), 16–17.

4. John Clark Marshman, *The Life and Times of Carey, Marhman, and Ward: Embracing the History of the Serampore Mission* (London: Longman, Brown, Green, Longmans, and Roberts, 1859), 223.

5. Ibid., 228.

The steam engine was introduced, as well as other scientific endeavors, to serve the cause of the Mission for human betterment.

Writing about the Indigo question, which became an issue in the latter half of the nineteenth century (1860), Abhijit Dutta remarked that prior to that time the missionaries had played a pivotal role in analysing the Indigo System. Dutta states that Carey, unlike other planters, refrained from oppressing the cultivators, and thus earned their confidence, but this proved detrimental to the Indigo business at Muduabatty, and led to its closure and so ended Carey's employment. Carey used his post to get near the poverty-stricken peasantry, and thus to get acquainted with their life and evils, and to spread the message of Christ. Their humanitarianism endeared the missionaries to the millions, states Dutta.[6] The missionary objective was the spiritual as well as physical transformation of the people.

Carey's was an integrated approach. The material aspect was not segregated from the spiritual. Issues and problems addressed included the slave trade, marriage and polygamy, caste, militarism, and politics. Horticulture and agriculture were part of his missionary aim "to enrich men with God's best." A savings bank, benevolent school and leper hospital all were part of an effort to enrich people materially as well spiritually. "In every way he tried to elevate the people not only by preaching the Gospel but also by applying the principles of the Gospel in daily life."[7]

Horticulture and Carey's missionary work, says Binoy Bhusan Roy, were twin expressions of a single aim, to enrich humanity with God's loveliest and best. Carey's engagement with nature and his participation in the Asiatic Society were aspects of his efforts "to transform the East's deep rooted religions by grafting into their stocks the rich Evangel of Jesus."[8]

At Serampore, Carey experimented with hybrid seeds and new crops. A. K. Ghosh comments that Carey was far ahead of his times in his advocacy of organic fertilizer (manure), rotation of crops, irrigation, soil conservation, productive use of fallow land, new varieties of seed and improving livestock. An Agricultural Society of

---

6. Abhijit Dutta, *Christian Missionaries on the Indigo Question in Bengal (1855–1861)* (Calcutta: Minerva Associates Publications, 1989), 152.

7. Aalbertinus Hermen Oussoren, "William Carey, Especially His Missionary Principles" (PhD diss., Universitas Libera Reformata at Amsterdam, 1945), 196.

8. Binoy Bhusan Roy, "William Carey and the Asiatic Society," in *Carey's Obligation and India's Renaissance*, ed. J. T. K. Daniel and R. E. Hedlund (Serampore: Council of Serampore College, 1993), 250, 247.

India was created, with Carey as president, which imported improved seed varieties (sugarcane from Mauritius, tobacoo and cotton from America). Carey initiated a catalogue of 3500 species cultivated in the Royal Botanic Garden and the formation of an Agro-Horticultural Society with a farm.

"Carey's most significant contribution to Agriculture and Horticulture was through the Agro-Horticultural Society of India that he established in 1820," states biologist George Michael.[9] As a conservationist Carey presented a plan for preserving old forests and planting new ones—"perhaps the earliest known plan in India for afforestation."[10] In beginning the first paper-manufacturing unit in India and in other new ventures, Serampore gave direction toward India's industrialization. India's printing industry, for example, had its birth at Serampore.

Science and education, theology and Bible come together in one common concern for the good of humanity in its totality in the work of Carey and Serampore. A major component was the production of Bengali literature beginning with Carey's translation of the Bible into Bengali. Carey's Bengali New Testament, the first book of prose published in the Bengali language, was the beginning of a vernacular cultural movement in Bengal.

BIBLE TRANSLATION

The chief instrument for missionary work was the written Word of God. Therefore the Bible was to be translated. In this Carey and the Serampore missionaries followed the example of Ziegenbalg and the Pietists at Tranquebar who had translated the Bible into Tamil—the first known Bible translation into an Indian language.

Today the Bible has been translated into more Indian languages than any other book.[11] During his lifetime, Carey and his co-workers translated the Bible into twenty-nine Indian languages. (Carey probably should have been nominated as Father of the Bible Translation Movement). Carey's Bengali New Testament was first published

---

9. George Michael, "Carey the Natural Historian," in Daniel and Hedlund, *Carey's Obligation and India's Renaissance*, 265.

10. A. K. Ghosh, "William Carey: The Botanist," in Daniel and Hedlund, *Carey's Obligation and India's Renaissance*, 261–62.

11. N. R. Ray, "William Carey—A Linguist with a Difference," in Daniel and Hedlund, *Carey's Obligation and India's Renaissance,* 154.

in 1801 and he continued revising throughout his life. By 1832, the entire Bengali Bible was completed, his eighth edition of the New Testament and the fifth edition of the Old Testament.[12] These are but part of an extensive literary contribution. By 1832, two years before his death, 212,000 volumes in forty languages had been published by the Serampore Press.

Carey's colossal literary contribution went far beyond Bible translation to the publication of tracts, pamphlets, newspaper and other periodicals, as well as translation of the *Ramayana* into English and into Bengali. "As early as 1802, Carey completed, in four volumes, the Bengali *Mahabharata* and the *Ramayana* in five volumes."[13]

The message of the Bible must also be demonstrated. It was to be illustrated by the life of the missionaries; hence the need for medical and other benevolent works.

CONTRIBUTIONS TO LEARNING

Carey apparently envisioned Serampore College as a centre for learning various Indian and Asian languages. Grammars, dictionaries and other language aids in more than fifty languages were collected at Serampore where they still are preserved in the Carey Library.[14]

Carey had a passion for developing the languages of India including the preservation of Sanskrit. Serampore birthed a linguistic renaissance in India.[15] As early as 1804, Carey delivered a public lecture in Sanskrit at Fort William College. In 1806, he composed a Sanskrit Grammar for student use. Later, he followed a six-volume Sanskrit Dictionary (which was destroyed in a disastrous 1812 Serampore fire) and an unpublished polyglot vocabulary. The entire Bible was translated by Carey into Sanskrit.

When Serampore College was founded in 1818, Sanskrit was made a compulsory subject. The Library of the College contained fourteen Sanskrit books and sixty-five Sanskrit manuscripts for use by its stu-

---

12. Christopher Arangaden, "Carey's Legacy of Bible Translation," in Daniel and Hedlund, *Carey's Obligation and India's Renaissance*, 178.

13. Kalidas Nag, "Carey's Contribution to Bengali Literature," in *The Story of Serampore and Its College*, ed. Wilma S. Stewart (Serampore, India: The Council of Serampore College, 1961), 98.

14. S. K. Chatterjee, "William Carey and the Linguistic Renaissance in India," in Daniel and Hedlund, *Carey's Obligation and India's Renaissance*, 157–75.

15. Ibid.

dents and teachers.[16] At Serampore College Sanskrit was required, and English was permitted, but Bengali was prerequisite for all further study.[17] It is said that Bengali is closer to Sanskrit than is true of any other modern Indian language.[18]

While Sanskrit was important for classical studies, Serampore promoted the vernacular as the medium of instruction. In doing so they struck a via medium between the Orientalists who wanted study of Sanskrit classics for the perpetuation of the classical tradition and the Anglicists who wanted Western education in English. Over a hundred schools were organized throughout Bengal, and many English books were translated into Bengali in order to provide "modern" education in the local vernacular.

Formation of vernacular schools required vernacular textbooks. Serampore became a production centre. Missionaries[19] wrote some of the early textbooks which were printed by the Serampore Mission Press. Textbooks included chemistry, geography, mathematics, medicine, science, philosophy and other subjects. Vernacular education was a distinct Serampore contribution to cultural revitalization among the common people in modern India. Serampore and Carey in numerous ways contributed to cultural renewal.

SCHOOLS FOR GIRLS

A singular Serampore contribution was to the education of girls. Chatterjee states that the Serampore missionaries pioneered the introduction of modern education for girls in Bengal. The beginning of a social reform movement helped to overcome local conservatism. The first Female Juvenile School was organized in Calcutta in 1819 followed by a number of such schools in Calcutta. Support was raised from England. Beginning in 1821, female schools were organised in Serampore under the leadership of William Ward, John Mack and especially Hannah Marshman who bore the major responsibility. Eventually, the Mission's girls' schools extended over a wide area as

---

16. Indira Mukhopadhayay, "William Carey's Contributions for the Promotion of Sanskritic Studies," in Daniel and Hedlund, *Carey's Obligation and India's Renaissance*, 193–201.

17. Mukhopadhayay, "William Carey's Contributions," 199.

18. Kalidas Nag, "Carey's Contribution to Bengali Literature," in Stewart, *Story of Serampore*, 100.

19. See, for example, Sunil Kumar Chatterjee, *Rev. John Mack (The First Professor of Science in Modern India)*, (Calcutta: Spark Publishing Concern, 1998).

far as Allahabad, Benares, Chitaganj, Dacca, Jessore as well as Calcutta and Serampore. Hundreds of girls were enrolled.

Eventually the schools declined, but by then other missions, for example, the London Missionary Society (LMS) and Church Missionary Society (CMS) were involved in female education. More important, the example of Hannah Marshman and Serampore provided inspiration for later educationists to launch a "crusade against illiteracy among the women of the villages of Bengal."[20] The inspiration continues today with the initiation of schools in remote villages and programmes to eradicate illiteracy throughout India.

WOMEN'S RIGHTS

The emancipation of women through education was accompanied by other reform efforts. The campaign against suttee (widow burning) has been mentioned. In his study of socio-economic aspects of suttee (sati) and the role of Raja Rammohan Roy, Benoy Bhusan Roy notes that William Ward, in efforts to get suttee suppressed, corresponded with a Miss Hope of Liverpool with an appeal "to the ladies of Britain and America to take the causes of the females of India as their own cause and save them from their miseries." William Ward described suttee in his letter, and in this way supplemented the efforts of Carey and the other Baptist missionaries who were "very much active to start a movement against it."[21]

The first volume of Ward's *History, Literature and Mythology of the Hindoos* includes detailed descriptions of practices such as rituals related to death including suttee, vulgar dances connected with certain temples and festivals, the burning of lepers, infanticide, caste practices, marriage patterns, as well as descriptions of common features of life such as houses and musical instruments. A preface of forty pages is an appeal to British humanity to do something to correct and prevent cruel practices seen in Bengal.

Ward's publication, however, was much more than an appeal for legislation for social change. It is a valuable description of religious life and social customs in Bengal in the early nineteenth century.

---

20. S. K. Chatterjee, *Hannah Marshman: The First Woman Missionary in India* (Calcutta,: Sri Sunil Chatterjee, 1987), 89.

21. Benoy Bhusan Roy, *Socioeconomic Impact of Sati in Bengal and the Role of Raja Rammmohan Roy* (Calcutta, 1987), 6, 7.

The third volume, on religion, describes beliefs about God and various objects of worship: gods, goddesses, humans, animals, birds, trees, fish, books, and stones. Volume 4 depicts temples, images, priests, temple worship, rites and ceremonies, doctrines and sects. It is volume 2, however, which contains a valuable compendium of Indian literature and philosophy translated into English along with exerpts on law, astronomy, medical works, poetry, ethics, history, geography, and other aspects of learning.[22]

CONCLUSION

Through their multi-faceted activities, Carey and the Serampore Mission contributed to a cultural renewal in Bengal which joined with other movements for social reform and political awakening throughout India. They certainly were not the sole makers of the movement toward modern Independent India, but they performed an essential catalytic function in which Serampore College was one important component.

In Bengal converts were never many, despite the favourable climate of the 1830s; they continued to come in a small but steady stream and at great cost. In his study of the subject, Copley mentions the significant influence of individual missionaries, but he also notes the proto-nationalism of Bengali Christians and a growing social conscience among them.[23] Examples include Krishna Mohan Banerjea and Lal Behari Dey as well as others.[24] The seeds of nationalism, encouraged by the radical humanism and spiritual egalitarianism exemplified at Serampore, combined together with other forces and agencies, in the twentieth century were to grow into movements of vitality and liberation culminating in India's re-birth as an Independent democracy.

---

22. William Ward, *History, Literature & Mythology of the Hindoos, Including a Minute Description of Their Manners and Customs and Translation from Their Principal Works*, 3rd ed., 4 vols. (Delhi: Low Price Publication, repr. 1990 [1817–1820]).

23. Antony Copley, "The Conversion Experience of India's Christian Elite in the Mid-Nineteenth Century," *Journal of Religious History* 18 (1994): 52–74. Also his more recent *Religions in Conflict: Ideology, Cultural Contact and Conversion in Late Colonial India* (Delhi: Oxford University Press, 1997), 86, 213–16.

24. Copley, *Religions in Conflict*, 220–38.

SOURCES FOR FURTHER REFERENCE

Carey, William. *An Enquiry into the Obligation of Christians to Use Means for the Conversion of the Heathens.* Leicester, UK: Ann Ireland, and other Booksellers, 1792. (A facsimile edition with introduction by Ernest A. Payne was published by Carey Kingsgate Press, London, in 1961).

Chatterjee, S. K. *Felix Carey (A Tiger Tamed).* Calcutta: Pustak Bipani, 1991.

———. *Hannah Marshman: The First Woman Missionary in India.* Calcutta: Sri Sunil Chatterjee, 1987.

———. "Missiological Resources at the Carey Library and Research Centre in Serampore." *Dharma Deepika* 1, no.1 (June 1995): 69–78.

———. "William Carey and the Linguistic Renaissance in India." In *Carey's Obligation and India's Renaissance*, edited by J. T. K. Daniel and R. E. Hedlund. Serampore, India: Council of Serampore College, 1993.

Copley, Antony. "The Conversion Experience of India's Christian Elite in the Mid-Nineteenth Century." *Journal of Religious History* 18 (1994): 52–74.

———. *Religions in Conflict: Ideology, Cultural Contact and Conversion in Late Colonial India.* Delhi: Oxford University Press, 1997.

Daniel, J. T. K., and R. E. Hedlund, eds. *Carey's Obligation and India's Renaissance.* Serampore, India: Council of Serampore College, 1993.

Dharmaraj, Jacob S. *Colonialism and Christian Mission: Postcolonial Reflections.* Delhi: ISPCK, 1993.

Drewery, Mary. *William Carey: A Biography.* Grand Rapids: Zondervan, 1979.

Dutta, Abhijit. *Christian Missionaries on the Indigo Question in Bengal (1855–1861).* Calcutta: Minerva Associates Publications, 1989.

Frykenberg, Robert Eric. *Christianity in India: From Beginnings to the Present.* New York: Oxford University Press, 2008.

George, Timothy. *Faithful Witness: The Life and Mission of William Carey.* Birmingham, AL: New Hope, 1991.

Hedlund, Roger E. "Carey, A Missiologist before Time." *Indian Church History Review* 27, no. 1 (June 1993): 29–49.

Hedlund, Roger E. "Christian Missionary Records in Calcutta." *Dharma Deepika* (December 1995): 79–80.

———. "The Literary and Social Contribution of William Carey and the Serampore Mission to Modern India." Paper presented at the Seminar on Christian Literature and Its Social Contribution, School of Philosophy, Tamil University, Thanjavur, November 22–23, 1999.

———. "William Carey's American Connections: Implications for the Serampore Mission, Indigenous Christiaity and India's Renaissance." PhD thesis, University of Madras, Chennai, 2003.

Mangalwadi, Ruth, and Vishal Mangalwadi. *Carey, Christ, and Cultural Transformation: The Life and Influence of William Carey.* Carlisle, Cumbria, UK: OM Publishing, 1997.

Marshman, John Clark. *The Life and Times of Carey, Marshman, and Ward: Embracing the History of the Serampore Mission.* London: Longman, Brown, Green, Longmans, and Roberts, 1859.

Oddie, Geoffrey A. *Popular Religion, Elites and Reform: Hook-Swinging and Its Prohibition in Colonial India, 1800–1894.* New Delhi: Manohar, 1995.

Payne, Ernest A. "Carey's 'Enquiry'." *Evangelical Review of Theology* 17 (1993): 309–15.

Potts, Daniel D. *British Baptist Missionaries in India 1793–1835: The History of Serampore and Its Missions.* New York: Cambridge University Press, 1967.

Smith, Christopher A. "The Legacy of William Ward and Joshua and Hannah Marshman." *International Bulletin of Missionary Research* 23, no. 3 (July 1999): 120–29.

Stanley, Brian. *The History of the Baptist Missionary Society 1792–1992.* Edinburgh: T & T Clark, 1992.

Stewart, Wilma S., ed. *The Story of Serampore and Its College.* Serampore, India: The Council of Serampore College, 1961.

Tennent, Timothy C. *Building Christianity on Indian Foundations: The Legacy of Brahmabandhav Upadhyay.* Delhi: ISPCK, 2000.

Ward, William. *History, Literature & Mythology of the Hindoos, Including a Minute Description of Their Manners and Customs and Translation from Their Principal Works.* 3rd ed. 4 vols. Reprint of the Serampore original by Low Price Publication, Delhi, 1990 (1817–1820).

6.

Ramabai Dongre Medhavi

Change Agent in Modern Indian History

A century before the start of the modern Indian missionary movement, Pandita Ramabai provides a model of indigenous missionary leadership.[1] In many ways, Pandita Ramabai was far ahead of the missionary movement of her day and ours.

Only today we are beginning to consider partnership possibilities, whereas Ramabai's Mukti Mission was truly international under Indian leadership (an Indian woman) a hundred years ago. By 1913, at least twenty foreigners were serving at Kedgaon.[2] A recent missiology textbook devotes a paragraph to Ramabai and makes the succinct statement, "Missionaries from England and the United States assisted in her charitable endeavors."[3] Personnel as well as funds came from America, Australia, Britain, New Zealand and Sweden.[4] From the inception, volunteers were attracted from the West, and served under Ramabai's capable leadership—that at the height of the colonial era!

---

1. An excerpt from my essay "Evangelical Christians and Social Transformation," in *Integral Mission, The Way Forward: Essays in Honour of Dr. Saphir P. Athyal*, ed. C. V. Mathew (Tiruvalla, India: CSS, 2008).

2. Kenneth Scott Latourette, *The Great Century in Northern Africa and in Asia*, vol. 4 of *A History of the Expansion of Christianity* (New York: Harper & Brothers, 1944), 188.

3. A. Scott Moreau, Gary R. Corwin and Gary B. McGee, *Introducing World Missions: A Biblical, Historical, and Practical Survey* (Grand Rapids: Baker Academic, 2004), 139.

4. Latourette, *The Great Century*, 196.

INDIGENOUS MISSIONARY LEADERSHIP

Neither subservient nor patronizing, in Pandita Ramabai we find a prototype for what must happen in mission today: Americans and Europeans, Koreans and Filipinos working under Indian-Asian-African-Latina/o leadership.

> Ramabai summoned U.S. Protestants to simple faith, moral vision, and humanitarian action. She challenged and prodded them by word and example to recognize and act upon the fundamental unity that overarched their divisions. They responded with prayer, personnel, and funds to one who followed an Anglo-American spiritual trajectory but refused to be co-opted by a Western agenda.[5]

HINDU AND CHRISTIAN

An important component was Ramabai's respectful attitude toward Hinduism. Her own passage into Christian faith was in stages beginning with conversion to the reformist Brahmo Samaj whose monotheism she later came to perceive as Christian in origin. Although she no longer accepted or practiced Hindu religious beliefs, she never reviled the Hindu heritage received from her devout parents. Ramabai was from a family of professional expounders of the Puranas, and her father was an adherent of one of the *bhakti* sects of Hinduism.[6] Ramabai regarded herself as both Hindu and Christian.[7] An initial intellectual conversion to the truth of Christianity was followed years later by an intense spiritual awakening. From this further conversion stems Ramabai's evangelical identity combining intense spirituality with a vigorous social engagement. Her interest in Keswick Holiness brought openness to the subsequent revival movement with accompanying Pentecostal manifestations. Pente-

---

5. Edith L. Blumhofer, "From India's Coral Strand: Pandita Ramabai and U.S. Support for Foreign Missions," in *The Foreign Missionary Enterprise at Home: Explorations in North American Cultural History*, ed. Daniel H. Bays and Grant Wacker (Tuscaloosa, AL: The University of Alabama Press, 2003), 170.

6. Nicol MacNicol, *Pandita Ramabai: A Builder of Modern India* (Calcutta: Association Press, 1926), reprinted with an introduction by Vishal Mangalwadi as *What Liberates a Woman? The Story of Pandita Ramabai, A Builder of Modern India* (New Delhi: Nivedit Good Books, 1996), 42, 54.

7. Robert E. Frykenberg, "Pandita Ramabai Saraswati: A Biographical Introduction," in *Pandita Ramabai's America: Conditions of Life in the United States*, ed. Robert E. Frykenberg (Grand Rapids: Eerdmans, 2003), 21, 36.

costal religious experience shows affinity to the *bhakti* expressions of the devotional Hinduism in which Ramabai was nurtured. The mystical tradition is common in both.[8]

Convert to Christ that she was, she declined to engage in negative polemics and endeavoured to maintain a policy of religious neutrality in her Home for Widows. Without apology she exposed the deplorable condition of Hindu women, and, in the spirit of a true reformer, did everything in her power to bring about change. To accomplish this objective she spoke in Hindu temples on behalf of women, and in 1889, became the first woman to address the Indian National Congress.[9] Innovative and courageous, her exploits carried her beyond the barriers imposed by tradition, religious prejudice and territorial boundaries.

Ramabai's Hindu heritage as well as her Christian faith contributed to her achievements.[10] Pointing out that Christ came to fulfil, not to destroy, Ramabai urged upon Christian missionaries the importance of studying the sacred writings of India in order to appreciate something of the religious values which have sustained the Hindus through the ages. She wrote, "I, who have adopted the Christian faith, and entered sympathetically into the elevated spiritual teachings of that faith, am anxious that my Christian friends should know, too, what is good and true and beautiful in the teachings of our books."[11]

In her conversion Ramabai neither rejected her own cultural background nor identified with Western observances. It is not surprising that the Mukti Church at Kedgaon emerges as an indigenous creation, distinct from "missionary" Christianity. Historically it is significant that here is an early expression of women's ministry and leadership.

---

8. This apparently was remarked upon by L. P. Larsen who was not attracted to mysticism in any form. See Eric J. Sharpe, "Lars Peter Larsen, 1862–1940: India's Enduring 'Great Dane'," in *Mission Legacies: Biographical Studies of Leaders of the Modern Missionary Movement*, ed. Gerald H. Anderson, Robert T. Coote, Norman A. Horner and James M. Phillips (Maryknoll, NY: Orbis Books, 1994), 300.

9. Blumhofer, "India's Coral Strand," 162.

10. Latourette, *The Great Century*, 196.

11. Pandita Ramabai, "Indian Religion," in *Pandita Ramabai through Her Own Words: Selected Works*, ed. Meera Kosambi (New Delhi: Oxford University Press, 2000), 121.

AN EARLY FEMINIST?

Historian M. D. David describes Pandita Ramabai as "the first liberated woman of modern India who broke the shackles of the age old orthodox religious rituals and practices that dehumanized women, especially high caste Brahmin widows."[12] This being true, might not Ramabai qualify as India's earliest feminist? Long before the advent of today's modern feminist movement, Ramabai was an advocate for women's equal rights and freedom. How so?

Born the youngest daughter in a Maratha Chitpavan Brahman family, her father Anant Shastri Dongre was an erudite scholar, orthodox Hindu, devout God-seeker, and reformer who educated his wife as well as his daughter—highly unusual and generally quite unthinkable in the high caste Brahman community of that time and place. Her father passed on to his daughter both his piety and his passion for learning. His deathbed declaration, "I have given you into the hand of one God; you are His, and to Him alone you must belong, and serve Him all your life," is to be understood as a prayer fulfilled in the life and experience of Ramabai.[13]

Brahmanic caste practices of the time denied a number of basic human rights to people of lower castes, and practices pertaining to women were particularly degrading; for example, polygamy, child marriage, and prohibition of widow remarriage, as well as suttee in the case of higher castes.[14] According to historian M. D. David, it was Protestant Christianity whose reformist zeal stimulated a need for cultural change in nineteenth century India leading eventually to reform of socio-religious practices such as suttee and child marriage as well as greater sensitivity towards human rights.[15] Schools and colleges begun by the missionaries contributed to the drive for social reform, economic betterment, social and spiritual advance, uplift of backward tribes, and amelioration of womanhood in India.[16]

Maharashtra has produced a number of important social reformers. Among them Jyotiba Govind Phule (1827–1890) and his wife Savitribai Phule (1831–1897) deserve special mention. Phule preceded

---

12. M. D. David, "Pandita Ramabai: The First Champion of Empowerment of Indian Women," in *Indian & Christian: The Life and Legacy of Pandita Ramabai*, ed. R. E. Hedlund, Sebastian Kim and Rajkumar Boaz Johnson (Chennai, India: MIIS, 2011), 30.
13. S. M. Adhav, *Pandita Ramabai* (Madras, 1979), 5.
14. David, "Pandita Ramabai," 35.
15. Ibid., 36–37.
16. Ibid., 38.

Ambedkar and Gandhi by about a century. Unlike Ambedkar and Gandhi, both of whom were university graduates, Phule never had opportunity for a university education, yet both Ambedkar and Gandhi called Phule their guru.[17] Savitribai Phule is known as India's "Mother of Modern Education" whose educational approach was in sharp contrast to the Brahminical priestly system by which women and low castes (Shudras) had no right to education.[18] "Jyotirao and Savitribai Phule were the first-ever Indians to open a school for girls and for low-caste children. Savitribai Phule was the first-ever Indian woman teacher of the low-caste/without-caste girl child."[19] Both were important nineteenth century social reformrs in Maharashtra.

Savitribai Phule is considered one of the first-generation modern Indian feminists who, along with her husband and social leader Mahatma Jyotiba Phule, worked among the down-trodden and lowest castes.[20] It is not incidental that Savitribai drew inspiration from the Judeo-Christian worldview so that an evangelical Protestant-shaped worldview molded her educational approach.[21] Despite her courageous leadership and noble accomplishments, it seems odd that "Savitribai Phule fails to find any mention in the history of modern India."[22]

This omission can hardly be accidental, and seems similar to the later marginalization of Pandita Ramabai in spite of her stellar achievements. Both women were activists as well as brilliant scholars, and both have been "discovered" by present-day feminists. Savitribai Phule "was in the forefront of a socio-cultural struggle that challenged the tendency to focus only on higher social groups—brahman and allied castes. She encouraged a reversal of traditional subservient roles of women and depressed castes."[23] Therein no doubt is found the reason for this great woman's absence among the reformers' hall of fame. Savitribai worked with Jotirao when he started a series of five schools in 1849, with the school for girls as the climax. She took

---

17. Thom Wolf, *India Progress Prone: The Baliraja Proposal of Mahatma Phule* (New Delhi: University Institute, 2008), 26–27.

18. Thom Wolf and Suzana Andrade, *Savitribai: India's Conversation on Education* (New Delhi: University Institute Publications, 2008), 11, 16.

19. Wolf and Andrade, *Savitribai*, 16.

20. David, "Pandita Ramabai," 41.

21. Wolf and Andrade, *Savitribai*, 41.

22. Braj Ranjan Mani, "Introduction," in *A Forgotten Liberator: The Life and Struggle of Savitribai Phule*, ed. Braj Ranjan Mani and Pamela Sardar (New Delhi: Mountain Peak, 2008), 7.

23. Ibid., 9.

part boldly in all the social revolutionary activities, throwing open her own well to Untouchables in 1868, serving as the president of the Satyashodhak Samaj, and carrying on its work even after her husband's death.[24]

Portrayal of Ramabai as a proto-feminist seems amply justified.[25] Pandita Ramabai, in an anti-women era, launched a "pro-woman movement." The possibility of women entering the public sphere did not even exist until Ramabai did exactly that.[26] Publication of her first book, *The High-Caste Hindu Woman*,[27] was a huge success, profits from its sales providing start-up funds toward alleviating the plight of Hindu child widows.[28]

INTERNATIONAL MISSION PROJECT

"Ramabai's international career was launched in the USA," states Meera Kosambi.[29] Ramabai's American encounter was to prove formative for her international mission project. Her first public address in 1886, in which she told the story of Indian womanhood, brought acclaim. Overnight, Pandita Ramabai became a national sensation. Her name was heard and seen across the length and breadth of America. What she did and said was followed closely. Articles poured forth by the hundreds, especially in women's magazines. Invitations and speaking engagements multiplied. In lecture tours across the land Ramabai told her story and challenged Americans to help their less fortunate sisters in India.[30]

---

24. Gail Omvedt, "A Teacher and a Leader," in *A Forgotten Liberator: The Life and Struggle of Savitribai Phule*, ed. Braj Ranjan Mani and Pamela Sardar (New Delhi: Mountain Peak, 2008), 30, 31.

25. Gauri Viswanathan, *Outside the Fold: Conversion, Modernity, and Belief*, (New Delhi: Oxford University Press, 1998), 118.

26. David, "Pandita Ramabai," 54.

27. Pundita Ramabai Sarasvati [Dongre Medhavi], *The High-Caste Hindu Woman* (Philadelphia: Jas. B. Rodgers Printing Co., 1888 [1887]), with introduction by Rachel L. Bodley, xxiii–iv, 119.

28. According to A. B. Shah, "Introduction," in *Letters and Correspondence* (Bombay: Maharashtra State Board for Literature and Culture, 1977), xx, "10,000 copies . . . were sold out before Ramabai left the US . . . and brought her a profit of Rs. 25,000 [over $8,000]." Cited by Robert Eric Frykenberg, "Pandita Ramabai and World Christianity" in *Indian & Christian: The Life and Legacy of Pandita Ramabai*, ed. R. E. Hedlund, Sebastian Kim and Rajkumar Boaz Johnson (Chennai, India: MIIS, 2011), 173.

29. Meera Kosambi, "Introduction," in Ramabai, *Pandita Ramabai through Her Own Words*, 21.

30. Frykenberg, "Pandita Ramabai Saraswati," 26.

Her experiences, observations, and contacts in the West were to be utilised in an indigenous endeavour, the first of its kind under direction of an Indian woman. During this very time Swami Vivekananda was engaged in his famous mission tour as a proponent of Hinduism in America. The Swami also launched a campaign to discredit Ramabai, "seeking to blunt or nullify Ramabai's impact on North America. Wherever he went, he denigrated what she had said and done."[31] Perhaps it was the Swami's onslaught that prompted Ramabai to warn Westerners against being misled by false information. "The teachers of false philosophies and lifeless spiritualities will do no good to our people. Nothing has been done by them to protect the fatherless and judge the widow."[32] The Pandita urged the women of America and England to visit India to "live in our sacred cities' like the poor beggar-women in their dirty huts, "hearing the stories of their miserable lives, and seeing the fruits of the 'sublime' philosophies."[33]

During her two-year stay in America, Ramabai travelled extensively, observing and gathering information. These impressions she shared first in lectures at Bombay (Mumbai) and Pune, then later in print.[34] In her book, Ramabai devotes several pages describing care for the blind, mute, lame, and crippled people in America, as well as hospitals, orphanages, industrial schools, and prison reform. By advocating these traits Ramabai appears to be preparing the ground for her international mission proposal.

To her Indian audience, Ramabai explained that the political leaders and moral teachers of the United States had focused on the importance of education for all including the women of America.[35] She was pleased with the public school system, and with its teachers, which she had observed. Here we see something of her engagement with the American experience that was to find expression in her mission to the women of India.

Ramabai also was impressed with the freedom of religion as practised in America, supported through voluntary contributions (in contrast to the establishment religion of the Church of England supported by the Crown). She described the work of the Women's Christian Temperance Union, which was to have a leading partici-

31. Ibid., 37.
32. Ramabai, *Pandita Ramabai through Her own Words*, 290.
33. Ibid., 294.
34. Pandita Ramabai, "Conditions of Life in the United States," in *Pandita Ramabai's America*, translated by Kshitija Gomes, ed. Robert Eric Frykenberg (Grand Rapids: Eerdmans, 2003).
35. Ibid., 174.

patory role in Ramabai's Indian venture toward the needs of women in India. Clearly, Ramabai was paving the way for her soon-to-be international mission project. In her spiritual formation, Ramabai was inspired by the experiences of Hudson Taylor, George Muller and John G. Paton and the "faith mission" movement. The principles of the China Inland Mission especially seem to have impressed her. The faith mission ideal was put into practice in the formation of Mukti Mission at Kedgaon. From its inception the Mukti Mission Church at Kedgaon was engaged in missionary activity. As early as 1898 under the guidance of Minnie Abrams a mission band with twenty-five members was formed along the lines of the Student Volunteer Movement.[36]

In Ramabai's model we see components of Bible translation, of mission to the educated, to academics, to the Hindu intelligentsia and to members of the political structure as well as to the marginalised and downtrodden. Her comprehensive approach seems far in advance of much of what transpires today in the name of Christian mission. Ours seems fragmentary by comparison, hers was wholistic a century ahead of our time.

MUKTI MISSION

At Kedgaon the faith mission ideal was put into practice in the formation of Mukti Mission. Mukti sent money to the China Inland Mission, to Armenia, and to help other missions in India. At an early stage the Mukti Mission Church engaged in missionary sending and support. Ramabai taught her people to give, and money flowed from the Mukti widows and orphans to missionary work in China and Korea.[37] Mukti provides an unprecedented example of foreign mission support *from* India.

Ramabai's message in America had included a practical proposal for a residential school for high-caste widows to be created in India. Upon her return home she planned to begin one such institution, as a trial, for which money was needed. "Therefore I invite all good women and men of the United States to give me their help liberally in whatever way they may be able for a period of about ten years."[38]

36. "Pandita Ramabai," in *Indian Christians: Biographical and Critical Sketches* (Madras, India: G. A. Natesan & Co., 1928), 218.
37. Blumhofer, "From India's Coral Strand," 167.
38. Ramabai, *Pandita Ramabai through Her Own Words*, 178.

Her support-raising was highly successful. Publication in 1887 of her book, *The High-Caste Hindu Woman*, "aroused a widespread interest in the unhappy lot of the women of India and in the work that the author proposed to do in their behalf."[39] Some ten thousand copies were sold, and proceeds from sale of the book helped finance the work at Kedgaon.

CHILD WIDOWS

Ramabai envisioned sheltering and educating child widows for a useful living as "teachers, governesses, nurses and housekeepers."[40] Influential Hindus would manage these homes, but well-qualified American women would be recruited as assistants and teachers.

Upon her return to India she did indeed launch such an institution. A letter from Bombay tells of meeting the Advisory Board and the opening of *Sharada Sadan* in Bombay. Within two and half months eighteen pupils were enrolled. The institution was secular. But in her private devotions Ramabai read the Bible and prayed in Marathi, which the girls understood.[41] A considerable amount of correspondence from *Sharada Sadan*, Bombay, tells the stories of the child widows enrolled. Correspondence mentioned various visitors at *Sharada Sadan*, among them a Miss Hamlin from America.[42] An increase in number of inhabitants was reported, along with the relocation of *Sharada Sadan* to a more suitable location in Pune. Soon, however, Ramabai's letter revealed "black clouds" of misunderstanding at Pune, and attempts "to pull this school down."[43] It became evident that the erstwhile reformist supporters were concerned not with social reform but with religious reform, and they severed their connection with the Sadan. From then onward, Ramabai no longer had the support of the general Hindu public. "Anti-Christian and Hindutva sentiments prevailed."[44]

---

39. John Clair Minot, "Ramabai Dongre Medhavi," in *Heroines of Modern Religion*, ed. Warren Dunham Foster (New York: Sturgis & Walton, 1913), 213.
40. Ramabai, *Pandita Ramabai through Her Own Words*, 177.
41. Pandita Ramabai to Dorothea Beale (May 30, 1889), in *The Letters and Correspondence of Pandita Ramabai*, compiled by Sister Geraldine and edited by A. B. Shah (Bombay: Maharashtra State Board for Literature and Culture, 1977), 185.
42. Pandita Ramabai to Sister Geraldine (December 6, 1889), in ibid., 250.
43. Pandita Ramabai to Sister Geraldine (July 2, 1891), in ibid., 262.
44. Frykenberg, "Pandita Ramabai Saraswati," 35.

AT KEDGAON

Ramabai's purpose did not falter. When the Hindus failed to support the *Sharada Sadan*, Ramabai reorganized and made plans for self-support. She purchased 100 acres at Kedgaon to develop a farm.[45] The farm flourished. Since the Hindus did not give the needed funds, Ramabai resorted to other means. Her opponents did create a Hindu *Sharada Sadan*, which was closed to non-Brahman widows, and not "secular" as envisioned by Ramabai.

Ramabai's critics, states Frykenberg,

> seem never to have realized that her conscience, grounded in deeply held convictions concerning each person's inherent right to freedom and liberty, would never have allowed her to take advantage of her position in such a way as to exert coercion or to make attempts to proselytize. She did not believe that genuine conversion was something that human agency alone could accomplish: only God could truly change and inwardly transform the human condition. Also, therefore, her critics never quite realized that Ramabai saw herself as both Hindu and Christian.[46]

In other words, the prejudiced opposition from the Brahmin community necessitated the call for Christian support. Not surprisingly the Ramabai Association was restructured as an explicitly Christian mission.

FAMINE RELIEF

In India, a devastating famine occurred in 1899. Funds were raised in England for building a Mercy Home (*Krupa Sadan*) to provide shelter for famine-stricken villages and women.[47] Other new institutions were the Boys' Home (*Sadanand Sadan*) and the Home for the Blind (*Bartan Sadan*).[48] By the turn of the century nearly two thousand needy persons were being cared for by only sixteen paid teachers and eighty-five of her own women and girls.[49]

---

45. Sister Geraldine from Wantage (1894), *Letters and Correspondence*, 215.
46. Frykenberg, "Pandita Ramabai Saraswati," 36.
47. Sister Geraldine, "Introductory Notes" (1899), *Letters and Correspondence*, 357.
48. Frykenberg, "Pandita Ramabai Saraswati," 42.
49. Sister Geraldine, "Introductory Notes" (1900), *Letters and Correspondence*, 362.

Famine relief at Kedgaon was one aspect of meeting human needs. But there was more. "Complete rehabilitation called for dealing with the effects of emotional and psychological trauma as well. . . . *This massive rescue operation profoundly altered Ramabai's work.*"[50] Correspondence speaks of famine victims, lepers, fallen women.[51] The advent of plague and famine necessitated rescue work. In her letters and reports, Ramabai mentions the names of coworkers, Kashibai and Bhimabai and others, themselves converts from Hinduism, serving as Bible women and as rescue workers reaching out to the famine victims.[52] Mukti Church, founded in 1899 by Ramabai, became a channel of new life for many. Hundreds of women became followers of Christ and were baptized at Mukti Church.

REVIVAL

The 1905 Revival at Mukti was an important event. First of all was its impact in the spiritual formation of the residents. A first person account is given by Ramabai's daughter Manoramabai:

> On the 19th June, a marvellous Pentecostal outpouring of the Holy Spirit began at Mukti and continued for more than six weeks. A large number of girls and women have been deeply convicted of sin and filled with joy of pardon, and many have received the cleansing and fullness of the spirit for life and service.[53]

A detailed account of the Revival given by Minnie Abrams describes sorrow for sin intermingled with joy. "Some who had been shaken violently under the power of conviction, now sang, praised, danced for joy. Some had visions, others dreams."[54] Abrams discusses power for witness and mentions the bestowal of gifts such as faith, healing, tongues, prophecy and discernment of spirits. Abrams's interpretation is reminiscent of the Wesleyan theology of the Holiness Movement.[55] That roots of the Pentecostal Movement in India

50. Frykenberg, "Pandita Ramabai Saraswati," 41 (emphasis mine).
51. Pandita Ramabai to Sister Geraldine (November 25, 1896), *Letters and Correspondence*, 336.
52. Sister Geraldine, "Introductory Note" (1898), *Letters and Correspondence*, 356.
53. Manoramabai to Sister Geraldine (1905), *Letters and Correspondence*, 390.
54. Minnie F. Abrams, *The Baptism of the Holy Ghost & Fire* (Kedgaon, India: Pandita Ramabai Mukti Mission, 1905 [2000]), 2.
55. According to Edith Blumhofer, Ramabai never embraced speaking in tongues, and Abrams rarely experienced it; see Blumhofer, "India's Coral Strand," 168.

are traced to Mukti establishes a further importance of the Revival as one of the origins of Pentecostalism in India.

Revival brought changes in the life of Mukti. Prayer meetings and evangelism, already part of the Mukti activities, intensified and became the heart of the community. Praying bands were established, voluntary groups of young women who dedicated themselves to pray five hours a day, "or as long as the Spirit led them to pray," for the revival of other Christians, and to engage in evangelistic outreach. "It was reported that by 1911 more than 150 villages were visited by the bands and that they established twelve different centres."[56]

Initially the revival at Mukti appears to have been well received by church and mission leaders. Before long, however, there was criticism and controversy. The heart of the controversy had to do with the exercise of "spiritual gifts at Mukti during the revival meetings," particularly the gift of speaking in tongues.[57] Both Pandita Ramabai and Minnie Abrams responded by writing "extensive articles to explain that the special features of the revival were from God and that they were in accordance with the Christian scriptures and tradition."[58] Ramabai perceived the criticism as "an intrusion by western missionaries" and argued that the missionaries should learn the "religious inclination" and "emotional side" of the Indian nature.[59] Sebastian Kim points out that there were two phases of the Mukti revival movement, one starting in June 1905, the other in February 1907, with a significant difference between them, that the speaking in tongues occurred only in the second (February 1907) phase and was described as a "greater outpouring of the Holy Spirit" or "greater blessings."[60]

Minnie Abrams[61] understood the gift of tongues as a "Pentecostal baptism" and essential component of the spiritual revival, which was given in answer to prayer for power to witness. Pandita Ramabai, who did not regard tongue speaking as the only sign of Holy Spirit

---

56. Sebastian C. H. Kim, "Pandita Ramabai's Conversion towards Mukti: In Search of Companionship, Integrity and Faith," in Hedlund, Kim, and Johnson, *Indian & Christian*, 26.
57. Ibid.
58. Ibid.
59. Ibid.
60. Ibid.
61. See Darrin J. Rodgers, "Abrams, Minnie F.," in *The Oxford Encyclopaedia of South Asian Christianity*, ed. R. E. Hedlund, Jesudas Athyal, Joshua Kalapati and Jessica Richard (New Delhi: Oxford University Press, 2012), 4.

baptism, defended those who received it and were helped thereby to live better lives and also display the attribute of "perfect divine love."[62]

Characterised by emotional phenomena, the impact of the awakening was long-lasting in terms of conversions and changed lives. Ramabai channeled the enthusiasm of the believing community into famine relief work as well as social rehabilitation. In this way the spiritual awakening had an enduring influence in Maharashtrian society.

CONCLUSION

In 1897, Ramabai invited Minnie Abrams, a Methodist "Holiness" missionary from America, to minister at Kedgaon. In 1905, a spiritual revival at Mukti was to reverberate far beyond Kedgaon. It has been suggested that Pentecostalism in India has roots in Maharashtra at the Ramabai Mukti Mission, Kedgaon. The revival spread as the Mukti bands carried the message throughout the Maratha country. Characterised by emotional phenomena, the impact of the awakening was long-lasting in terms of conversions and changed lives. Ramabai channeled the enthusiasm of the believing community into famine relief work as well as social rehabilitation.

Mukti Church continues today. The legacy of ministry to needy women and children continues. Training of members for ministry in the power of the Holy Spirit continues to be a distinctive emphasis. Mukti Church bears the Ramabai imprint of social vision combined with spiritual fervour. Mukti Church is a unique indigenous legacy of one of India's greatest women, Pandita Ramabai Saraswati, one of the makers of modern India.

SOURCES FOR FURTHER REFERENCE

Abrams, Minnie F. *The Baptism of the Holy Ghost & Fire*. Kedgaon, India: Pandita Ramabai Mukti Mission, reprint 2000 (1905).

Adhav, S. M. *Pandita Ramabai*. Madras, India: Christian Literature Service, 1979.

---

62. Kim, "Pandita Ramabai's Conversion towards Mukti," 28.

Anderson, Gerald H., Robert T. Coote, Norman A. Horner, and James M. Phillips, eds. *Mission Legacies: Biographical Studies of Leaders of the Modern Missionary Movement*. Maryknoll, NY: Orbis Books, 1994.

Chakravarti, Uma. *Rewriting History: The Life and Times of Pandita Ramabai*. New Delhi: Zubaan (Kali for Women imprint), 2013 (1998).

Dongre, Rajas Krishnarao, and Josephine F. Patterson. *Pandita Ramabai: A Life of Faith and Prayer*. Madras: Christian Literature Service, 1963.

Frykenberg, Robert E., ed. *Pandita Ramabai's America: Conditions of Life in the United States*. Grand Rapids: Eerdmans, 2003.

Hedlund, Roger E., Sebastian Kim Sebastian, and Rajkumr Boaz Johnson, eds. *Indian & Christian: The Life and Legacy of Pandita Ramabai*. Chennai: MIIS, 2011.

Kosambi, Meera, ed. *Pandita Ramabai through Her Own Words: Selected Works*. New Delhi: Oxford University Press, 2000.

MacNicol, Nicol. *Pandita Ramabai: A Builder of Modern India*. Calcutta: Association Press, 1926.

Natesan, G. A. *Indian Christians: Biographical and Critical Sketches*. Madras, India: G. A. Natesan & Co., 1928.

Ramabai, Pandita. *The Letters and Correspondence of Pandita Ramabai*. Compiled by Sister Geraldine and edited by A. B. Shah. Bombay: Maharashtra State Board for Literature and Culture, 1977.

―――. *A Testimony of Our Inexhaustible Treasure*. Kedgaon, Pune, India: Pandita Ramabai Mukti Mission, 1977 (1907).

Sengupta, Padmini Sathianadhan. *Pandita Ramabai Saraswati*. New York: Asia Publishing House, 1970.

Viswanathan, Gauri. *Outside the Fold: Conversion, Modernity, and Belief*. New Delhi: Oxford University Press, 1998.

7.

Evangelical Christians and Social Transformation

Who is an evangelical?[1] What does it mean to be evangelical? According to the Radical Followers of Jesus from Latin America, being evangelical is more than a question of doctrine. The radical discipleship answer in terms of mission in a context of poverty resonates well in Asia which faces similar challenges. In an exposition of "The Biblical Basis for Integral Mission in the Context of Poverty," Esteban Voth concludes, "If the Church works for justice by means of its varied social relationships, the image of God may one day be restored in the poor."[2] That hope is appealing in the Asian context of massive poverty.

SIGNS OF HOPE

We live in a world of need in which human ideologies—Marxism, capitalism, globalization—have been weighed in the balances and found wanting. "Marxism has passed away.... The market economy

---

1. Portions of this chapter are from my essay "Evangelical Christians and Social Transformation," in *Integral Mission, The Way Forward: Essays in Honour of Dr. Saphir P. Athyal*, ed. C. V. Mathew (Tiruvalla, India: CSS, 2008).

2. Esteban Voth, "The Biblical Basis for Integral Mission in the Context of Poverty," in *The Local Church, Agent of Transformation: An Ecclesiology for Integral Mission*. Edited by Tetsunao Yamamori and C. René Padilla (Buenos Aires: Ediciones Kairos, 2004), 97.

has arrived, but the poor are even poorer, and the life of the majority of the people of the world has deteriorated," remarks Pedro Arana-Quiroz.[3] Yet, as C. René Padilla states, there are signs of hope: "The church that is committed to the poor becomes a sign of the new creation that burst into history in the person and work of Jesus Christ—a sign of hope in the midst of despair."[4] Churches are called to community action, to engagement with the hardships of everyday life and thus to resist becoming self-centered ecclesiastical ghettos.[5] An Evangelical Church "is a Church for sinners" and will be involved in ministry to drug addicts, HIV/AIDS afflicted, the homeless and others.[6]

God has destined the Church to serve as his agent of transformation in society. How is this to happen? For the Church to fulfill its Divine destiny requires transformation of the Church. This begins with transformed minds of believers. Transformed churches begin to influence their communities. God's agenda includes the physical and social as well as the spiritual restoration of humankind. God is concerned for the whole person and the whole humanity.

NON-WESTERN MAJORITY WORLD

The demise of social engagement in evangelical churches in the West was a reaction to theological liberalism prevailing during the fundamentalist-modernist controversy of the early twentieth century. Today however the social vision has been restored in the practice as well as the rhetoric in sections of evangelical Christianity worldwide, especially in the vibrant Christianity of the contemporary non-Western majority world of Africa, Asia and Latin America.[7]

Earlier evangelicals were deeply involved in social issues. Carey, Marshman, Ward and the Serampore Mission, we have seen, were engaged in a broad scope of activities aimed at alleviating human misery and building hope for a just and equitable society. Evangelical

---

3. Pedro Arana-Quiroz, "Integral Mission in the Framework of Grace, World, and Church," in Yamamori and Padilla, *The Local Church*, 189.

4. C. René Padilla, "Vignettes of a Servant Church," in Yamamori and Padilla, *The Local Church*, 270.

5. Josué Fonseca, "Integral Mission in Worship," in Yamamori and Padilla, *The Local Church*, 293.

6. Padilla, "Vignettes of a Servant Church," 293.

7. See Bob Moffitt with Karla Tesch, *If Jesus Were Mayor: Transformation and the Local Church* (Phoenix: Harvest, 2004).

Christianity in India has been an agent of transformation and social compassion. Carey from earlier history and Ramabai from more recent times are two examples. This reality is further documented by studies of various indigenous expressions of Christianity throughout the Region. A striking case in point is the contemporary "first century" Christianity of India's bordering Hindu nation of Nepal[8] where healing and exorcism are important dimensions of Christian witness in the animistic context of Tantric Hinduism and Tibetan Buddhism. Indigenous Christianity in South Asia is contextual, evangelical, socially aware, and has proven adaptable and resilient. Christian witness is carried out through a variety of creative means.

Investigation reveals empowerment activities among slum dwellers and street children, liberation of backward communities and tribals, encouragement of women's movements and Christ *Bhaktas*, use of indigenous communication media, employment of local proverbs and sayings, as well as the more traditional roles of community development, Bible translation, village schools, and church planting, all of which play a part in community transformation.[9]

SOCIAL VISION RECOVERY

Writing about evangelicals' recovery of social dimensions of the gospel, Jacob Thomas (of the Union Biblical Seminary faculty in Pune) pointed to the emergence of World Vision International, Tear Fund, World Concern, EFICOR and other expressions of compassion. He notes that Evangelicals from India and the developing world have a far greater concern than relief services and the alleviation of suffering. The greater issue is to struggle with questions about the evil structures of society which have pushed masses of humanity to the periphery of history.[10] Integrity of the gospel demands that evangelicals grapple with the root causes of poverty.

---

8. Ramesh Khatry, "Religious Freedom in Nepal Then and Now," in *Missiology for the 21st Century: South Asian Perspectives*, ed. R. E. Hedlund and Paul Joshua Bhakiaraj (Delhi: ISPCK, 2004), 414–29.

9. Roger E. Hedlund, "Creative Ministries of New Christian Movements," a paper prepared for the Fellowship of Indian Missiologists (FOIM) Workshop on Creative Ministries, Mount Abu, Rajastan, August 14–18, 2002.

10. Jacob Thomas, "The Church's Response to the Poor—Evangelical Tradition," in *Good News to the Poor: The Challenge to the Church*, ed. Sebastian C. H. Kim and Krickwin C. Marak (Delhi: ISPCK, 1997), 196.

From his pastoral experience among university students and graduates in Asia, Vinoth Ramachandra finds that people who have known only an individualistic gospel, find it difficult to appreciate an integral gospel. They fail to see how one's political views, economic behavior, daily work or social involvement have anything to do with the gospel.[11] Yet, in the Greco-Roman world, the claim "Jesus is Lord" was primarily a political claim. "The good news of the in-breaking reign of God in Jesus to heal, renew and recreate his broken world is far, far bigger than a message of individual salvation." Integral mission is more than a matter of "right techniques," it springs from an integral gospel. "We live within a global economic system that stimulates greed, massive waste, the destruction of nature and the exploitation of our fellow human beings." This is the context in which the gospel challenges the falsity of global capitalism, the world in which followers of Christ are called to live, not as vagabond tourists, but as sojourners, as resident aliens (1 Pet 2:11).[12]

Evangelical spokespersons tend to be activists rather than deep thinkers. Perhaps. Nevertheless the Christian mission requires theological reflection. It is rewarding and revealing to engage in theological dialogue from the perspective of the poor.[13] Dehumanizing poverty is an affront to the image of God which is found in every human. The poor, in evangelical perspective, are not only the victims of evil structures and systems, through no fault of their own they are deprived of God's love and compassion. The root cause of poverty is human sinfulness, not infrequently manifested in acts of selfishness and greed which deprive the poor of their basic rights to an abundant life. Rich and poor alike are in need of Christ's redemption.[14]

BIBLICAL HOLINESS

God's identity with the poor and oppressed is seen in Scripture. "You are the sons and daughters of the Lord your God. . . . You are a people holy to the Lord your God, and the Lord has chosen you to be a people for his own possession, out of all the peoples that are on the

---

11. Vinoth Ramachandra, *Church and Mission in the New Asia: New Gods, New Identities* (Singapore: Trinity Theological College, 2009), 16.
12. Ibid., 16, 18, 43, 48, 49.
13. This is achieved by Jayakumar Christian in his landmark study, *God of the Empty-Handed: Poverty, Power and the Kingdom of God* (Monrovia: MARC World Vision, 1999).
14. Ibid., 67–73.

face of the earth."[15] "Remember that you were a slave in the land of Egypt, and the Lord your God redeemed you."[16] God's reclamation of his Old Testament People from slavery and their priestly reinstallation is replicated in the New Testament declaration:

> But you are a chosen race, a royal priesthood, a holy nation, God's own people, that you may declare the wonderful deeds of him who called you out of darkness into his marvelous light. Once you were no people but now you are God's people; once you had not received mercy but now you have received mercy.[17]

That impoverished peoples have risen to claim their spiritual inheritance is a fact of history and a contemporary reality. Many have found new human dignity through a new identity in Christ. Evangelization begins a process of spiritual recovery whereby those of no social status have discovered their true identity of equality and self-esteem as the children of God and full citizens of his Kingdom. This is mission as evangelical transformation.

EVANGELICAL CATHOLICS

Protestant evangelicalism has a Catholic counterpart, and the evangelical movement is heir to the medieval spirituality of the German mystic Thomas á Kempis (1380–1471)—whose *Imitation of Christ* became a devotional classic for Protestants as well as for Catholics[18]—as well as of the great artist-scientist Leonardo Da Vinci (1452–1519), the mystical Bernard of Clairvaux (1090–1153),[19] and especially St. Francis of Assisi (1182–1226)[20] and other Catholic luminaries. An example from India is none other than the late blessed Mother Teresa, whose love for Jesus was legendary. Responding to a public official's question, Mother Teresa replied, "I am convinced

---

15. Deut 14:1–2.
16. Deut 15:15.
17. 1 Pet 2:9–10.
18. Mark A. Noll, *The Rise of Evangelicalism: The Age of Edwards, Whitefield and the Wesleys* (Downers Grove, IL: IVP Academic, 2003), 61.
19. "Bernard of Clairvaux" in *ChristianHistory.net* available from http://tinyurl.com/ybaaoo4c.
20. St. Francis of Assisi, 2015, the Biography.com website. Available from http://tinyurl.com/y9ex49ut.

that faith in Christ is the best thing to have in the world. I would like for all to know and love Christ at least as much as I love him."[21]

Evangelical Catholicism is defined by George Wiegle as "a Catholicism of radical conversion, deep fidelity, joyful discipleship, and courageous evangelism. Evangelical Catholics put friendship with the Lord Jesus at the center of everything: personal identity, relationships, activity."[22] Evangelical Catholics have experienced Pentecost, are touched by the fire of the Holy Spirit. "Radically converted Christians have become men and women marked by tongues of fire, animated by the Spirit."[23] Evangelical Catholicism comes with high expectations: For the laity more than an hour of weekly worship. For clergy far more attention to preparation for preaching the Word of God.[24] The starting point for Evangelical Catholicism is its confession of faith in Jesus Christ, for "friendship with Jesus Christ is at the center of Evangelical Catholicism."[25] It is noted that this confession brings Evangelical Catholics into fuller communion with Evangelical Protestants who also affirm orthodox Christian beliefs.[26] Evangelical Catholic proclamation is a call to "repent and believe" and to accept the invitation to enter the Kingdom "here and now, through ongoing conversion of heart and way of life."[27] In the case of Mother Teresa, on board a train bound for Darjeeling, this became a "call within a call" by which she knew what she wanted to do for the rest of her life, namely to consecrate herself "to help the poor, living among them."[28]

In his biography of Pope John Paul II, George Wiegle describes his as "The Evangelical Papacy."[29] In his proclamation of the gospel, John Paul offered the Kingdom of God "as an encounter with the person of Jesus of Nazareth, the image of the visible God."[30] As understood by John Paul, the Second Vatican Council (1962–1965) was intended to

21. Mother Teresa, *Mother Teresa: In My Own Words*, compiled by José Luis González-Balado (New York: Gramercy Books, 1996), 101.
22. George Wiegle, "The Rise of Evangelical Catholicism," *First Things,* March 2013, 33–40.
23. George Wiegle, *Evangelical Catholicism, Deep Reform in the 21st-Century Church* (New York: Basic Books, 2013), 19.
24. Ibid., 21.
25. Ibid., 31.
26. Ibid., 38.
27. Ibid., 34.
28. Mother Teresa, *In My Own Words*, ix.
29. George Wiegle, *The End and the Beginning: Pope John Paul II--The Victory of Freedom, the Last Years, the Legacy* (New York: Doubleday, 2010).
30. Ibid., 473.

prepare the Church "for a springtime of evangelization at the beginning of the third millennium of its history."[31] The Church's "New Evangelization" was John Paul's response, and it was

> both Christocentric and mission oriented: all the baptized were called to the task of evangelization, which required every baptized Catholic to develop a personal relationship Ewith Jesus Christ as Lord and Savior, and to commit themselves to being instruments by which others came to know Christ.[32]

The New Evangelization appears to require the renewal of the Catholic Church, which might well have been the Holy Father's intent. As Wiegle sees it, "The New Evangelization requires a Church sure of its identity and confident of the truths it bears" which include "both the proclamation of the Gospel and the Church's work for justice in the public square."[33]

Wiegle's *Evangelical Catholicism* is a call for radical reform including reform of the papacy. The latter requires also the reform of the Roman Curia and the College of Cardinals in light of realities of the postmodern world as well as of the rapid growth of Catholicism in the global South. A number of valuable suggestions are offered including a need to reconsider commitment to dialogue with "liberal Protestant bodies that seemed to be achieving very little, while opening new lines of conversation with the evangelical, fundamentalist, and Pentecostal Protestants who were manifestly the growing Protestant communities of the twenty-first century and beyond."[34]

Is Pope Francis's visit to a Pentecostal pastor in Caserta (southern Italy near Naples) a step in that direction, and a sign of welcome change? Time will tell. In various ways Pope Francis seems to be sending signals that his pontificate may be marked by change, that transformation trumps tradition. One of his early acts was to establish a commission of cardinals charged with radical overhaul of the Catholic Church's central structures; he appears to favour a shared rather than autocratic approach to authority, his new appointments of cardinals from lesser-known dioceses in Asia, Africa, and Oceania intended to empower the Church at the margins.[35] Speculating as to

31. Ibid., 445.
32. Ibid., 446.
33. Wiegle, *Evangelical Catholicism*, 232.
34. Ibid., 256.
35. See Eamon Duffy, "Who Is the Pope?," *The New York Review of Books*, February 19, 2015.

possible impact of a pending visit to Washington, DC, *Time* magazine noted that the political and economic messages of Pope Francis were "upending politics around the globe" and included such issues as climate protection, nuclear weapon abolition, immigration rights and closure of the Guantanamo Bay detention centre.[36]

As George Wiegle reminds us, "Evangelical Catholicism enters the public square with the voice of reason, grounded in gospel conviction." It does so for the purpose of mission. "Evangelical Catholicism awaits with eager anticipation the coming of the Lord Jesus in glory, and until that time, Evangelical Catholicism is ordered to mission—to the proclamation of the Gospel for the world's salvation."[37]

IDENTITY CONFUSION

Despite a positive engagement in mission to a needy world, a considerable confusion persists as to the identity of today's Christians. Who are India's Christians? Confusion of identity derives from India's colonial history. The colonial powers—whether Danish, Dutch, French, Portuguese or British—generally paid little attention to religion except for efforts to propagate Christianity which they opposed. Historians have noted that the Europeans were looked upon as Christians, whereas in reality they often were the worst possible representatives of the Christian faith. European missionaries moreover were viewed as agents of colonialism and therefore sometimes treated with contempt. A similar attitude expressed toward Indian Christians is a carry-over of hatred toward European colonialists—presumably Christians—erstwhile conquerors, exploiters, rulers.[38] The misperception "that Christianity is essentially European and that European religion has traditionally been Christian"—neither of which is true[39]—has caused considerable confusion leading to persecution of higher-caste converts to Christ.[40]

During the so-called mass conversions of the 1930s, conversion

---

36. Elizabeth Dias, "Kiss the Ring," *Time*, June 1, 2015, 33–35.

37. Wiegle, "Rise of Evangelical Catholicism," 39.

38. Eleanor Zelliot and Maxine Berntsen, eds., *The Experience of Hinduism: Essays on Religion in Maharashtra* (Albany: State University of New York Press, 1988), 142–71.

39. Robert Eric Frykenberg, ed., *Christians and Missionaries in India: Cross-Cultural Communication since 1500* (Grand Rapids: Eerdmans, 2003), 5.

40. Mohan D. David, "Mission, Inter-Cultural Encounter and Change in Western India: A Case Study of Local in Relation to Global Church History," *Mission Studies* 16, no. 1 (1999): 10–25.

became a political issue and was strongly opposed by Mahatma Gandhi who was aware of the political implications of the conversion of the Depressed Classes (today's Dalits).[41] Mass conversions taking place all over India were viewed as "a new threat not only to communal harmony but to the very concept of the nationalist movement."[42] In Gandhi's viewpoint, "religion and politics were inseparable," and Gandhi became increasingly hostile toward liberation of the "untouchables" through conversion to Christianity, which he regarded as "the religion of the oppressors."[43] Conversion, in Gandhi's understanding, represented the "arrogance" of the missionaries, which drew Gandhi into conflict with his friend the highly-respected Methodist evangelist E. Stanley Jones.[44] Jones's "long association with and admiration of Gandhi was well known."[45] Jones endeavoured to persuade Gandhi "to meet and experience" Christ—an invitation the Mahatma did not accept.[46] Nevertheless they remained friends. Eventually Gandhi declared that India had "no need of conversion from one faith to another."[47] According to Gandhi "religion was embodied in the religious heritage of one's forefathers," that is, it is a matter of birth, whereas for Stanley Jones it was a matter of human rights, a choice, "the individual right to share one's faith and choose one's religion."[48]

However, as Gandhi's grandson observes, "It was Ambedkar who made conversion a hot topic."[49] The leader of India's "Untouchables" parted company with Gandhi over the latter's opposition to equal rights for the Harijans (today's Dalits). "The complex nature of religious conversion in India was exposed more clearly in the debate between M. K. Gandhi and B. R. Ambedkar," their conflict "a prototype of the struggle between the caste Hindus and the 'outcastes' in

---

41. Sebastian C. H. Kim, "The Politics of Conversion during the British Raj: 'Mass Movements' in the 1930s and Their Impact on Indian Politics and the Church," *Dharma Deepika* 17, no. 2 (July–December 2013): 6–25.
42. Ibid., 8.
43. Ibid., 9.
44. According to his grandson, Rajmohan Gandhi, Gandhi developed close relationships with several Christian ministers and evangelists, among whom E. Stanley Jones is named, "without conceding a need to become a Christian" (Rajmohan Gandhi, *Gandhi: The Man, His People, and the Empire* [Berkeley: University of California Press, 2007], 404).
45. Kim, "The Politics of Conversion," 9.
46. Ibid., 9, 10.
47. Ibid., 10.
48. Ibid., 11.
49. Rajmohan Gandhi, *Gandhi: The Man*, 376.

India."[50] Hindu opposition to proposed reforms convinced Ambedkar of the futility of the drive for equality and change. At Yeola, Maharashtra, on October 13, 1935, Ambedkar made the sensational announcement that he would leave Hinduism: "I had the misfortune of being born with the stigma of an untouchable. It is not my fault. But I will not die a Hindu for this is in my power."[51] Gandhi was not pleased. In a rejoinder to the missionaries and to John R. Mott, the American founder of the YMCA, Gandhi asked, "Would you, Dr. Mott, preach the Gospel to a cow?"[52] This unfortunate remark reveals something of the apprehension of many Hindus "at the thought of 'losing' some of their numbers."[53] In a related aside, Gandhiji's grandson Arun Gandhi castigates the arrogance of the British:

> The British, with their pernicious divide-and-rule politics, exploited the caste system to perpetuate their rule of India. They could easily have eliminated the caste system by modernizing the country's sanitation system, educating the oppressed, and elevating them from a life of poverty and destitution. However, not only did they not modernize the sanitation; they did not even supply the millions employed to carry buckets of feces and urine with the tools to do their work with some small portion of dignity. Often these workers had to carry leaky buckets for long distances on their heads.[54]

Ambedkar, meanwhile, had published a booklet on "Annihilation of Caste" in which he systematically critiqued the Hindu caste system.[55] Gandhi, however, admired the caste system.[56] As novelist and social critic Arundhati Roy states, "Democracy hasn't eradicated caste. It has entrenched and modernized it. This is why it's time to read Ambedkar."[57] Furthermore "History has been kind to Gandhi" who was deified by millions during his lifetime, but "unkind to Ambedkar" and has hidden away his writings.[58] Yet

---

50. Kim, "The Politics of Conversion," 11.
51. Ibid., 13.
52. Rajmohan Gandhi, *Gandhi: The Man*, 378.
53. Ibid., 379.
54. Arun Gandhi, *Legacy of Love: My Education in the Path of Nonviolence* (El Sobrante, CA: North Bay Books, 2003), 93.
55. Kim, "The Politics of Conversion," 14. See B. R. Ambedkar, *Annihilation of Caste: The Annotated Critical Edition*, ed. and annotated by S. Anand, with an introduction, "The Doctor and the Saint," by Arundhati Roy (New Delhi: Navayana Publishing, 2013).
56. Roy, "The Doctor and the Saint," 26.
57. Ibid., 37.
58. Ibid., 40, 43.

Ambedkar played a vital role in conceptualising and producing the Indian Constitution.[59]

> Ambedkar's main concern was to privilege and legalise "constitutional morality" over the traditional, social morality of the caste system. Speaking in the Constituent Assembly on December 17, 1946, he said, "Constitutional morality is not a natural sentiment. It has to be cultivated. We must realize that our people have yet to learn it. Democracy in India is only a top-dressing on an Indian soil which is essentially undemocratic."[60]

Apparently Ambedkar was "seriously disappointed with the final draft of the Constitution," which he considered "a work in progress."[61] In his booklet, Ambedkar commented that "the path of social reform . . . is strewn with many difficulties," and in India "has few friends and many critics" (2.1).[62]

Meanwhile Protestant leaders found it necessary to express their views on conversion which they defined in spiritual terms as a "change of heart from sin to God which is brought about by Christ alone."[63] In light of their deep spiritual hunger, V. S. Azariah defended the legitimacy of evangelisation among the restless Depressed Classes.[64] It is to be noted that many of the Christians in Dornakal were products of conversion movements in Andhra Pradesh among Malas and Madigas, movements ignited by new converts and spread through networks of relationships, especially of family and caste. Here as elsewhere in India the most effective agents for the spread of Christianity were not the missionaries but the Indian Christians who spread the gospel informally among their own people.[65] Records reveal that conversions during the first four decades of the twentieth century were at a faster rate in Andhra than in almost any other South Asian region. "Between 1921 and 1931, an average of 12,855 converts joined the church each month. The Indian Christian population of India and Burma increased at a rate of 32.5 percent

---

59. Ibid., 44.
60. Ibid., 45.
61. Ibid., 46.
62. Ambedkar, *Annihilation of Caste*, 210.
63. Kim, "The Politics of Conversion," 16.
64. Ibid., 17.
65. Susan Billington Harper, *In the Shadow of the Mahatma: Bishop V. S. Azariah and the Travails of Christianity in British India* (Grand Rapids: Eerdmans, 2000), 182.

during this decade."[66] The Anglican Christian population of Dornakal Diocese increased from 56,681 in 1912 to 225,080 in 1941.[67] "By 1933, roughly 80 percent of India's Protestant Christians were mass movement converts from depressed class backgrounds."[68]

Dual identity of India's Christians is a somewhat confusing reality, frequently misunderstood. One unfortunate misperception is the notion that India's Christians owe allegiance to some alien power or institution. History, however, reveals that despite intrusions from the West and from Christians of the West, from cultures that were alien and foreign, most Christians of India have continued to retain their own distinct cultural identities. These identities have remained, in most respects, clearly and predominantly Indian.[69]

CONCLUSION

Robert Frykenberg observes that Gandhi's 1937 attack on Bishop V. S. Azariah's efforts to bring the gospel to the outcaste Malas and Madigas at Dornakal as "anti-national" has stuck fast, and is used to implicate Indian Christians as alien, anti-national, unpatriotic and engaged in fraudulant conversion.[70] Then as now, the charge is unfair and untrue.

In Dornakal, conversion proved "an effective instrument for improving the status of depressed class groups." The evidence has shown that conversion movements to Christianity were less a means of rejecting Hinduism and the prevailing caste system than a means by which subordinate groups tried to elevate their rank in the social hierarchy by accommodating and, sometimes, transforming the values of dominant, non-Christian groups.[71] Then as now the vibrant Christianity of the non-Western majority world of Africa, Asia and Latin America offers hope to the disenfranchised and oppressed. As we have seen, Evangelical Christianity in India has been an agent of transformation and social compassion.

66. Ibid., 184.
67. Ibid.
68. Ibid., 185.
69. Frykenberg, *Christians and Missionaries*, 2.
70. Ibid., 7.
71. Susan Billington Harper "The Dornakal Church," in *Christians, Cultural Interactions, and India's Religious Traditions*, ed. Judith M. Brown and Robert Eric Frykenberg (Grand Rapids: Eerdmans, 2002), 210.

SOURCES FOR FURTHER REFERENCE

Ambedkar, B. R. *Annihilation of Caste: The Annotated Critical Edition.* Edited and annotated by S. Anand, with an introduction, "The Doctor and the Saint," by Arundhati Roy. New Delhi: Navayana Publishing, 2013.

Brown, Judith M., and Robert Eric Frykenberg, eds. *Christians, Cultural Interactions, and India's Religious Traditions.* Grand Rapids: Eerdmans, 2002.

Christian, Jayakumar. *God of the Empty-Handed: Poverty, Power and the Kingdom of God.* Monrovia, CA: MARC World Vision, 1999.

Frykenberg, Robert Eric, ed. *Christians and Missionaries in India: Cross-Cultural Communication since 1500.* Grand Rapids: Eerdmans, 2003.

Gandhi, Arun. *Legacy of Love: My Education in the Path of Nonviolence.* El Sobrante, CA: North Bay Books, 2003.

Gandhi, Rajmohan. *Gandhi: The Man, His People, and the Empire.* Berkeley: University of California Press, 2007.

Harper, Susan Billington. "The Dornakal Church on the Cultural Frontier." In *Christians, Cultural Interactions, and India's Religious Traditions*, edited by Judith M. Brown and Robert Eric Frykenberg, 183–211. Grand Rapids: Eerdmans, 2002.

_____. *In the Shadow of the Mahatma: Bishop V. S. Azariah and the Travails of Christianity in British India.* Grand Rapids: Eerdmans, 2000.

Hedlund, Roger E. "Indigenous Christianity." In *Missiology for the 21st Century: South Asian Perspectives*, edited by Roger E. Hedlund and Paul Joshua Bhakiaraj. Delhi: ISPCK, 2004.

Hedlund, Roger E., and Paul Joshua Bhakiaraj, eds. *Missiology for the 21st Century: South Asian Perspectives.* Delhi: ISPCK, 2004.

Kim, Sebastian C. H. "The Politics of Conversion during the British Raj: 'Mass Movements' in the 1930s and Their Impact on Indian Politics and the Church." *Dharma Deepika* 17, no. 2 (July–December 2013): 6–25.

_____. *In Search of Identity: Debates on Religious Conversion in India.* New Delhi: Oxford University Press, 2003.

Kim, Sebastian C. H., and Krickwin Marak, eds. *Good News to the Poor: The Challenge to the Church.* Delhi: ISPCK, 1997.

Moffitt, Bob, with Karla Tesch. *If Jesus Were Mayor: Transformation and the Local Church*. Phoenix: Harvest, 2004.

Noll, Mark A. *The Rise of Evangelicalism: The Age of Edwards, Whitefield and the Wesleys*. Downers Grove, IL: IVP Academic, 2003.

Ramachandra, Vinoth. *Church and Mission in the New Asia: New Gods, New Identities*. Edited by Kimhong Hazra, with responses from Simon Chan, Melba P. Maggay, and Martin L. Sinaga. Centre for the Study of Christianity in Asia, Annual Lectures 2007. Singapore: Trinity Theological College Publications, 2009.

Wiegle, George. *The End and the Beginning: Pope John Paul II—The Victory of Freedom, the Last Years, the Legacy*. New York: Doubleday, 2010.

———. *Evangelical Catholicism, Deep Reform in the 21st-Century Church*. New York: Basic Books, 2013.

———. "The Rise of Evangelical Catholcism," *First Things,* March 2013, 33–40.

Yamamori, Tetsunao, and C. René Padilla, eds. *The Local Church, Agent of Transformation: An Ecclesiology for Integral Mission*. Buenos Aires: Ediciones Kairos, 2004.

Zelliot, Eleanor, and Maxine Berntsen, eds. *The Experience of Hinduism: Essays on Religion in Maharashtra*. Albany: State University of New York Press, 1988.

8.

Indigenous Churches of South Asia and Beyond

Independent Christianity experienced explosive growth in Asia, Latin America and Africa throughout the twentieth century.[1] Global Christianity today is centred in these three regions. This rapidly spreading Christianity is indigenous to Asia, Africa, and Latin America. It is a vibrant faith, much of it Pentecostal or Charismatic, with considerable appeal to the poor and the marginalised.

INDIA

At an early time, Christianity came to South Asia, where it adapted itself to the prevailing culture. A notable example is the Thomas Christianity of India. According to tradition, the Apostle Thomas preached, died and was buried in South India, and the community of Thomas Christians originated in the mission of St. Thomas in India.[2] Historically, indigenous Christianity has a two-thousand year tradition in South Asia. Cult and culture combined to preserve a Christian community which is authentically Christian as well as thoroughly

---

1. Based on the author's article, "Indigenous Churches," in the *Encyclopedia of Pentecostal and Charismatic Christianity*, ed. Stanley M. Burgess (New York: Routledge, OnLine, 2006).

2. Leslie W. Brown, *The Indian Christians of St Thomas* (Cambridge: Cambridge University Press, 1982 [1956]). Indian reprint of the 1982 revised text issued by the St. Thomas Service and Community Centre, Chennai.

Indian. The Thomas Christians have been an integral part of the social and religious fabric of the region for nearly two thousand years. Evidence also indicates that ancient Christianity once existed in the larger region of what is now Pakistan[3] and Afghanistan[4] prior to the advent of Islam.

Ancient South Asian Christianity has experienced countless rebirths. Attempts were made in Tamil Nadu (Roberto de Nobili,[5] Vedanayagam Shastriar,[6] Krishna Pillai[7]), in Bengal (Keshub Chunder Sen[8]), and in Maharashtra (Narayan Vaman Tillak[9]) to express historic Christianity through Indian cultural forms. Among the countless others who in various ways appropriated the gospel in an Indian mode were Sadhu Sundar Singh,[10] R. C. Das[11] at Varanasi, Subba Rao[12] in Andhra, Devadas[13] of the Bible Mission at Guntur, Bro. Bakht Singh.[14]

In Maharashtra, Pandita Ramabai (1858–1922)[15] was a notable social activist and radical advocate of women's rights and

---

3. Charles Amjad-Ali, "Pakistan," in *The Oxford Encyclopaedia of South Asian Christianity*, ed. R. E. Hedlund, Jesudas Athyal, Joshua Kalapati and Jessica Richard (New Delhi: Oxford University Press, 2012), 516–25.

4. J. Dudley Woodberry, "Afghanistan," in Hedlund et al., *Oxford Encyclopaedia of South Asian Christianity*, 7–8.

5. P. Peter Raj, "Robert de Nobili: An Indigenous Foreigner," in *Christianity Is Indian: The Emergence of an Indigenous Community*, ed. R. E. Hedlund (Delhi: ISPCK, 2004 [2000]), 101–11.

6. Michael Faraday, "Vedanayagam Shastriar," in Hedlund et al., *Oxford Encyclopaedia of South Asian Christianity*, 723–24.

7. A. J. Appasamy, *Tamil Christian Poet: The Life and Writings of H. A. Krishna Pillai* (London: Lutterworth Press, 1966).

8. K. P. Aleaz, "Sen, Keshub Sunder," in Hedlund et al., *Oxford Encyclopaedia of South Asian Christianity*, 619–20.

9. Plamthodathil S. Jacob, "The Indigenous Christian Spirituality of Narayan Vaman Tilak," in Hedlund, *Christianity Is Indian*, 23–58.

10. P. Surya Prakash, "Contribution of Sadhu Sundar Singh to the Indigenous Christian Movement in India," in Hedlund, *Christianity Is Indian*, 113–27.

11. H. L. Richard, ed., *R. C. Das: Evangelical Prophet for Contextual Christianity* (Delhi: ISPCK for CISRS, 1995).

12. H. L. Richard, *Exploring the Depths of the Mystery of Christ: K. Subba Rao's Eclectic Praxis of Hindu Discipleship to Jesus* (Bangalore: Centre for Contemporary Christianity, 2005).

13. P. Solomon Raj, "Father Devadas of the Bible Mission at Guntur," *Dharma Deepika* (June 1995); also "Bible Mission of Devadas," in Hedlund et al., *Oxford Encyclopaedia of South Asian Christianity*, 85–86.

14. T. E. Koshy, *Brother Bakht Singh* (Secunderabad, India: OM Books, 2005. Also M. Premanendham, "God-Chosen Movement for India," in Hedlund, *Christianity Is Indian*, 331–44.

15. See chapter 6 in this book, "Ramabai Dongre Medhavi: A Change Agent in Modern Indian History." For further information see the compilation R. E. Hedlund, Sebastian Kim, and Rajkumar Boaz Johnson, eds., *Indian and Christian: The Life and Legacy of Pandita Ramabai* (Delhi: ISPCK, 2011).

egalitarianism. A Marathi Chitpavan Brahmin convert to Christianity, and an articulate spokesperson on behalf of suppressed Hindu women, her advocacy has earned her a place of honour in modern Indian history. In her conversion Ramabai neither rejected her own cultural background nor identified with Western customs. Mukti Church at Kedgaon emerged as an indigenous creation, distinct from "missionary" Christianity, an early expression of women's ministry and leadership. Mukti Church continues today. The legacy of ministry to needy women and children continues. Mukti Church bears the Ramabai imprint of social vision combined with spiritual fervour. India has many more examples.

The Indigenous Churches of India (the official name of the assemblies associated with Bro. Bakht Singh) must be mentioned, as well as numerous independent local assemblies and several break-away denominations in Andhra Pradesh. At Madras the indigenous Laymen's Evangelical Fellowship[16] is an example of a significant holiness revival movement. Similar new churches are found in other parts of India. The largest cluster consists of numerous indigenous Pentecostal[17] fellowships. Some are off-shoots of the Indian Pentecostal Church of God[18] (IPC) based in Kerala, others have emerged from the more exclusive Ceylon Pentecostal Mission[19] (CPM). At Mumbai the Charismatic New Life Fellowship[20] is an indigenous house church movement that owns no property but has thousands of members functioning in cell churches throughout the city. Many of India's Christians are from humble backgrounds. Numbers of Dalits, Tribals, and the poor are finding dignity and hope in a new identity as disciples of Jesus Christ.

SRI LANKA

An unusual demonstration of Christian indigeneity is found in the career of Fr. Joseph Vaz (1651–1711), a Brahman convert in Goa,

16. Whitson Paul, "The Laymen's Evangelical Fellowship: An Indigenous Christian Movement in India," in Hedlund, *Christianity Is Indian*, 411–27.

17. Roger E. Hedlund, *Quest for Identity: India's Churches of Indigenous Origin* (Delhi: ISPCK, 2000), 81–88.

18. Sara Abraham, "The Indigeneity of the Indian Pentecostal Church of God," in Hedlund, *Christianity Is Indian*, 439–50.

19. Paul C. Martin, "A Brief History of the Ceylon Pentecostal Church" in Hedlund, *Christianity Is Indian*, 429–37.

20. Hedlund, *Quest for Identity*, 193–96.

ordained a priest, served first in Kanara, then returned to Goa where he launched a "native" Oratorian Congregation and departed secretly to Ceylon (Sri Lanka) which he entered incognito disguised as a beggar (ca. 1685). The Catholic Church in Ceylon was under severe persecution by the colonial Dutch. Vaz trained underground local missionaries and lay leaders, creating an inculturated Sri Lancan liturgy, literature and indigenous Church.[21] Vaz is credited to have saved the underground Catholic Church from extinction. The persecuted Church which he re-established, survived its isolation from Rome for 140 years. Joseph Vaz was canonized by Pope Francis on January 14, 2015, the "Apostle of Ceylon/Sri Lanka."

Sri Lankan Christian indigeneity has further affinity to that of India as is illustrated by the history of Pentecostalism in Sri Lanka. The Ceylon Pentecostal Mission began as a breakaway from the Assemblies of God led by Alwin R. de Alwis and Pastor Paul in 1923.[22] The CPM espoused an ascetic approach to spirituality. Ministers were not to marry and should wear white. They disdained the use of medicine and gave central importance to the doctrine of the second coming of Christ. Testimonies of miraculous healing attracted Buddhists and Hindus, and the wearing of white was appropriate culturally in Sri Lanka where Buddhist devotees wore white to visit the temples. The CPM also instituted indigenous forms of worship.[23]

The CPM laid the foundation for other Pentecostal ministries not only in Sri Lanka and India but beyond with branches today in several countries. While exact membership figures are not available, in 1998 there were 848 branches reported worldwide (including 708 in India) and nearly 5,000 full-time ministers.[24] In addition, there are numbers of independent assemblies and movements which have severed connections with the CPM. Some of these are prominent, such as the Apostolic Christian Assembly[25] in Tamil Nadu, founded by Pastor G. Sundram, led today by Pastor Sam Sundaram, and many more.

---

21. Don Alexis Dassanayake, "Vaz, Joseph," in Hedlund et al., *Oxford Encyclopaedia of South Asian Christianity*, 722.

22. G. P. V. Somaratna, *Walter Clifford: Apostle of Pentecostalism in Sri Lanka* (Nugegoda, Sri Lanka: Margaya Fellowship, 1997).

23. G. P. V. Somaratna, *Origins of the Pentecostal Mission in Sri Lanka* (Nugegoda, Sri Lanka: Margaya Fellowship, 1996).

24. Ibid., 30, 34, 40.

25. Hedlund, *Quest for Identity*, 138–40.

NEPAL

Nepal[26] is of particular note. Christianity in modern-day Nepal is in its first century. Prior to 1950, there were no Nepali Christians residents in Nepal. The story of the Church in Nepal is a record of efforts by Nepali Christians to reach their own people. Nepal was closed to the outside, but Nepali people managed to seep out into India where a number of them were converted and became active evangelists. These Nepali Christians organized their own Gorkha Mission. Contacts developed along the border, and there were excursions into Nepal as well, but there was no place for Christians in Nepal.

Revolution in 1950 brought change and the first decade of the Church in Nepal. St. Xavier's School was started by the Catholics in 1951. Christian worship began in Kathmandu in 1953. Three Mar Thoma missionaries founded the Christa Shanti Sangh Ashram and took up residence in Kathmandu in 1953. Secret believers eventually were baptized. In 1953, the Nepal Evangelist Band received permission to open a hospital at Pokhara. In 1954, the United Mission to Nepal received permission to begin medical work. Other agencies followed, but primarily the story of the Church in Nepal is a record of Nepali Christians, many of them women, penetrating their country with the gospel.

The Nepali Church from its inception has been indigenous in character and outlook with emphasis on local leadership development. Discipleship schools and Bible schools were organized during the 1970s and 1980s. Kathmandu today has numerous small Bible training institutes, one or two seminaries, and at least one fledgling Christian university. The Association for Theological Education in Nepal (ATEN) serves to provide library resources to meet the need of the growing Christian movement for training.

In 1991, there were more than 50,000 baptized believers in Nepal. The exact number of Christians is not known, but in 1996 it was estimated at about 200,000 Christians in Nepal, and more recently as many as 500,000 were reported, as well as response in the diaspora

---

26. Ibid., 45–46. Also Cindy Perry, *A Biographical History of the Church in Nepal* (Wheaton, IL: Wheaton Graduate School, 1989); Ramesh Khatry, "The Church in Nepal," in *Church in Asia Today: Challenges and Opportunities*, ed. Saphir Athyal (Singapore: Asian Lausanne Committee for World Evangelization, 1996); Jan Minderhoud, "The Christian Presence in Nepal before 1951," in *Indian Church History Review* 24 (December 4, 1990): 144–64.

86   CHRISTIANITY MADE IN INDIA

Nepali community in Northern India, Bhutan and other countries.[27] The witness of the gospel has advanced despite persecution, imprisonment and other hardships.

The indigenous Christianity of Nepal has been described as Pentecostal or Charismatic in character from its very inception. Even before Nepal opened its doors in 1951, Pentecostal missionaries in India were active on the Nepal border. Some of the converts were trained at the North India Bible Institute of the Assemblies of God at Hardoi. In Nepal converts were exposed to Pentecostal teaching. Besides the Assemblies of God, the Agape Fellowship and many independent churches are Pentecostal or Charismatic.[28]

Healing and exorcism[29] are important dimensions of Christian witness in the animistic context of Tantric Hinduism and Tibetan Buddhism. Christianity in Nepal is in its first century, a church completely indigenous in origin.

TAIWAN

In East Asia the translation of the Gospel proceeds in a vast plurality of cultures, languages and competing ideologies in which the church inculturates itself. Several examples may be noted. In Taiwan the True Jesus Church[30] has a distinctive understanding of Christ, which is somewhat less than Trinitarian but which stresses the unity of God and the full deity of Christ and his unity with the Father. The Church holds five cardinal doctrines: Baptism by immersion, Holy Communion, Feet Washing, Baptism of the Holy Spirit and Sabbath (Saturday) as the day of worship. This church experienced rapid growth and has expanded into other countries. The denomination is highly organized with participation from every local congregation. The laity, not the professional clergy, is the foundation of the church. The church is fully self-supporting. The True Jesus Church is Taiwan's third largest denomination.

27. Cindy L. Perry, *Nepali around the World: Emphasizing Nepali Christians of the Himalayas* (Kathmandu: Ekta Books, 1997).
28. Bal Krishna Sharma, "Nepal, Charismatic/Pentecostal Movement," in Hedlund, 482–83.
29. Michael Bergunder, "Miracle Healing and Exorcism in South Indian Pentecostalism," in *Global Pentecostal and Charismatic Healing*, ed. Candy Gunther Brown (New York: Oxford University Press, 2011).
30. Allen J. Swanson, *Taiwan: Mainline vs. Independent Church Growth* (Pasadena, CA: William Carey Library, 1970); Swanson, *The Church in Taiwan: Profile 1980* (Pasadena, CA: William Carey Library, 1981).

The Assembly Hall Church[31] is the second largest Protestant denomination in Taiwan. Origins are shrouded in mystery; the history unwritten, but these believers are the followers of Watchman Nee and Witness Lee. Organisation is simple with no synods, conventions, committees, or headquarters, in spite of which the Assembly Hall is more highly organized than most denominations. The local church is the centre of it all. Great emphasis is placed on lay training for evangelism. There is no clergy-laity distinction. Theologically the Assembly is both millenarian and Trinitarian with its own distinctive interpretation of the Trinity. A strict millenial outlook tends to an other-worldly separatism.

In addition to these two indigenous denominations, Taiwan has a large number of independent "local" churches with no outside affiliation or mission relationships. These too are a significant part of the Christian expression in Taiwan.

JAPAN

Christianity remains a relatively insignificant minority faith in Japan where its perceived "Westernness" has been its major roadblock to acceptance and growth. The story of Christianity in Japan is replete with rejection of transplanted churches perceived as manifestations of an alien faith. But a recent study of twelve Japanese indigenous Churches tells a different story. The Christian message in Japanese garb[32] is creatively appropriated in these indigenous Christian movements.

Concern for the ancestors is a central issue among the Japanese.[33] Traditional Protestant Christianity, however, fails to address this question. Protestant missionary theology and practice represent a discontinuity with customary Japanese beliefs. Leaders of indigenous Japanese Christian movements take a different approach which gives attention to questions of household salvation and the possibility of ministry to the spirit world. Functional alternatives are found to

---

31. Swanson, *Mainline vs. Independent Church Growth*, 189.

32. Mark R. Mullins, *Christianity Made in Japan: A Study of Indigenous Movements* (Honolulu: University of Hawai'i Press, 1998).

33. Michael Pye, "Japanese Ancestor Veneration in Comparative Perspective," *Dharma World* 34 (July–September 2007), available at http://tinyurl.com/yak5saca.

traditional religious observances such as ancestor veneration.[34] Exorcism of malignant spirits, purification rituals, and vicarious baptism are further examples of Japanese inculturation of Christianity.

The Spirit of Jesus Church[35] is one such Japanese church which in less than twenty years in the post-war period grew to the second largest Protestant church in Japan stressing lay witness and house meetings. Perhaps the best known Japanese indigenous tradition is the Nonchurch Movement of Uchimura Kanzo. The Way, Christ Heart Church, the Holy Ecclesia of Jesus, and the Original Gospel Movement are among other indigenous Japanese Christian churches.[36]

SOUTH KOREA

In South Korea, Christianity entered the core of Korean culture, identified with nationalism, and has produced the world's largest Christian congregations. Korean Christianity is predominantly Presbyterian.[37] Outwardly "Western" in ornate basilicas with pipe organs and vested choirs, Korean Christianity has its own distinctive indigenous forms including a proliferation of break-away Presbyterian denominations and other local expressions.

Korean Christianity is a study not only in independence and indigeneity but in Korean contextuality and leadership dynamics expressed in a succession of break-away movements. Not surprising, one finds Korean Presbyterian Churches in other countries where Koreans have engaged in mission. Large Korean churches of various denominations are found in North America, and Korean missionaries have been sent to several countries of Africa, Asia, Latin America and the Pacific. Christianity in Korea appears distinctly Korean, and Korean Christianity is aggressively missionary.[38]

---

34. Mark R. Mullins, "What About the Ancestors? Some Japanese Christian Responses to Protestant Individualism," *Studies in World Christianity* 4, no. 1 (1998): 41–64.

35. Mullins, *Christianity Made in Japan*, 141.

36. Mullins, "What About the Ancestors?," 32.

37. John H. Conner, "When Culture Leaves Contextualized Christianity Behind," *Missiology* (January 1991): 21–29. Also, Jean-Jacques Bauswein and Lukas Vischer, eds., *The Reformed Family Worldwide* (Grand Rapids: Eerdmans, 1999), 294–334.

38. Phillip Connor, "6 Facts about South Korea's Growing Christian Population," Pew ResearchCenter, available at http://tinyurl.com/ydc7aok9.

CHINA

Cut off and under persecution for forty years, the Church in China became fully indigenous and has experienced explosive growth.[39] The "Chinese-ness" of the Church is visible, and they no longer have foreign connections. In parts of China where Christians were few during the missionary era, today tens of thousands of Christians are reported.[40] While the visible church disappeared under the Cultural Revolution, the Christian faith survived in small house group meetings. House churches had also been characteristic of earlier, pre-revolutionary indigenous movements such as the True Jesus Church, the Little Flock, the Independent Church, and the Jesus Family. Under repression, the house churches proved flexible and became the training ground for an emerging lay leadership of the indigenous Chinese Church.[41]

AFRICA

Nowhere has the contextual initiative been more evident than in Africa with its abundance of African Instituted Churches (AICs). Indigenous Christianity thrives in Africa, with thousands of distinctly African denominations.[42] A recent source mentions "about 15,000 different AICs in sub-Saharan Africa as a whole."[43] Previously viewed as sub-Christian sects or cults, the African Instituted Churches today are understood as authentic Christian churches initiated by Africans and having African characteristics.[44] Aspects of an African worldview, ignored by Western theology, are taken seriously in the AICs.[45]

---

39. David Aikman, *Jesus in Beijing: How Christianity Is Transforming China and Changing the Global Balance of Power* (Washington, DC: Regnery Publishing, 2003). Also Jean-Pierre Charbonnier, *Christians in China: AD 600 to 2000* (San Francisco: Ignatius Press, 2007).

40. David H. Adeney, *China: The Church's Long March* (Eastbourne, UK: MARC, 1988).

41. Alex Jürgen Thumm, "Christianity's Sleeping Giant: Churches—Both Legal and Illegal—Are Booming in China," available at http://tinyurl.com/ycpq293z.

42. David Barrett, *Schism and Renewal in Africa* (Nairobi: Oxford University Press, 1968).

43. Henning Wrogemann, *Intercultural Hermeneutics*, Intercultural Theology vol. 1 (Downers Grove, IL: IVP Academic, 2016), 175.

44. Harold W. Turner, *History of an African Independent Church: The Church of the Lord (Aladura)* (Oxford: Clarendon Press, 1967).

45. John S. Pobee and Gabriel Ositelu II, *African Initiatives in Christianity: The Growth Gifts and Diversities of Indigenous African Churches; A Challenge to the Ecumenical Movement* (Geneva: World Council of Churches, 1998).

Creed is less important than curing.[46] Causation must be considered. The ancestors, spirits and divinities, dreams and visions, prophecy and divination are taken seriously.[47] African healing traditions, an oral liturgy, African music and dance, a narrative theology, and the inclusion of dreams and visions are important elements in African Christianity found also in modern Pentecostalism.

The African expression is significant in light of the world-wide emergence of Pentecostalism as the twenty-first century's dominant expression of Protestant Christianity. African Pentecostalism has its own distinctive character much more in common with the rest of the developing world than with the West, not least in its appeal to the disadvantaged and underprivileged. Pentecostal spirituality has proven itself culturally adaptable and has incarnated itself into an African expression of Christianity.[48]

Pentecostalism is one type of indigenous Christianity. But not all indigenous Christian expressions are Pentecostal. The distinctive African experience finds parallels in Asia and Latin America.

LATIN AMERICA

Until recently the Latin American phenomenon was largely unrecognised but consists of fully indigenous churches developed exclusively with Latin American leadership and funds, an autochthonous movement primarily among the poor.[49] In the Roman Catholic context the base ecclesial communities are an indigenous Christian movement independent from church and state, not officially separated from the Catholic Church, often functioning without priests, and essentially self-governing.[50] Among the Protestants, the "Grass-Roots" churches that are the outcome of Latin American revival movements are more indigenous in ministry and style and are experiencing spontaneous growth among the urban poor. Pentecostal Churches are the fastest growing.

The Pentecostals are more contextual than other churches and

---

46. Robert C. Mitchell, "Christian Healing," in *African Independent Church Movements*, ed. Victor E. W. Hayward (London: Edinburgh House Press, 1997).

47. G. C. Oosthuizen, *Afro-Christian Religions* (Leiden: E.J. Brill, 1979).

48. G. C. Oosthuizen, *Pentecostal Penetration into the Indian Community in South Africa* (Durban, 1975).

49. Emilio Antonio Nuñez C. and William David Taylor, *Crisis and Hope in Latin America* (Pasadena, CA: William Carey Library, 1996).

50. Ibid., 286–87.

actualize the genius and ideals of Protestantism among the marginalised. In Central America, emphasis on the Holy Spirit is an important distinction of indigeneity in Pentecostal and other Evangelical Churches. These "Grass-Roots" churches[51] are spontaneous Christian fellowships found in every Latin American country, churches arising through local initiative independent of traditional mission structures. Considerable diversity exists, but there is one common feature: they are Latino/a incarnations of the Gospel of Christ.[52]

NORTH AMERICA

Indigenous expressions can be found in every region of the world where Christianity has taken firm root, including North America. The Baptist, Methodist and Pentecostal denominations of North America are examples of culturally assimilated Churches of the Great Tradition, whereas Jehovah's Witnesses, Christian Science and the Latter Day Saints are prime species of heretical fringe sects of the Little Tradition. The Seventh Day Adventists are an interesting case of a quasi-marginal American Church moving into the mainstream of the Christian tradition.

In North America the Great Tradition consists of Baptists, Mennonites, and Methodists, as well as Catholics, Lutherans, and Presbyterians. Pentecostals who originated in North America were looked upon as sectarian, but have entered the mainstream of church life in North America and are in process of doing so in South America and other regions of the world, including Asia. As Andrew Walls has remarked, the greatest missionary achievement of the nineteenth century was the Christianizing of the United States.[53]

CONCLUSION: CHRISTIAN WITNESS

Indigenous Christianity has proven adaptable and resilient. Christian witness involves empowerment activities among slum dwellers and

---

51. M. Berg and P. Pretiz, *Spontaneous Combustion: Grass-Roots Christianity, Latin American Style* (Pasadena, CA: William Carey Library, 1996).

52. William R. Read, Victor M. Monterroso and Harmon A. Johnson, *Latin American Church Growth* (Grand Rapids: Eerdmans, 1969).

53. Andrew Walls, "The American Dimension in the History of the Mission Movement," in *Earthen Vessels: American Evangelicals and Foreign Missions, 1880–1980*, ed. Joel A. Carpenter and Wilbert R. Shenk (Grand Rapids: Eerdmans, 1990).

street children, liberation of backward communities and tribals, encouragement of women's movements and Christ Bhaktas, use of indigenous communication media, employment of local proverbs and sayings, as well as the more traditional roles of community development, Bible translation, village schools, and church planting.

Churches of indigenous origins (CIOs) tend to be "grass-roots" expressions of a popular Christianity of the "Little Tradition." Indigenous Christianity is an authentic signature of faith wherever the gospel has taken root. From Jerusalem outward the gospel has continued to translate itself into local cultures. The phenomenon was true of what are now the established Christian traditions of America and Europe and is true as well of the emerging Christianity of Asia, Africa, Latin America and the Pacific region.

But why study the emerging new movements? To a consideration of this intriguing question we turn next.

SOURCES FOR FURTHER REFERENCE

Abrams, Minnie F. *The Baptism of the Holy Ghost & Fire*. Kedgaon, India: Pandita Ramabai Mukti Mission, 1999 (1906).

Adeney, David H. *China: The Church's Long March*. Eastbourne, UK: MARC, 1985.

Aikman, David. *Jesus in Beijing: How Christianity Is Transforming China*. Washington: Regnery Publishing, 2003.

Anderson, Allan, and W. Hollenweger, eds. *Pentecostals after a Century: Global Perspectives on a Movement in Transition*. Sheffield, UK: Sheffield Academic Press, 1999.

Berg M., and P. Pretiz. *Spontaneous Combustion: Grass-Roots Christianity, Latin American Style*. Pasadena, CA: William Carey Library, 1996.

Carpenter, Joel A., and Wilbert R. Shenk, eds. *Earthen Vessels: American Evangelicals and Foreign Missions, 1880–1980*. Grand Rapids: Eerdmans, 1990.

Hedlund, Roger E. "Emerging Indigenous Christianity in India and Asia (Nineteenth and Twentieth Centuries)." In *Transkontinentale Beziehungen in der Geschichte des Ausereuropäischen Christentums/ Transcontinental Links in the History of Non-Western Christianity*, edited by Klaus Koschorke. Wiesbaden, Germany: Harrassowiz Verlag, 2002.

———. *Quest for Identity: India's Churches of Indigenous Origin*. Delhi: ISPCK, 2000.

Hedlund, Roger E., ed. *Christianity Is Indian*. Delhi: ISPCK, 2004 (2000).

Lambert, Tony. *The Resurrection of the Chinese Church*. London: Hodder & Stoughton, 1991.

Mullins, M. R. *Christianity Made in Japan: A Study of Indigenous Movements*. Honolulu: University of Hawaii Press, 1998.

Mundadan, M. *History of Christianity in India*. Vol. 1. Bangalore: Church History Association of India, 1989.

Perry, C. *A Biographical History of the Church in Nepal*. Wheaton, IL: Wheaton Graduate School, 1989.

———. *Nepali around the World*. Kathmandu: Ekta Books, 1997.

Raj, Selva J., and Corinne G. Dempsey, eds. *Popular Christianity in India: Riting between the Lines*. Albany: State University of New York Press, 2002.

Rooney, J. *Shadows in the Dark*. Rawalpindi, Pakistan: Christian Study Centre, 1984.

Sanneh, L. *Translating the Message*. Maryknoll, NY: Orbis Books, 1991.

Somaratna, G. P. V. *Origins of the Pentecostal Mission in Sri Lanka*. Nugegoda, Sri Lanka: Margaya Fellowship, 1996.

Tennent, T. C. *Building Christianity on Indian Foundations*. Delhi: ISPCK, 2000.

Wrogemann, Henning. *Intercultural Hermeneutics*. Intercultural Theology, Vol. 1. Downers Grove, IL: IVP Academic, 2016.

9.

Why Study New Movements?

The Importance of India's New Christian Movements

INTRODUCTION

History has known numbers of new religious movements.[1] Not infrequently such groups have been branded as cults (false and dangerous) or as sects (heretical or deviant). As Rodney Stark states it, however, all major world religions began in obscurity and might have been considered cults.[2] From a Christian perspective, for example, the religion of Muhammad might well have been regarded a Christian deviation or sect. More commonly it is marginal Christian groups such as Christian Science, Jehovah's Witnesses and Mormons (the Church of Jesus Christ of Latter Day Saints) which are classed as cults.[3] Historically Christianity has had its share of disputes and divisions caused by theological differences, others due to movements of

---

1. Originally published as appendix 1 by Roger E. Hedlund in *The New Wine-Skins: The Story of the Indigenous Missions in Coastal Andhra Pradesh, India*, by P. Solomon Raj (Delhi: ISPCK, 2003), 141–62.

2. "Foreword" by Rodney Stark in *New Religions as Global Cultures: Making the Human Sacred*, by Irving Hexham and Karla Poewe (Boulder, CO: Westview Press, 1997), ix.

3. A considerable anti-cult literature has accummulated, e.g., Charles Braden, *These Also Believe: A Study of Modern American Cults and Minority Religious Movements* (New York: Macmillan Co., 1949), Elmer T. Clark, *The Small Sects in America* (New York: Abingdon-Cokesbury Press, 1949); Gordon Lewis, *Confronting the Cults* (Phillipsburg, NJ: P & R, 1966); Walter Martin, *The Kingdom of the Cults* (Minneapolis: Bethany, 2003); William Petersen, *Those Curious New Cults* (New Canaan, CT: Keats, 1982); and J. K. van Baalen, *The Chaos of Cults* (Grand Rapids: Eerdmans, 1962).

social, political or nationalist protest[4]—not unlike similar currents in India today.

NEW RELIGIOUS MOVEMENTS

Western Christians in recent decades have been confronted by an array of previously unknown religious groups from Asia,[5] which are looked upon as new cults, counter-culture fringe groups, alternative religions or new religious movements. Some scholars include new Christian groups among these movements.[6] Wilbert Shenk in fact uses the term "New Religious Movements" (NRMs) to designate the kind of independent-indigenous "small churches" which are part of the Christian movement in Andhra Pradesh today.[7] To classify these groups as "cults" is pejorative and demeaning. To view them as New Religious Movements is both cordial and promising for dialogue. Shenk shows the connectedness of the NRMs to the missionary movement with which they appear in tension. They combine Christian elements with forms and ideas from the traditional religion and thus create a new religious entity.[8]

It may be questioned, however, whether the Andhra groups under investigation really constitute New Religious Movements so much as distinctive renewal movements within Christianity. Do the new groups perpetuate pre-Christian practices and beliefs which overshadow or contradict Christian identity? Do they combine ideas borrowed from outside the Christian tradition to such an extent that they embody a new vision in contradistinction to that of Christianity? That might appear to have been the case with Mormonism (LDS) in North America. But can it be said of Andhra Pradesh groups such as the Bible Mission of Devadas? Mormonism might be considered a new religious movement which was founded upon a new mythology, the revelations of Joseph Smith and his Scriptures.[9] The

---

4. See A. H. M. Jones, *Were Ancient Heresies Disguised Social Movements?* (Fortress Press, Philadelphia, 1966).
5. TM, ISKON, Rajnish and numerous gurus from India as well as the "Moonies" from Korea among others.
6. John A. Saliba, *Understanding New Religious Movements* (Grand Rapids: Eerdmans, 1995), 21.
7. Wilbert R. Shenk, *Changing Frontiers of Mission* (Maryknoll, NY: Orbis, 1999).
8. Ibid., 59–60.
9. Hexham and Poewe, *New Religions as Global Cultures*, 153.

Seventh Day Adventist Church, by way of contrast, growing out of the prophetic writings of Ellen White, did not part company with historic Christianity but is viewed rather as a restoration movement, or a deviant Christian denomination, or as Evangelical Christianity with some distinctives or peculiarities—according to one's preference or prejudice!

The new churches in Andhra Pradesh, it seems to me, are best seen as authentic Christian attempts to respond to the local worldview and culture by addressing weaknesses in the Christian traditions inherited from Western missionaries, filling gaps, meeting needs.

These new groups should be studied because they are new and because they are Christian. Arising "from the soil," they are both indigenous and spontaneously contextual. Sharing the worldview of the people, they express a theology of the people. Their experience knows nothing of the questions faced by Luther and Calvin in the sixteenth century, nor those of Geneva and Rome today. Issues faced in the villages and towns of Andhra are concerned with everyday problems: the need for security and human dignity, the problems of poverty and sickness, food and water scarcity. Theirs is a spiritual realm of good and evil spirits, gods and goddesses, demons and unstabilising influences—issues not addressed in theology textbooks. Yet these are the real experiences of the people for which they are seeking satisfactory solutions.[10]

The theology of the new movements is found not in the textbook and lecture hall, but in the faith experience of the people and is expressed in story and song. The lyrical theology of the Telugu hymnal has been commented upon by scholars.[11] Some of the founders of new church movements in Andhra, such as Devadas, were song writers. The hymn book of the Bible Mission contains 120 hymns by Devadas, sixteen of them incorporated into the Telugu hymnal used by churches of all denominations.[12] Study of new movements will require evaluation of the lyrical theology and the narrative theology found in songs and sermons.

---

10. Paul Hiebert found that much of village religion in South India had little to do with Hinduism but focused on local spirits residing in trees, rivers, rocks and hills. New converts struggled with questions of spirits, magic, divination and ancestors for which the Great Tradition Christian missionaries lacked answers. See Paul G. Hiebert, R. Daniel Shaw, and Tite Tiénou, *Understanding Folk Religion: A Christian Response to Popular Beliefs and Practices* (Grand Rapids: Baker Books, 1999), 9.

11. R. R. Sundara Rao, *Bhakti Theology in the Telugu Hymnal* (Madras, India: CLS, 1983).

12. P. Solomon Raj, *A Christian Folk-Religion in India* (Frankfurt: Lang, 1986), 164.

It is not surprising that many of the new small churches of Andhra are considered Pentecostal. They share a narrative (story) approach characteristic of Pentecostal theology in other parts of the world.[13] Pentecostal theology is said to be a theology of the Book of Acts, which is essentially narrative theology. Neglect of the Holy Spirit in traditional Christianity along with a failure to provide a biblical worldview regarding the spirit world are also factors leading to new independent movements of Pentecostal type in India as in other parts of the world.[14]

LITTLE TRADITION CHRISTIANITY

The "Small Indigenous Missions" which are the focus of the present study belong to the so-called Little Tradition[15] of Indian Christianity. The Little Tradition represents the practices and beliefs of Christian adherents which may be at variance with the dogmas and rituals of recognized Great Tradition Christianity. Churches of the Little Tradition may be looked upon as Christian expressions of popular folk religion, an equation which, can be questioned. In India the Little Tradition consists of lesser-known churches and recent new movements of Indian origin in contrast to the historic denominations and institutions constituting the Great Tradition in Indian Christianity.

The history of Christianity generally is written from the standpoint of the Great Tradition. Usually it is the story of Western Christianity, whereas the history of Christianity in the East is neglected and not

---

13. See Japie LaPoorta's study of the role of narrative theology in Pentecostalism in "Unity or Division: A Case Study of the Apostolic Faith Mission of South Africa," in *The Globalization of Pentecostalism: A Religion Made to Travel,* ed. Murray W. Dempster, Byron D. Klaus, and Douglas Petersen (Oxford: Regnum, 1999), 151–69.

14. Paul A. Pomerville, *The Third Force in Missions* (Peabody, MA: Hendrickson, 1985), 74, 75.

15. "Little Tradition" is a term coined by Robert Redfield and applied to India by Milton Singer and cultural anthropologists at the University of Chicago. See Robert Redfield, *Peasant Society and Culture* (Chicago: University of Chicago Press, 1967), and Milton Singer, *When a Great Tradition Modernizes: An Anthropological Approach to Indian Civilization* (New York: Praeger Publishers, 1972). Redfield states, "In a civilization there is a great tradition of the reflective few, and there is a little tradition of the largely unreflective many." The two traditions intersect and are interdependent. One is the tradition of the philosopher, the other that of the little people. One is literary, the other oral. "Great and little tradition can be thought of as two currents of thought and action, distinguishable, yet ever flowing into and out of each other" (Redfield, *Peasant Society and Culture,* 41–43).

well known.[16] Seldom is it written from the underside.[17] Yet the greatest growth of the Church today is taking place in the East and the South, in countries and peoples of Africa, Latin America, and Asia, frequently among poor and disenfranchised, marginalised populations. "The emergence of independent Churches around the world expressing indigenous forms of Christianity is undermining the equation of Christianity with Western culture."[18] India is no exception.[19] Asian incarnations of the gospel are embodied in various indigenous movements of the sub-continent including Nepal where an indigenous church has emerged within the past fifty years through Nepali initiative despite persecution and repression.[20] India itself has seen numerous attempted incarnations of the Christian faith, some highly successful, others less so. Therefore the study of new religious movements of Christian origins is timely and promising.

A majority of India's Christians are from the oppressed, the products of Tribal and Dalit conversion movements.[21] Conversion movements in India not infrequently have been movements of social protest, the response of Dalits and the poor to the call to a counter-culture, movements of affirmation in quest of dignity and equality. Numerous "Messianic" movements among tribal and other subaltern communities are examples of social protest movements which did not become explicitly Christian.[22] In India today, however, in North as well as South, a number of subaltern movements are taking place in which oppressed peoples are finding dignity in a new identity as disciples of Jesus Christ. For many, upward mobility resulted from

16. Samuel Hugh Moffett, *A History of Christianity in Asia*, vol.1 *Beginnings to 1500*, 2nd ed. (Maryknoll, NY: Orbis Books, 1998), xiii.
17. Roger E. Hedlund, "Christian History from the Under Side: Indian Instituted Churches & Indigenous Christianity, keynote address, Conference on Subaltern Perspectives on Seminary Training, Centre for Dalit Solidarity, Dharmaram College, Bangalore, October 23, 1998.
18. Paul G. Hiebert, "Missiological Education for a Global Era," in *Missiological Education for the 21st Century*, ed. J. Dudley Woodberry, Charles Van Engen, and Edgar J. Elliston (Maryknoll, NY: Orbis Books, 1996), 36.
19. Roger E. Hedlund, "Indian Instituted Churches: Indigenous Christianity Indian Style," *Mission Studies* 16, no. 1 (1999): 26–41.
20. Ramesh Khatry, "The Church in Nepal," in *Church in Asia Today: Challenges and Opportunities*, ed. Saphir Athyal (Singapore: Asian Lausanne Committee for World Evangelization, 1996); Cindy Perry, *A Biographical History of the Church in Nepal* (Wheaton, IL: Wheaton Graduate School, 1989); Jan Minderhoud, "The Christian Presence in Nepal Before 1951," *Indian Church History Review* 24 (December 2, 1990): 144–64.
21. Estimates vary from perhaps 70 percent to as much as 80–90 percent.
22. Stephen Fuchs, *Rebellious Prophets: A Study of Messianic Movements in Indian Religions* (New York: Asia Publishing House), 1965.

conversion by which the downtrodden discovered new dignity and hope.[23] Not all conversions are among the oppressed, of course, nor are all the emerging churches of indigenous origins to be so classed, but nevertheless subaltern categories are prominent in the broad sweep of diversity among India's indigenous Christian movements.

PROMINENCE AND NEGLECT

Reasons to study the Lesser Tradition are many. These new churches are important. They exist, and they represent a contemporary "grassroots" development. To some extent they are becoming prominent. They deserve to be known and understood. Are they any less Christian than the better-known churches of the Great Tradition? Is popular Christianity any less biblical in its faith and practices? Are the new small churches to be dismissed as heretical cults and schismatic sects? Or are they, in fact, distinctly Indian expressions of orthodox Christian faith? That, it appears is a strong possibility. If for no other reason than their growth and spread, these new developments are important to our understanding of contemporary Christianity.

Yet they are neglected. For the most part the new small hcurches have been bypassed in the study of Christianity in India. Church history to a large extent is written in terms of Western Christianity. The multi-volume History of Christianity in India project of the Church History Association of India (CHAI) seeks to compensate this lacuna. Many churches of the Little Tradition represent an oral culture, however, which lacks the literary sources used by historiographers. It is necessary therefore to begin to collect and record the stories of the new indigenous bodies, their founders and leaders and adherents.

WORLD PHENOMENA

Indigenous Christianity is a world phenomenon.[24] Where it has taken root, the gospel has produced a wide diversity of expressions arising from the local culture. Hitherto scarcely noted in South Asia, numer-

---

23. Roger E. Hedlund, "Indian Christians of Indigenous Origins and Their Solidarity with Original Groups," *Journal of Dharma* 16, no. 1 (1999): 13–27.

24. The phenomenon is documented with examples from around the world in chapter 2 of my *Quest for Identity: India's Churches of Indigenous Origin, the "Little Tradition" in Indian Christianity* (Delhi: ISPCK, 2000).

ous studies have documented the development in other regions. Most notable is that of Africa which has given rise to numerous university theses, books and an ongoing spate of articles appearing in *Missionalia*,[25] published by the Southern African Missiological Society and the University of South Africa, as well as other periodicals. Previously viewed as sub-Christian sects or cults, the African Instituted Churches today are understood as authentic Christian churches initiated by Africans and having African characteristics. In like fashion, the newer Indian Indigenous Churches need to be studied, known, and understood.

Indigenous Christianity is a new field for academic research in South Asia. A few such studies have been carried out in other parts of Asia, e.g. Korea,[26] Indonesia,[27] Japan,[28] Taiwan,[29] and the Philippines.[30] But in India similar studies are rare. Solomon Raj's study of the Bible Mission of Devadas is the most notable exception.[31] In recent decades a movement around the late Subba Rao (1912–1981) attracted attention of writers (Kaj Baago, Robin Boyd, H. L. Richard). The Bakht Singh movement has been described in brief, inspirational accounts and a recent biography of the founder.[32]

Here and there mention is made of other independent movements in South India, but for the most part little is known about these

---

25. Numerous articles have appeared. See, e.g., Obed Ndeya Kealotswe, "Corporate Personality in the African Independent Churches in Southern Africa, with Special Reference to the 'Head Mountain of God Apostolic Church' in Botswana," *Missionalia* 27, no. 3 (November 1999): 299–312; Ulrich van der Heyden, "The Origins and Political-Religious Functions of an Independent Church: The Lutheran Ba-Pedi Church in the Nineteenth Century," *Missionalia* 27, no. 3 (November 1999): 377–89; Adrian Chatfield, "African Independency in the Caribbean, The Case of the Spiritual Baptists," *Missionalia* 26, no. 1 (April 1998): 94–115; and others.

26. Hong Young-gi, "The Backgrounds and Characteristics of the Charismatic Megachurches in Korea," *Asian Journal of Pentecostal Studies* 3, no. 1 (January 2000): 99–118.

27. Chris Sugden, *Seeking the Asian Face of Jesus* (Oxford: Regnum Books, 1997).

28. Mark R. Mullins, *Christianity Made in Japan: A Study of Indigenous Movements* (Honolulu: University of Hawai'i Press, 1998).

29. Allen J. Swanson, *Taiwan: Mainline vs. Independent Church Growth: A Study in Contrasts* (Pasadena, CA: William Carey Library, 1970).

30. A. Leonard Tuggy, *Iglesia Ni Cristo: A Study in Independent Church Dynamics* (Quezon City, Philippines: Conservative Baptist Publishing, 1976).

31. P. Solomon Raj, *A Christian Folk-Religion in India* (Frankfurt: Peter Lang, 1986).

32. T. E. Koshy, *Brother Bakht Singh of India: An Account of 20th Century Apostolic Revival* (Secunderabad, India: OM Books, 2003).

movements. The Indigenous Christianity Series[33] is an effort to disseminate findings and encourage further research.

NEW INSIGHT

Study of new churches and movements is important because of the fresh insights to be gained, including folk movements within historic mainline Churches. For example, popular (folk) Catholicism[34] has been studied extensively in Latin America, but less so in Africa and Asia. In South India the Mukkuvar Catholics incorporate elements of popular Hinduism while maintaining a Catholic affiliation which serves to preserve a distinct community identity.

> Their religion centers on illness, misfortune, and augmenting the fish catch.... The Catholic rituals are transformed to suit the Mukkuvar's conception of spirits and demonic deities and accustomed ways of relating to them.... In times of illness, a blessing is sought from the priest. Prolonged illness is treated with a long stay at a shrine or the village church. The priest is called to bless the fishing gear, and when there is a lean season for fishing the beach is blessed with a procession of the statue of St. Anthony.[35]

These and other cases reveal that popular Catholicism grapples with divination, witchcraft, ancestor veneration, spiritual power and protection, exorcism and healing but also with developmental issues, poverty and the status of the marginalised. Popular Catholicism is alive and flourishing.[36] In Andhra Pradesh an interesting example of Catholic "folk" religion was observed at Karunapuram near Warangal.[37] Here every Saturday a crowd of five thousand (5,000) women and men from all religions gather under one shelter at the Krista Jyothi Ashram. Numerous spiritual and physical healings are reported at this weekly retreat. Participants have been analyzed as 75 percent

---

33. The Indigenous Christianity Series, begun in 2000, is published by ISPCK on behalf of the Mylapore Institute for Indigenous Studies.

34. Thomas Barnat and Jean-Paul Wiest, eds. *Popular Catholicism in a World Church: Seven Case Studies in Inculturation* (Maryknoll, NY: Orbis Books, 1999).

35. Francis Jayapathy, "Southern India: Mukkuvar Catholicism," in Barnat and Wiest, *Popular Catholicism in a World Church*, 194.

36. Michael Amaladoss, "Toward a New Ecumenism,"in Barnat and Wiest, *Popular Catholicism in a World Church*, 272.

37. This indigenous gathering was observed by the writer during a visit on Saturday, September 4, 1999.

Hindus, 20 percent Catholic and Protestant Christians, and 5 percent Muslims and others. At these gatherings "non-Christians are evangelized and Christians re-evangelized."[38] During five and a half years approximately 800,000 persons have attended the ecumenical preaching and healing services conducted by a charismatic Catholic layman under the patronage of the Catholic Church.

At the Divine Word Centre, Medak, near Hyderabad, another type of Catholic indigeneity is found. Here Charismatic retreats have brought a new experience of the Word of God in the Roman Catholic Church. According to the Director, people hungry for the Word of God are drawn into a new spiritual experience. Many who come for healing are attracted to the Word of God, then are referred back to local parishes for baptism.[39]

Details differ, but the accommodation of local culture in popular Catholicism and its cordial relationship with official Catholicism are significant insights to be gained from the study of such movements. In India a number of Catholic scholars have shown interest in the quest for an authentic Indian Christian identity.[40] Religious manifestations such as these described above are popular expressions of cultural authenticity.

PENTECOSTAL EXPLOSION

It is important to study the new movements because they represent a major development in World Christianity. Within a century, from humble origins at Azusa Street in Los Angeles in 1906, the modern Pentecostal movement has grown to become a major global Christian tradition, second in number only to the Roman Catholics.[41] Today a quarter of all full-time Christian workers worldwide are Pentecostal-Charismatics.[42] Pentecostalism, from its beginning, has been a missionary religion.[43]

---

38. Report by Fr. D. Joseph, Director, Kristu Jyothi Ashram, August 27, 1999.
39. According to Fr. Christuraj James, SVD, interviewed at the Centre on April 4, 2000.
40. See, for example, A. M. Mundadan, *Indian Christians Search for Identity and Struggle for Autonomy* (Bangalore, India: Dharmaram Publications, 1984).
41. Russell P. Spittler, "Foreword," in *The Globalization of Pentecostalism*, ed. Murray W. Dempster, Byron D. Klaus, and Douglas Petersen (Oxford: Regnum Books, 1999).
42. Vinson Synan, *The Spirit Said "Grow": The Astounding Worldwide Expansion of Pentecostal and Charismatic Churches* (Monrovia, CA: MARC World Vision, 1992), 13.
43. This point is documented in several recent studies. See, for example, L. Grant McClung, ed., *Azusa Street and beyond: Pentecostal Missions and Church Growth in the Twentieth Century*

It is not surprising, then, that Pentecostal missionaries appeared in India almost immediately following the Azusa Street experience. Prior to that, however, Pentecostal manifestations were reported in India. "The outpouring of the Holy Spirit at the Mukti Mission of Pandita Ramabai in Pune, India, in June 1905 is normally regarded as the origin of the Pentecostal revival in South Asia."[44] An earlier manifestation of tongues and other charismatic gifts had been reported in 1860 at Tirunelveli in Tamil Nadu.[45] Revivals have been recorded in North East India from as early as 1897. Manifestations such as unison dancing, singing and praying were noted in the 1905 revival, whereas tongues, healing and prophecy were more recent phenomena,[46] associated with the Mizo so-called high revival of 1935.[47]

Today Pentecostal and other independent movements comprise the fastest growing sectors of the Church in several areas of India.[48] Hollenweger, who notes the Black oral roots of the modern Pentecostal movement, observes that it is strongest in areas of the world where oral communication predominates.[49]

The first major scholarly study of South Indian Pentecostalism[50]

(South Plainfield, NJ: Bridge Publishing, 1986); Vinson Synan, *The Holiness-Pentecostal Tradition: Charismatic Movements in the Twentieth Century* (Grand Rapids: Eerdmans, 1997); Gary B. McGee, *"This Gospel Shall Be Preached": A History and Theology of Assemblies of God Foreign Mission to 1959* (Springfield, MO: Gospel Publishing House, 1986); Murray A. Dempster, Byron D. Klaus, and Douglas Petersen, eds., *Called and Empowered: Global Mission in Pentecostal Perspective* (Peabody, MA: Hendrickson Publishers, 1991); Murray A. Dempster, Byron D. Klaus, and Douglas Petersen, eds., *Globalization of Pentecostalism: A Religion Made To Travel* (Oxford: Regnum, 1999).

44. Ivan Satyavrata, "Contextual Perspectives on Pentecostalism as a Global Culture: A South Asian View," in *The Globalization of Pentecostalism*, ed. Murray W. Dempster, Byron D. Klaus, and Douglas Petersen (Oxford: Regnum, 1999), 204. The phenomena are described by Miss Minnie F. Abrams who was present at Kedgaon at the time in a little book, *The Baptism of the Holy Ghost & Fire* (Kedgaon, India: Pandita Ramabai Mukti Mission, 1999 reprint).

45. Satyavrata, "Contextual Perspectives on Pentecostalism," 205. J. Edwin Orr documents the phenomena at Tirunelveli as well as at Mukti in *Evangelical Awakenings in Southern Asia* (Minneapolis: Bethany, 1975), 59–60 and 144–45; also Orr, *Evangelical Awakenings in India* (New Delhi: MSS, 1970), 33, 110–11.

46. T. Nongsiej, "Revival Movement in Khasi-Jaintia Hills," in *Churches of Indigenous Origins in Northeast India*, ed. O. L. Snaitang (Delhi: ISPCK, 2000), 29, 36.

47. C. L. Hminga, *The Life and Witness of the Church in Mizoram* (Serkawn, Lunglei, India: Baptist Church of Mizoram, 1987), 161–62.

48. See, for example, findings in fifteen cities of Tamil Nadu, in Roger E. Hedlund, *Evangelization & Church Growth Issues: Issues from the Asian Context* (Madras, India: Church Growth Research Centre, 1992), 202–11.

49. Walter J. Hollenweger, *Pentecostalism: Origins and Developments Worldwide* (Peabody, MA: Hendrickson Publishers, 1997), 20.

50. This is a definitive work by the German scholar Michael Bergunder of Halle University, *Die Südindische Pfingstbewegung im 20. Jahrhundert* (Frankfurt: Peter Lang, 1999). An English

touches the history of all known Pentecostal bodies in South India including those of indigenous origins as well as those of international (foreign missionary) extraction. Bergunder lists a total of seventy-one Pentecostal bodies in the four southern states. Andhra Pradesh has fourteen Pentecostal denominations, of which twelve appear to be indigenous in origin. In Karnataka, out of seven Pentecostal groups, six might be classed as indigenous in origin. In Kerala eleven out of fifteen Pentecostal bodies listed appear to be of indigenous origins. Tamil Nadu has the greatest number with thirty-three Pentecostal bodies, of which twenty-seven appear to be of indigenous origin.This is not an exhaustive listing of South Indian Pentecostals. New groups frequently appear, other groups are overlooked inadvertently by researchers and compilers. A similar investigation in North India would reveal parallel developments of new indigenous Pentecostal and Charismatic movements in Mumbai, in Punjab, and in Delhi as well as in Kolkata and West Bengal.

A common thread running through each of these Pentecostal churches is a conscious expression of their Indian identity and character. Their Pentecostal faith binds them to fellow-believers worldwide. Yet their life and witness at home and in the diaspora are indelibly marked by an Indian identity and character. Their expression of Indian Christian nationalism deserves publication.

QUESTIONS OF IDENTITY

India has numerous subaltern movements, Pentecostal as well as non-Pentecostal, which require study. Ecumenical Great Tradition Christianity frequently and pejoratively has tended to label such Little Tradition movements as sects, whereas they are better recognized as revival or renewal movements within the larger Christian movement. Documentation is urgent because of the oral traditions and theology of many.[51]

These Small Church Movements, or Indian Indigenous Churches, or whatever name we give them, can be classified according to three or more types. One distinct category focuses on healing (e.g., the movement around the late Subba Rao and the Bible Mission

translation appeared as *The South Indian Pentecostal Movement in the Twentieth Century* (Grand Rapids: Eerdmans, 2008).

51. P. B. Thomas, "Pentecostal Ecclesiology, Promises and Problems," *Jeevadhara: A Journal of Christian Interpretation* (July 1990): 286–301.

of Fr. Devadas). Brethren or "Baptistic" groups would include the movement around Bro. Bakht Singh, numerous local independent assemblies, and several small break-away denominations in coastal Andhra Pradesh. An example of a "Holiness" movement is the Laymen's Evangelical Fellowship (LEF). But the largest cluster would be numerous indigenous South Indian Pentecostal fellowships, denominations and organizations. In Tamil Nadu some of them are an outgrowth of the more radical Ceylon Pentecostal Mission, others in Kerala and Andhra have their roots in the Indian Pentecostal Church. These and other indigenous groups deserve careful observation and documentation. The fledgling Mylapore Institute for Indigenous Studies seeks to encourage serious academic research in the Indian context similar to that undertaken by Harold Turner at the Centre for New Religious Movements at Selly Oak in UK, which documented independent churches throughout the world.[52]

Questions have been raised concerning the authenticity of the new movements. This bears investigation. Are the new Small Church Movements fully Christian? Are they syncretic? Schismatic? Heretical? Questioners tend to be judgmental, especially where new groups are perceived as "break-away" deviations from the mainstream. Biases aside, some evaluation in light of the norms of historical Christianity may prove helpful. An example from the Philippines serves to illustrate. A Pentecostal study of an indigenous cult revealed an instance of syncretism in which traditional animistic religious ideas and practices were combined with Pentecostal beliefs. Visionary experiences took the place of Bible study and preaching resulting in unbiblical beliefs and practices.[53] Study of new movements in India likewise may prove enlightening. To what extent are pre-Christian concepts and practices perpetuated among the new independent churches? Careful investigation also may alert indigenous leaders against non-indigenous heresies brought to India by popular preachers from the West.[54] Careful investigation may prove beneficial.

---

52. See Harold W. Turner, *Bibliography of New Religious Movements in Primal Societies*, vol. 4, *Europe and Asia* (Boston: G.K. Hall, 1991).

53. Julie Ma, "Santuala: A Case of Pentecostal Syncretism," *Asian Journal of Pentecostal Studies* 3, no. 1 (2000): 61–82.

54. See, for example, "Healing and Kenneth Hagin," by Keith Warrington, *Asian Journal of Pentecostal Studies* 3, no. 1 (2000): 119–38.

DOCUMENTATION

Newer groups have important stories to tell before they are forgotten. One thinks, for instance, of the extensive movement related to the ministry of the late Bro. Bakht Singh (1903–2000). Apart from short devotional accounts, little or no history had been written until recently. Then in 2008 an authorized biography was published in India.[55] Yet the Assemblies associated with Bro. Bakht Singh view themselves as the original Indigenous churches in India.[56]

Today assemblies are found in many parts of India from Kalimpong to Kanyakumari, and also in Pakistan, but especially in Andhra Pradesh. The main centre is in Hyderabad at Hebron which is the headquarter of the Indigenous churches In India. The assemblies have no official hierarchical structure or paid clergy. Elders are set apart to guide the spiritual life of the local church. Annual All-India Holy Convocations have been a means of a nation-wide spread of the assemblies.[57] Worship in the assemblies is culturally indigenous, with elements derived from familiar local cultural practices. Some observers have remarked on the similarity to practices in the Gurdwaras of Punjab. Here is a distinctive North Indian cultural incarnation of the Christian faith in which biblical practices are adapted to the Indian experience. Devotional singing, testimonials, shared experiences, the congregation seated on mats on the floor with participation by all as moved by the Holy Spirit, and the central prominence of the Bible,[58] which is carefully expounded for about an hour (with translation as required): these are regular features of the assemblies gathered for Sunday worship.[59]

Already with the death of the founder a mythology has begun to develop: at his death in Hyderabad an earthquate took place, and a halo around the sun was observed at the time of his funeral. How important then to record events from the memories of those who

---

55. T. E. Koshy, *Bakht Singh of India: The Incredible Account of a Modern-Day Apostle* (Secunderabad, India: Authentic, 2008).

56. This information was offered by leaders at Hebron during my visit on September 6, 1999. That the movement is officially registered as the "Indigenous Churches in India," is not generally known.

57. R. R. Rajamani, *Monsoon Daybreak* (Bombay: GLS, 1971).

58. Members carry their Bibles to the service, participate by reading passages, and follow the exposition. This seems a significant functional substitute and Christian adaptation of the adoration of the Garanth in Sikh devotional practice.

59. As observed by the writer, services may continue for three or more hours. "It takes time to worship God," was the explanation quoted from Bro. Bakht Singh.

knew him, to document the genesis and impact of an extensive movement. Bible teaching is a hallmark of the Assemblies. The sermons of Bro. Bakht Singh remain in print and consist of simple Bible expositions.[60] This pattern is followed by other leaders.[61] Various aspects of the movement require documentation and study. Whatever weaknesses and strengths there may be, the ministry of Bro. Bakht Singh and the Assemblies is a remarkable indigenous Christian witness and a worthy subject for historiography.

Leaders of movements tend to be activists, not scholars and writers. Archives may not yet exist for many younger churches. But people can be consulted: founders, leaders, members. People who were there should be asked to tell their story. Research will entail extensive travel, visitation and interview. Where they exist, reports and records should be consulted and collected. Even oral communities have song books, hymnals, promotional literature, and cassettes. Photographs can be copied, stories and songs recorded. Archival deposits should be created. Study of indigenous organizations provides ample scope for archival projects embracing older as well as recent movements.[62] Church history cannot afford to be confined to retelling the stories of the well-known traditions of the past.

GROWTH

Christians will want to study the new small churches because they represent movement. Christianity is historical, but it need not be static or dormant. History shows that wherever Christianity spreads it introduces change, but in the very process, Christianity itself becomes changed. The new small churches of India also manifest change and development, proofs of the translatability of the gospel[63] in a plethora of contextual expressions.

---

60. See any of the 27 books of his sermons, e.g., *Behold I Will Do a New Thing* (Isa 43:19); *Come Let Us Build* (Nehemiah); *Our Inheritance* (Book of Joshua); *The Overcomers' Secret* (Studies in the Book of Daniel); *The Strong Foundation* (Heb 5:11–14; 6:1–3); *Walk Before Me* (Studies in the Life of Abraham); and others.

61. See, for example, Edwin Samuel, ed., *In the Day of Thy Power* (Madras: Jehovah-Shammah, 19830.

62. A visit to the Ramabai Mukti Mission at Kedgaon near Pune revealed an important archive being maintained by the Mission whereas there is no comparable archival deposit for the existing Marathi Churches of various denominations in the region.

63. Lamin Sanneh, *Translating the Message: The Missionary Impact on Culture*, (Maryknoll, NY: Orbis Books, 1991).

The new so-called small churches of the Little Tradition do not necessarily remain small. In Chennai, for example, the mother church of the Apostolic Christian Assembly, a notable movement of indigenous origin, attracts more than 13,000 worshipers to its Sunday morning bi-lingual service.[64]

In Kerala, the indigenous Indian Pentecostal Church of God is a major Pentecostal denomination with branches throughout India.[65] In Mumbai the New Life Fellowship is an indigenous urban movement which has grown to several thousand members found in more than 300 house churches and 500 house groups, plus 140 prayer cells and 122 composite celebration centres in rented facilities throughout the city.[66] Examples abound. Indian Christianity is incarnate in a diversity of cultures as the new movements demonstrate. Indigenous Christianity is vigorous. India in 1995 observed the twenty-fifth anniversary of the founding of the Church of North India and in 1997, celebrated the fiftieth anniversary of the merger which created the Church of South India. CSI and CNI are significant ecumenical milestones, rightly celebrated as creative achievements in indigenization. Simultaneously have arisen hundreds (perhaps thousands) of new entities arising spontaneously from the Indian soil. These diversified independent churches and structures should not be overlooked.[67] Diversity notwithstanding, Indian Christianity has in common with churches in other sections of the non-Western world "an indigenous, grassroots leadership; embeddedness in local cultures; and reliance on a vernacular Bible."[68]

As previously noted, not all indigenous groups are Pentecostal. Dana Robert calls for a judicious use of terms following careful research:

> Historians should take the lead in acknowledging the new Christianities as radically indigenous movements, not simply Pentecostalism or primal religiosity, or perhaps not even multicultural options within a global

---

64. This was observed during visits on February 13 and April 1, 2000, and confirmed in interviews with Pastor Sam Sundaram on March 30 and Pastor Kumar on April 1, 2000, at Chennai.

65. Information is from the published reports of the IPC and interview with the president, Pastor T. S. Abraham, at the IPC headquarter in Hebron, Kadambanad, Kerala.

66. Information provided by the lead pastors who were interviewed at the home of the founder, Pastor S. Joseph, at Mahim, Mumbai, on February 26, 1998.

67. See David B. Barrett and Todd M. Johnson, "Annual Statistical Table on Global Mission: 2000," *International Bulletin of Missionary Research* (January 2000): 24–25.

68. Dana Robert, "Shifting Southward: Global Christianity since 1945," *International Bulletin of Missionary Research* (April 2000): 50–58, at 56.

evangelicalism. Each movement should be studied from within its own internal logic, even as the universal nature of Christianity is recognizable in the construction of local identities. . . . As historians work within the tensions between the global and the local that characterize indigenous world Christianities today, we should recognize that each form of twenty-first century Christianity represents a synthesis of global and local elements that has its own integrity.[69]

In a carefully-researched study of African Initiated Churches, Allan Anderson distinguishes between types of Independent Churches which he designates African pentecostal (lowercase "p") in contradistinction to Classical Pentecostals.[70] Something similar might be helpful in the Indian situation.

DEMOGRAPHIC SHIFT

Why study the new movements? Because they are part of a dramatic "shift in the demography of world Christianity"[71] which today is predominantly in Asia, Africa and Latin America. Vitality today is found in these new centres. It is time to begin dialogue with these new expressions of Christianity. They are ecumenically important, not to be ignored. In Africa the AICs created their own associations and ecumenical structures.[72] In India, ecumenical and evangelical bodies should make every effort to include the frequently excluded Pentecostal and Independent churches. The church of the twenty-first century, from every indication, is destined to continued numerical growth and cultural diversity.[73] Its institutional expressions may become less prominent, its rootedness in the Indian soil increasingly evident. Indian Christianity will find greater commonality with the localized Christianity of other Asian countries, the Pacific, Africa, and Latin America, much of which is of a Pentecostal-Charismatic nature.

69. Ibid., 57.
70. Allan Anderson, *Zion and Pentecost: The Spirituality and Experience of Pentecostal and Zionist/Apostolic Churches in South Africa* (Pretoria: University of South Africa Press, 2000).
71. John S. Pobee and Gabriel Ositelu II, *African Initiatives in Christianity: The Growth, Gifts and Diversities of Indigenous Churches; A Challenge to the Ecumenical Movement* (Geneva: WCC Publications, 1998), 52.
72. Ibid., 57–59.
73. See the cover story of the November 2016 issue of *Christianity Today* devoted to "Incredible Indian Christianity" described in the subtitle as "the World's Most Colorful and Vibrant Christward Movement" in a well-researched article by Jeremy Weber, "Outpacing Persecution," with photography by Gary S. Chapman, 38–47.

Pentecostal Christianity is the second largest grouping of Christians in the world today, second only to the Roman Catholic Church. The new Christian movements increasingly may align themselves with the Pentecostals and the Catholics to the exclusion of traditional Protestants. The new independent church movements provide ample scope for creative investigation and writing. Indian church history scholars are challenged to identify and study specific new movements and to tell their story in academic publications. A few notable examples suggest what can be done. At the United Theological College, Bangalore, Sara Abraham wrote her MTh thesis on the indigenous Indian Pentecostal Church of God.[74] In 1971, Thomas Thangaraj published a well-researched article on the Hindu Christian Community based on his Serampore BD thesis.[75] Recently Fr. Felix Wilfred published an insightful analysis of how early Christian converts in Tamil Nadu came to terms with the dominant culture.[76] Each indigenous Christian movement has a story which needs to be told. New Small Church Movements are fragile. Often their stories represent the experiences of minorities and are vulnerable to distortion, exploitation and suppression. A recent article argues the strategic importance of minority historiography[77] without which our understanding of Christian history is incomplete.

This suggests an urgency to the historiographer's task in India at the present time. "Minority Christians themselves have a responsibility to help ensure their story is told in ways which do justice to their concerns and perspectives."[78] True, and in this pursuit the professional historiographer has an important role of advocacy for indigenous groups as well as intervention to preserve their narratives against attempts to expunge the record.[79] In this setting, historiography has as

74. "A Critical Evaluation of the Indian Pentecostal Church of God, Its Origin and Development in Kerala" (MTh thesis, Serampore University, March 1990).

75. M. Thomas Thangaraj, "The History and Teachings of the Hindu Christian Community Commonly Called Nattu Sabai in Tirunelveli," *Indian Church History Review* 1 (June 1971): 43–68.

76. Felix Wilfred, "Christianity in Hindu Polytheistic Structural Mould: Converts in Southern Tamilnadu Respond to an Alien Religion during 'the Vasco da Gama Epoch'," *Arch. de Sc. soc. des Rel.* 103 (July–September 1998): 67–86. This essay was reprinted by permission in *Dharma Deepika: A South Asian Journal of Missiological Research*, Issue 35, Vol. 16 (January–June 2012): 42–59.

77. John Roxborogh, "Minority Christians in the Church History Curriculum," *Evangelical Review of Theology* 24, no. 2 (April 2000): 159–66.

78. Ibid., 164.

79. Consider the implications of recent propagandistic statements by the RSS chief, Mr. K. S. Sudarshan, against India's Christians and other minorities as reported in the press: "A Dangerous

its correlary a concern for human rights as well as a passion for scholarly truth.

CONCLUSION

Solomon Raj wrote in his earlier study:

> The strength of the future church in India will not be in its hierarchical structures but it will be in its rank and file, in its ordinary members and in its humble faithful. Its leaders will be the more charismatic persons among them and not the presidents and the bishops who are elected and appointed to wield power and authority as the rulers of the world do. The future church in India will have minimal rules and adaptable constitutions and statutes to guide it, all these rules, constitutions and statutes being ever subject to the overall guidance of the Holy Spirit.[80]

The future is upon us now in a multitude of new groups. May all of us together be guided by God's Holy Spirit.

SOURCES FOR FURTHER REFERENCE

Anderson, Allan. *Zion and Pentecost: The Spirituality and Experience of Pentecostal and Zionist/Apostolic Churches in South Africa.* Pretoria: University of South Africa Press, 2000.

Bamat, Tomás, and Jean-Paul Wiest, eds. *Popular Catholicism in a World Church: Seven Case Studies in Inculturation.* Maryknoll, NY: Orbis Books, 1999.

Bergunder, Michael. *The South Indian Pentecostal Movement in the Twentieth Century.* Grand Rapids: Eerdmans, 2008.

Agenda," editorial, *The Hindu*, October 10, 2000; "Agree to a 'Swadesh' Church, says Sudarshan," *The Hindu*, October 14, 2000; "Integrate with the Culture of the Land, Sudarshan Tells Minorities," *The Hindu*, October 15, 2000; "Disturbing Aggressiveness," editorial, *The Hindu*, October 17, 2000; and a Congress rebuttal, "Let RSS Return to Mainstream," *The Hindu*, October 17, 2000.

80. P. Solomon Raj, *Christian Folk-Religion in India*, 340.

Braden, Charles S. *These Also Believe: A Study of Modern American Cults & Minority Religious Movements.* New York: Macmillan Co., 1949.

Clark, Elmer T. *The Small Sects in America.* New York: Abingdon-Cokesbury Press, 1949.

Dempster, Murray W., Byron D. Klaus, and Douglas Petersen, eds. *The Globalization of Pentecostalism: A Religion Made to Travel.* Oxford: Regnum, 1999.

Fuchs, Stephen. *Rebellious Prophets: A Study of Messianic Movements in Indian Religions.* New York: Asia Publishing House, 1965.

Hedlund, Roger E. *Evangelization & Church Growth: Issues from the Asian Context.* Madras, India: Church Growth Research Centre, 1992.

―――. *Indian Christianity: An Alternate Reading.* New Delhi: Christian World Imprints, 2016.

―――. "Indian Christians of Indigenous Origins and Their Solidarity with Original Groups." *Journal of Dharma* 24, no. 1 (1999): 13–27.

―――. "Indian Instituted Churches: Indigenous Christianity Indian Style." *Mission Studies* 16–1, no. 31 (1999): 26–41.

―――. *Quest for Identity: India's Churches of Indigenous Origin; The "Little Tradition" in Indian Christianity.* Delhi: ISPCK, 2000.

Hexham, Irving, and Karla Poewe. *New Religions as Global Cultures: Making the Human Sacred.* Boulder, CO: Westview Press, 1997.

Hiebert, Paul G. "Missiological Education for a Global Era." In *Missiological Education for the 21st Century,* edited by J. Dudley Woodberry, Charles Van Engen, and Edgar J. Elliston. Maryknoll, NY: Orbis Books, 1996.

Hiebert, Paul G., R. Daniel Shaw, and Tite Tiénou. *Understanding Folk Religion: A Christian Response to Popular Beliefs and Practices.* Grand Rapids: Baker Books, 1999.

Hminga, C. L. *The Life and Witness of the Church in Mizoram.* Serkawn, Lunglei, India: Baptist Church of Mizoram, 1987.

Hollenweger, Walter J. *Pentecostalism: Origins and Developments Worldwide.* Peabody, MA: Hendrickson Publishers, 1997.

Hong, Young-gi. "The Backgrounds and Characteristics of the Charismatic Mega-churches in Korea." *Asian Journal of Pentecostal Studies* 3, no.1 (January 2000): 99–118.

Jones, A. H. M. *Were Ancient Heresies Disguised Social Movements?* Philadelphia, PA: Fortress Press, 1966.

Koshy, T. E. *Brother Bakht Singh of India: An Account of 20th Century Apostolic Revival*. Secunderabad, India: OM Books, 2003.

Ma, Julie. "Santuala: A Case of Pentecostal Syncretism." *Asian Journal of Pentecostal Studies* 3, no. 1 (2000): 61–82.

McClung, L. Grant, ed. *Azusa Street and beyond: Pentecostal Missions and Church Growth in the Twentieth Century*. South Plainfield, NJ: Bridge Publishing, New Jersey, 1986.

Minderhoud, Jan. "The Christian Presence in Nepal Before 1951." *Indian Church History Review* 24, no. 2 (December 1990): 144–64.

Moffett, Samuel Hugh. *A History of Christianity in Asia*. Vol. 1, *Beginnings to 1500*. 2nd ed. Maryknoll, NY: Orbis Books, 1998.

Mullins, Mark R. *Christianity Made in Japan: A Study of Indigenous Movements*. Honolulu: University of Hawai'i Press, 1998.

Mundadan, A. M. *Indian Christians Search for Identity & Struggle for Autonomy*. Bangalore, India: Dharmaram Publications, 1984.

Perry, Cindy. *A Biographical History of the Church in Nepal*. Wheaton, IL: Wheaton College Graduate School, 1989.

Petersen, William J. *Those Curious New Cults*. New Canaan, CT: Keats, 1982.

Pobee, John S., and Gabriel Ositelu II. *African Initiatives in Christianity: The Growth, Gifts and Diversities of Indigenous Churches; A Challenge to the Ecumenical Movement*. Geneva: WCC Publications, 1998.

Pomerville, Paul A. *The Third Force in Missions*. Peabody, MA: Hendrickson, 1985.

Raj, P. Solomon. *A Christian Folk-Religion in India*. Frankfurt: Lang, 1986.

Rajamani, R. R. *Monsoon Daybreak*. Bombay: GLS, 1971.

Rao, Sundara R. R. *Bhakti Theology in the Telugu Hymnal*. Madras, India: CLS, 1983.

Redfield, Robert. *Peasant Society and Culture*. Chicago: University of Chicago Press, 1967.

Robert, Dana. "Shifting Southward: Global Christianity Since 1945." *International Bulletin of Missionary Research* (April 2000): 50–58.

Roxborogh, John. "Minority Christians in the Church History Curriculum." *Evangelical Review of Theology* 24 (April 2000): 159–66.
Saliba, John A. *Understanding New Religious Movements*. Grand Rapids: Eerdmans, 1995.
Sanneh, Lamin. *Translating the Message: The Missionary Impact on Culture*. Maryknoll, NY: Orbis Books, 1991.
Shenk, Wilbert R. *Changing Frontiers of Mission*. Maryknoll, NY: Orbis, 1999.
Singer, Milton. *When a Great Tradition Modernizes: An Anthropological Approach to Indian Civilization*. New York: Praeger Publishers, 1972.
Snaitang, O. L., ed. *Churches of Indigenous Origins in Northeast India*. Delhi: ISPCK, 2000.
Sugden, Chris. *Seeking the Asian Face of Jesus*. Oxford: Regnum Books, 1997.
Swanson, Allen J. *Taiwan: Mainline versus Independent Church Growth; A Study in Contrasts*. Pasadena, CA: William Carey Library, 1970.
Synan, Vinson. *The Holiness-Pentecostal Tradition: Charismatic Movements in the Twentieth Century*. Grand Rapids: Eerdmans, 1997.
———. *The Spirit Said "Grow": The Astounding Worldwide Expansion of Pentecostal & Charismatic Churches*. Monrovia, CA: MARC World Vision, 1992.
Thangaraj, M. Thomas. "The History and Teachings of the Hindu Christian Community Commonly Called Nattu Sabai in Tirunelveli." *Indian Church History Review* (June 1971): 43–68.
Tucker, Ruth A. *Another Gospel: Cults, Alternative Religions, and the New Age Movement*. Grand Rapids: Zondervan, 1989.
Tuggy, Leonard A. *Iglesia Ni Cristo: A Study in Independent Church Dynamics*. Quezon City, Philippines: Conservative Baptist Publishing, 1976.
Turner, Harold W. *Bibliography of New Religious Movements in Primal Societies*. Vol. 4, *Europe and Asia*. Boston: G.K. Hall, 1991.
Warrington, Keith. "Healing and Kenneth Hagin." *Asian Journal of Pentecostal Studies* 3, no. 1 (2000): 119–38.
Weber, Jeremy. "Outpacing Persecution." *Christianity Today*, November 2016, 38–47.

Wilfred, Felix. "Christianity in Hindu Polytheistic Structural Mould: Converts in Southern Tamilnadu Respond to an Alien Religion during 'the Vasco da Gama Epoch'." *Arch. de Sc. soc. des Rel.* 103 (July–September 1998): 67–86. Reprinted in *Dharma Deepika: A South Asian Journal of Missiological Research* (January–June 2012): 42–59. Used by permission.

10.

Religious Plurality and Christian Concerns

Insights from India

INTRODUCTION

Christians form a small statistical minority in India, and that with an uneven spread.[1] The predominantly Christian states of North East India (Mizoram, Nagaland, Meghalaya, and Manipur) comprise a comparatively small population of less than a million each. The bulk of India's Christians are located in coastal areas of South India: Kerala, Tamil Nadu, Andhra Pradesh, Karnataka, and Goa. Chennai must be the most "Christian" city of India in terms of number of churches (probably about 2000 congregations of all denominations and sizes, some of them large, most of them active) and the presence of Christians (possibly 12–15 percent of the population in some sections of the city), unlike any other city in South Asia.

A Christian foundation, however, involves much more than statistical Christianity. It has in view Christian principles and values, the ethics of Jesus. In that sense we might have a long way to go. Stanley Jones in his day said he had a two-fold mission in India: one was to communicate the message of Christ to non-Christians, the other was to convert the un-Christlike Christians! That's a challenge always before us anywhere in the world.

---

1. Originally a response paper for a Consultation on Christianity and Religious Plurality in Historical and Global Perspective sponsored by Calvin College and Fuller Theological Seminary, Pasadena, CA, April 25–27, 2003, in which I responded to papers by Prof. Ravi Tiwari, former colleague at Serampore College, Kolkata, and Prof. Joshua Kalapati, professor and head of the Department of Philosophy at Madras Christian College, Tambaram.

At the same time it's good to recognise the influence of Christ and Christianity far beyond the Church in India. We are reminded that Carey and Serampore contributed to India's social and cultural awakening, a movement leading to India's Independence and emergence as a modern democratic republic. A strong stream of influence indeed, but not the only one. Ram Mohan Roy, modern reformer and morning star of the Indian renaissance, shared many of the radical social beliefs of the missionaries with whom he sometimes cooperated and sometimes disputed.[2] Without doubt Ram Mohan Roy was deeply influenced by the teaching of Jesus and the work of the Christian missionaries. The educational mission of the Church of Scotland and other missions through numerous schools and colleges has been a formative influence in Indian society. Several years ago following a seminar at Rohilkhand University in Bareilley in North India, several professors and leaders publically declared their gratitude: "We all are the products of Christianity!"

The Christian contribution is not forgotten. The impact continues. Building India on Christian foundations is a formidable challenge, especially in the present context of *Hindutva*. Nevertheless considerable goodwill exists among people who are beneficiaries of the Christian institutions and ministries past and present.

Building Christian *theology* on Indian foundations is yet another challenge.[3] Hinduism is itself a pluralistic religion better seen as a league of Indian religions. It is this hospitable tolerance which feels threatened by Islam on the one hand and on the other by insensitive Christian approaches to evangelism. Hindu fundamentalism is a reaction to a perceived threat. Christian preaching and witness require sensitive language and action, dialogue, and openness to new forms of Christian witness including the possibility of new communities of faith outside the church.

From these challenging observations we turn to consider some of the issues and implications arising.

---

2. Roy could not accept the doctrine of the Trinity over which he disputed with Joshua Marshman who upheld this basis of orthodox Christianity. Marshman's dogmatism deterred Ram Mohan Roy from becoming a Christian, and he became instead a founder of Unitarianism in India and of the Brahmo Samaj, a monotheistic new Hinduistic religion.

3. Prof. Tiwari's paper was especially helpful in its sympathetic portrayal of Hindu sensitivities. Prof. Tiwari reminded us of his father, Prof. Yisu Das Tiwari, a Hindu convert to Christ who retained his sense of Indian spirituality and culture, a virtue found also in his son.

THE QUESTION OF HERMENEUTICS

Religious plurality has serious ramifications for the issue of biblical hermeneutics. In a multi-religious context, what does it mean to confess Jesus Christ as the Lord and only Saviour of humankind? Chris Wright argues that the question about salvation in other religions makes no sense in the light of biblical revelation. Religions do not save. God alone saves, and the Bible bears witness to God's salvific action. More specifically the Bible tells the story of God's salvation.

Other scriptures do not tell this unique story. "Using the Bible among the religions must therefore mean telling the story which makes it good news, not merely treating it as a quarry of religious ideas and ideals for comparison, admiration, or exchange."[4] How one interprets the Bible therefore is a serious issue. *Exegesis aims at recovering the original meaning of the text.*[5] It is helpful to bear in mind that the biblical authors lived and wrote in a context of religious plurality not unlike our own.[6] In such a setting the distinctiveness of the Christian belief system must be clearly enunciated.

In contrast, consider the interpretation of Christianity offered by a Vedantic explanation of reality as exemplified by Radhakrishnan who interpreted the resurrection of Jesus as a symbolic act. The literal sense of the Christian doctrine is set aside by a Vedantic hermeneutic which favours a spiritual interpretation. "The physical resurrection of Jesus is not the important thing but the resurrection of the Divine. The rebirth of man as an event that happens within his soul, resulting in a deeper understanding of reality and a greater love for God and man, is the true resurrection which lifts human life to an awareness of its own Divine context and purpose."[7] The essence of Vedanta is that all religions are ultimately one. Therefore Christian doctrines must be reinterpreted to fit into the Vedantic understanding of reality. The result is a sustained attack on Christianity and especially against the uniqueness of Jesus Christ. As Kalapati confirms, Radhakrishnan

---

4. Chris Wright, "Christ and the Mosaic of Pluralisms," in *Global Missiology for the 21st Century,* ed. William D. Taylor (Grand Rapids: Baker Academic, 2000), 77.

5. For an example of a scholar who found his way backward "from modern accommodation to classic Christianity," see Thomas C. Oden, *A Change of Heart: A Personal and Theological Memoir* (Downers Grove, IL: InterVarsity Press, 2014), 178, 212, 256–57.

6. Wright, "Christ and the Mosaic," 76, 77.

7. Radhakrishnan's commentary on *The Bhagavad Gita,* cited by Joshua Kalapati, *Radhakrishnan and Christianity: An Introduction to Hindu-Christian Apologetics* (Delhi: ISPCK, 2002), 99.

utilised the comparative methodology but ignored the distinct contrasts which constitute the essentials of Christianity.

For Radhakrishnan, "the Sanatana Dharma is the essence of all religious faiths." It is not surprising therefore that he wanted to absorb Christ and Christianity into the Advaitic framework.[8] Kalapati points out that Radhakrishnan's understanding of Jesus Christ was borrowed from aspects of theological liberalism compatible with Vedanta. The result is a human Jesus who is historic but less than true deity. In this deconstruction, the incarnation of Jesus was not an historic reality but an avatar. "While Radhakrishnan completely ignores nearly all the supernatural qualities of Jesus, he highlights some human propensities which were never there," painting a derogatory picture of Jesus.[9] By trivialising the unique sayings of Jesus (e.g., the "I Am" sayings of the Fourth Gospel), Radhakrishnan attempts to "domesticate Jesus into Advaitic mould."[10]

Kalapati writes, "Radhakrishnan develops his own distinction between the *Jesus of history* and the *Christ of faith*. He commends the idea of the Christ of faith because it perfectly resembles his Vedantic Christ, but the historic Jesus he perceives to be a stumbling block." How important, then, a hermeneutic that is faithful to the meaning of the biblical text yet cognisant of the religious context of the reader. According to Radhakrishnan, "The saving knowledge of God is not the knowledge of and faith in Jesus as a historic person portrayed in the Gospels. Christ is not to be equated with the historic Jesus. Christ is the spirit of the Supreme, the Eternal Word. The manifestation of this Word in history is not limited to Jesus."[11]

Finally, Radharishnan proposes that Christians "should disown all uniqueness attributed to Jesus in order to be closer to Hinduism"—a proposition which no Christian can accept.[12] Yet that is the conclusion to be drawn from Radhakrishnan's hermeneutic and exposition. Radhakrishnan's Vedantic hermeneutic is unacceptable for a distinctly Christian theology which finds its essential uniqueness in Jesus Christ.

---

8. Kalapati, *Radhakrishnan and Christianity*, 116.
9. Ibid., 85.
10. Ibid., 87.
11. Quoted by ibid., 66.
12. Ibid., 115.

CHRISTOLOGY

The person, life and mission of Jesus Christ are at the heart of Christian theology and missiology. The incomparabiliy of Jesus Christ is a critical issue for a theology of religion/s in today's pluralistic world. Through their daily encounter with other faiths Asian and African theologians are particularly well-equipped to understand the distinctive meaning of Jesus Christ, as Samuel Escobar observes.[13] For example, Vinoth Ramachandra of Sri Lanka develops an evangelical Christology in dialogue with the religions in which he critiques the theologies of Samartha, Pieris, and Pannikar but avoids arrogance by presenting a biblical position which "defies classification under the customary categories of exclusivist, pluralist, and inclusivist."[14]

Faith in the uniqueness and universality of Jesus Christ is "basic to a proper appreciation of religious pluralism," states M. M. Thomas.[15] Pannenberg likewise considers disastrous the tendency of pluralists to relativize Christian truth claims. "The Christian has the promise of God in Christ. The other religious traditions do not provide that particular promise."[16] The uniqueness and universality of Christ are the substance of New Testament theology. Other religions offer insights which might enrich our understanding of redemption. But the Bible declares Jesus unique, "the one mediator between God and humans, the man Christ Jesus, who gave himself a ransom for all" (1 Tim 2:5–6). The cross and the resurrection were central to Jesus's mission. Here is the starting point of Christian faith. "Had Jesus not risen from the dead, Christianity could only have consisted in a group of his friends keeping alive the memory of his teaching and reproducing as best they could his example. Jesus would still be one of the great religious geniuses of humankind, but he would not be

---

13. Samuel Escobar, "Evangelical Missiology: Peering into the Future at the Turn of the Century," in *Global Missiology for the 21st Century*, ed. William D. Taylor (Grand Rapids: Baker Academic, 2000), 118.

14. Vinoth Ramachandra, *The Recovery of Mission* (Grand Rapids: Eerdmans, 1996), 275, cited by Escobar, "Evangelical Missiology," 118.

15. M. M. Thomas, "A Christ-Centered Humanist Approach to Other Religions in the Indian Pluralistic Context," in *Christian Uniqueness Reconsidered: The Myth of a Pluralistic Theology of Religions*, ed. Gavin D'Costa (Maryknoll NY: Orbis, 1990), 49.

16. Wolfhart Pannenberg, "Religious Pluralism and Conflicting Truth Claims: The Problem of a Theology of the World Religions," in D'Costa, *Christian Uniqueness Reconsidered*, 104.

the Lord."[17] Easter Christology is an explicit Christology which was characteristic of the New Testament *kerygma*.[18]

Theology today must take seriously the issue of the world religions, and a Christian theology cannot escape its essential Christological core. Contemporary theologizing may be helped by reference to the early church fathers[19] who grappled with issues and challenges of a pluralistic context not unlike our own.[20]

Confession of Jesus Christ as Lord is an issue of conversion. In the early centuries of the church conversion was a costly affair embracing the ultimate witness of martyrdom as a strong possibility. Conversion in India today has become a political event with punitive implications, as both Kalapati and Tiwari have shown. Nevertheless conversion is essential to biblical Christianity. "There cannot be an imitation of Christ in the biblical sense without a new birth."[21] Conversion in evangelical understanding is essentially a spiritual event with transformational ramifications. "Personal encounter with Jesus Christ changes people radically."[22] Conversion to Jesus Christ entails a life of discipleship centered in the historic, living, incarnate One who lived and died and arose from the dead. A theology of the cross and resurrection is at the heart of biblical Christology.

The mission of Jesus as the Suffering Servant is the source of the evangelical doctrine of redemption and the call to conversion which is the spiritual basis for the formation of the Christian community.[23]

ECCLESIOLOGY

Early missionaries in India included scholars who made important contributions to the understanding of Indian cultures. The Jesuit scholar, Roberto de Nobili (1577–1656), is one example. In a study

---

17. James Dupuis, *Who Do You Say I Am? Introduction to Christology* (Maryknoll, NY: Orbis, 1994), 54.

18. Ibid., 57, 61.

19. As a result of Thomas Oden's return to classic Christianity, see the resulting Ancient Christian Commentary on Scripture (29 volumes), the Ancient Christian Doctrine series (5 volumes) and the Ancient Christian Texts series (more than 12 volumes). Also Cyril C. Richardson, ed., *Early Church Fathers* (New York: Simon & Schuster Touchstone, 1996).

20. For further discussion on the critical issue of Christology in a pluralistic context see my essay, "Christ the Essential Core," in *God and the Nations: A Biblical Theology of Mission in the Asian Context* (Delhi: ISPCK, 1997, 2002), 187–201.

21. Escobar, "Evangelical Missiology," 116.

22. Ibid., 117.

23. Ibid., 116.

of de Nobili's *Responsio*, Anchukandam complains that "The Catholic Church in India has not yet been able to present itself to the Indians in an acceptable Indian form."[24] This being so, the work of de Nobili four centuries ago seems all the more relevant today. The *Responsio* is de Nobili's scholarly vindication of his adaptation policy which had occasioned a bitter debate. The controversy was critical for the precarious future of a neophyte Church.

Historian Latourette expressed the opinion that Nobili's mission met with considerable success. The Madura Mission reported some forty thousand (40,000) Christians, which had increased to ninety thousand (90,000) by the start of the century, although some sources suggested as many as one hundred fifty thousand (150,000) or two lakhs (200,000).[25]

Bengal produced its own scholars who responded creatively to the Christian challenge. Among them none was more controversial than the flamboyant Keshub Chundra Sen (1838–1884) who struggled to comprehend and express Christ in Indian terms. Attracted to Jesus, Keshub never identified with mainline institutional Christianity. Christian writers therefore have regarded him a Hindu. A leader of the Brahmo Samaj, he became head of a Brahmo faction which he named the Church of the New Dispensation and utilised to propagate Christian ideas and values. His method was borrowed from Hindu tradition. "Keshub made it abundantly clear that he had chosen Christ as his Lord, but there is no evidence that Keshub's master was necessarily attached to the Christian religion."[26] He used Hindu symbols, sometimes combined with Christian concepts. His concern was with "disseminating the spirit of Christ in India." Keshub hoped to unite East and West. He wanted India to come to Christ, "to the feet of my sweet Jesus." He urged the missionaries to stop presenting Christ as an Englishman because the picture of a foreign Christianity is repugnant to Indians and "hinders the progress of the true spirit of Christianity in this country."

Keshub's attempt represents a spontaneous response to the gospel from within Hindu society expressed in Indian culture and symbol. At a time when Christianity was seen as part of an aggressive

---

24. Thomas Anchukandam, *Roberto de Nobili's Responsio (1610): A Vindication of Inculturation and Adaptation* (Bangalore, India: Kristu Jyoti Publications, 1996).

25. Kenneth Scott Latourette, *Three Centuries of Advance, AD 1500–AD 1800*, vol. 3 of *A History of the Expansion of Christianity* (New York: Harper & Bros., 1939), 262.

26. David C. Scott, ed., *Keshub Chunder Sen* (Madras, India: CLS, 1979), 1–42.

European civilization, Keshub urged his contemporaries to distinguish Christianity from Western customs. To Keshub, Christ came as an Asian kinsman to fulfil the Hindu longing for union with God.

Another important Bengali figure was Brahmabandhab Upadhyaya (1861–1907)[27] who went beyond Keshub by membership in the Catholic Church. A Hindu by birth, he became a Christian by spiritual rebirth, calling himself a Hindu Catholic. Hindu in custom, spiritually a Christian, Upadhyaya believed the best in the Hindu character is made better by Christ. He distinguished sadhana dharma from samaj dharma, that is, culture is different from faith.

In a provocative study, Staffner cites the examples of Upadhyay, Keshub and other Hindu converts to support his thesis that converts to Christ must be able to remain socially part of the Hindu community.[28] To Staffner the essence of Christianity is a faith in Jesus Christ as Saviour, received, not through rituals or ceremony, but through personal faith in Christ's promises. The entrance card to following Christ is not baptism but confession of our sinfulness and of his forgiveness. God gives himself to us in Jesus Christ. The correction to our self-centredness is in spiritual re-birth (John 3:3) whereby we become part of a new creation (2 Cor 5:17). This transforming Presence is available to all through the gift of the Holy Spirit which comes through invitation, not rituals.

Notable in the examples above is the absence of any clear expression of ecclesiology, at least not in the traditional expression of the Christian faith community. Staffner, for instance, understands Hinduism as a culture with room for many religions, Christianity as a spirituality which can be incarnated in any culture. Staffner's study assumes the validity of a theoretical Hindu-Christian synthesis without defining the contours of the Christian faith expression within the Hindu Samaj. Is this sufficient?

The Church has been problematic for many Hindu converts. It was so for Bengali converts in the nineteenth century as well as for others. The result has been the existence of secret followers of Christ in some localities. One remarkable instance is a group of women converts in Sivakasi, South India, who were not permitted to openly practice their faith. "These Sivakasi women are Christians of a very clear

---

27. For a study of Upadhyaya, see Timothy C. Tennent, *Building Christianity on Indian Foundations: The Legacy of Brahmabandhav Upadhyay* (Delhi: ISPCK, 2000).

28. Hans Staffner, *Jesus Christ and the Hindu Community: Is a Synthesis of Hinduism and Christianity Possible?* (Anand, Gujarat, India: Gujarat Sahitya Prakash, 1988).

character, who live daily the teaching that they have been given."[29] Sustained by the Bible, prayer and sacraments these women have transmitted the faith over several generations despite difficulties and persecution.

Quite different is the response of K. Subba Rao (1912–1981), the "Christ-centred Healer of Andhra Pradesh."[30] Subba Rao was born a Hindu of Kamma caste in Godavari District. At any early age he became an atheist and opposed all religion, especially the sadhus and priests. Having lost his health through reckless living, in 1942, Subba Rao had a vision of Christ, which became the decisive event in his life. Subba Rao was healed, and eventually began a ministry of healing which attracted multitudes. According to H. L. Richard, "Subba Rao remained a faithful devotee and servant of Christ within the Hindu community until his death."[31] Nevertheless, despite his confession of Christ, Subba Rao rejected the church, its sacraments, teachings, and clergy.[32] His writings consisted largely of attacks on baptism, on the church, and Christianity as a religion. His rejection of Christianity and the church must be seen as part of his critique of all religions. It also appears that Subba Rao had very little knowledge of the Bible, was interested in experience rather than doctrine, and interpreted Christ in ambiguous advaitic categories.[33] Despite these shortcomings, H. L. Richard commends Subba Rao's as a truly contextual ministry. "That Subba Rao appeared more Hindu than Christian is a positive rather than negative point. He is in the tradition of the apostle Paul who appeared more Gentile than Jewish."[34] Possibly so.

As reported by David Barrett, the Subba Rao movement had 300,000 followers in 1966.[35] It was my impression that the movement had dissipated since the death of the guru. However H. L. Richard

---

29. Andrew Wingate, "The Secret Christians of Sivakasi, Tamil Nadu: One Pattern of Conversion in a South Indian Town," *Religion and Society* 33, no. 1 (March 1986), 84.

30. H. L. Richard, "The Christ-Centred Healer of Andhra Pradesh," unpublished, undated paper, ca. 1995.

31. Ibid., 3.

32. See Kaj Baago, *The Movement around Subba Rao: A Study of the Hindu-Christian Movement around K. Subba Rao in Andhra Pradesh* (Bangalore, India: CISRS, 1968). Baago's study is frequently cited in H. L. Richard's paper (above) as well as in the study of Indian Christian theology.

33. H. L. Richard, "The Christ-Centred Healer."

34. Ibid., 11.

35. David B. Barrett, ed., *World Christian Encyclopedia* (Nairobi: Oxford University Press, 1982).

reports numerous devotees of Christ remaining as well as twenty groups meeting in various places including a registered society and prayer hall at Vijayawada.[36]

In the early part of the twentieth century the "Rethinking Christianity" group at Madras had raised the theoretical possibility of a "Churchless Christianity." More recently, based on research carried out at the Gurukul Lutheran Theological College and Research Institute, Herbert Hoefer revived this thinking through a study of non-baptised believers in Christ (NBBCs) in Tamil Nadu.[37] The study reports thousands of believers in Jesus Christ outside the institutional church. Theirs is a Hindu style of worship that Hoefer believes may lead eventually to "a truly indigenous form of Christianity" in India.[38] More recently, Hoefer explains that Hindu devotees of Jesus see little meaning in the church:

> The Jesu bhakta typically feels no particular need to participate in public worship. The Hindu tradition of bhakti worship takes place primarily in the home and in private. The church's rites seem like external shells.[39]

The Bible and the Christian sacraments are important to Jesus *bhaktas*, but most have met Jesus through direct encounter. Therefore they see less need for the church or its clergy and sacraments:

> If the Jesu bhakta decides to take Holy Baptism, it is essentially an act of commitment to his [sic] Master. It is not a joining of another social community or a rejection his [sic] caste. If s/he participates in Holy Communion, it is a spiritual communion with the Lord and a spiritual affirmation of the Christian fellowship. It is not participation or membership in an organization.[40]

Not everyone will agree with Hoefer's postulate, which implies a fundamental failure of the Christian mission in India. Emil Chandran responds that there were approaches which identified with Indian culture and have contextualized the life of faith. Chandran cites the examples of de Nobili in the past and of the Friends Missionary

---

36. H. L. Richard, "The Christ-centred Healer," 3.
37. Herbert E. Hoefer, *Churchless Christianity: A Report of Research among Non-baptised Believers in Christ in Rural and Urban Tamilnadu, India, with Practical and Theological Reflections* (Madras, India: Gurukul Lutheran Theological College and Research Institute, 1991.
38. Ibid., 207.
39. Herbert Hoefer, "Jesus, My Master: 'Jesu Bhakta' Hindu Christian Theology," unpublished paper, Portland, OR, April 2002.
40. Ibid., 4–5.

Prayer Band, the Pentecostals and independent church movements of the present.[41] Chandran holds that "Christian faith cannot be genuinely and fully accommodated into a Hindu frame work."[42]

Theologians generally will protest that some form of the church is a biblical and historical necessity. Some sort of institutionalised form is evident from the time of Jesus which has been a source for continuity and order. The church, states Kevin Giles, "is both a theological reality and a social reality."[43] Quite a number of Indian expressions of Christian faith exist. Perhaps the full flower of Indian ecclesiology is yet to develop, but glimpses can be seen in numerous Indian instituted church models.[44]

INSIGHTS FROM INDIA

Sometimes referred as "father" of Indian Christian theology, Brahmabandhav Upadhyay provides a model for constructing Christian theology on Indian foundations. Upadhyay utilised the terminology of the Upanishads to restate the doctrine of the Trinity in familiar Indian categories while remaining faithful to historic Christian belief.[45] Upadhyay's achievement is an early example of contextual theologising, largely unsurpassed.

Upadhyay believed there were "fragments of divine revelation present in the indigenous scriptures of India" much as the early church fathers, such as Justin Martyr, found seeds of the word (*logos spermatikos*) in Greek philosophy.[46] Upadhyay's work was courageous and creative. His "Hymn to the Incarnate Logos" is Christian and Trinitarian, "Christian worship grown from the seeds of the Indian tradition and planted in the indigenous soil of India."[47] Upadhyay not only explored Indian categories for stating Christian beliefs, he also interacted with Eastern ideas which he found incompatible with

---

41. Emil Chandran, "Response to Herbert Hoefer's paper, 'Jesus, My Master: Jesu Bhakta Hindu Christian Theology'," Nairobi, Kenya, Daystar University, May 2003.

42. Ibid.

43. Kevin Giles, *What on Earth Is the Church? An Exploration in New Testament Theology* (Downers Grove, IL: InterVarsity, 1995), 188.

44. See Roger E. Hedlund, *Quest for Identity: India's Churches of Indigenous Origin* (Delhi: ISPCK, 2000).

45. Tennent, *Building Christianity on Indian Foundations*, 224.

46. Timothy C. Tennent, "Trinity and Saccidananda in the Writings of Brahmabandhav Upadhyaya," *Dharma Deepika* 1 (January–June 2003): 7.

47. Tennent, *Building Christianity on Indian Foundations*, 255.

Christian faith. He objected strongly to the Hindu notion of *karma* and to the doctrine of transmigration of souls which he regarded a monstrous and debilitating evil.[48]

Meaningful dialogue requires recognising contrasts as well as commonalities. As Tennent points out, there is a great gulf between Christian theology and Vedantic theism. He takes as an example Ramanuja's theism which fails to distinguish between the Brahman who receives worship and the devotee who offers worship. "For a Christian, this is an ontological confusion of the highest magnitude."[49] An informed theologising is required which will recognize pitfalls along the way.

Kalapati and Tiwari urge the formation of Christian foundations apropos to theology and society in a context of plurality. An unexpected model is found in a Hindu who has been looked upon as more Christlike than many Christians, M. K. Gandhi (1869–1948). A recent study states that

> Gandhi was captivated by the person and message of Christ. . . . While Gandhi remained fundamentally a Hindu in outward things, he was more Christlike than most Christians, with his inner life more and more transformed toward Christ. In many ways Gandhi, a non-Christian, helped to Christianize unchristian Christianity, yet his influence for Christ on Hindus and Muslims was even greater.[50]

Methodist missionary E. Stanley Jones was supportive of Gandhi.[51] As an evangelist, Jones likewise sought to convert the un-Christlike church as well as present Christ to educated Hindus.[52] Jones believed in conversion. Gandhi did not. Jones utilised indigenous institutions such as the ashram and engaged in "round table discussions" (before the era of dialogue) with Indian intellectuals. Jones stated that this format brought out the best in religion and that Christ began to emerge, despite the deficiencies of Christianity as a system.

Stanley Jones's method was straight forward and open, out of his own experience to present Christ to the needs of persons. Jones understood that conversion is a process. He concluded that India

---

48. Ibid., 283.
49. Timothy C. Tennent, *Christianity at the Religious Roundtable: Evangelicalism in Conversation with Hinduism, Buddhism, and Islam* (Grand Rapids: Baker Academic, 2002), 58.
50. Paul-Gordon Chandler, "Mazhur Mallouhi: Gandhi's Living Christian Legacy in the Muslim World," *International Bulletin of Missionary Research* 27, no. 2 (April 2003): 54.
51. E. Stanley Jones, *Mahatma Gandhi: An Interpretation* (New York: Abingdon Press, 1948).
52. E. Stanley Jones, *The Christ of the Indian Road* (New York: Abingdon Press, 1925).

was beginning to walk with the Christ of the Indian road.[53] Gandhi opposed the conversion work of the missionaries, telling them rather to engage in deeds of compassion and humble service. Despite his rejection of explicit identification with Christianity, Gandhi is seen by some to have presented "an Eastern face of Christ to India. By his life, Gandhi helped Indians to visualize Christ walking down Eastern roads, dwelling among Eastern villagers in lowly poverty, simplicity and love."[54]

This portrayal of Gandhi is significant for Hindus in the present context of tension. On the one hand advocates of *Hindutva* manifest a militancy which is very out of keeping with the nonviolent *ahimsa* of the Mahatma as well as of the gospel of Christ. On the other hand, contemporary movements for Dalit liberation also find inspiration in the transforming power of the gospel but ignore the example of Gandhi in favour of the advocacy of Ambedkar, the late champion of the Untouchables who opposed Gandhi's Harijan project in favour of a movement of conversion away from Hinduism. Ambedkar too was greatly influenced by Christianity and by Christian missionaries such as E. Stanley Jones. Numerous scholars[55] today repudiate Gandhian castism. The evils of caste were pointed out by Ambedkar, but Gandhi upheld the caste system which he considered integral to Hindu society.[56]

> Gandhi only wanted to remove untouchability so that millions of dehumanized people—whom he patronizingly renamed Harijan (literally, children of God)—could remain forever within the fold of Hinduism as servile creatures.[57]

Gandhi's synthesis of *varna*, culture and patriotism, was both upper casteist and ahistorical, rooted in an imaginary past, states Braj Mani, "the Gandhian non-violence entailed acceptance of the apparent and indirect forms of coercion implicit in the caste system."[58]

A challenge for Christian mission today is to uphold the rights of

---

53. Ibid., 223.
54. Chandler, "Mazhur Mallouhi."
55. In his recent book, *Knowledge and Power: A Discourse for Transformation* (New Delhi: Manohar Publishers, 2014), 296, Braj Ranjan Mani names Gail Omvedt, G. Aloysius, Kancha Ilaiah, Uma Chakravarti, Meera Nanda, and Christophe Jaffrelot as some of those who challenge the basic tenets of Brahmanism.
56. Ibid., 206, 251.
57. Ibid., 253.
58. Ibid., 257.

the oppressed to humanisation, as well as to confront oppressors with the need to repent and to communicate Jesus Christ to all.

TOWARD A CONCLUSION

Whither next? In a recent effort to move beyond the current stalemate in the debate about theology of religions, Amos Yong explores the possibility of a pneumatological approach. "Christian theology of religions is the attempt to reflect on the relationship between God and the phenomenon of the religions from the standpoint of Christian faith."[59] Pneumatology in no way displaces Christology. To the contrary, pneumatology upholds the centrality of Christ. "No one can say 'Jesus is Lord' except by the Holy Spirit" (1 Cor 12:3). Neither one is subordinate to the other. The Spirit witnesses to Christ. The Spirit also grants discernment.

> "By this you know the Spirit of God: every spirit that confesses that Jesus Christ has come in the flesh is from God, and every spirit that does not confess Jesus is not from God. And this is the spirit of the antichrist, of which you have heard that it is coming; and now it is already in the world." (1 John 4:2–3)

This discernment relates to the meaning of Jesus Christ and is available for a Christian theological evaluation of the religions.[60] The goal is "the ongoing activity of discerning the Holy Spirit and the diversity of spirits in the world of the religions."[61]

A pneumatological theology of religions is significant in light of the growth and development of Pentecostal churches in much of the world, including India. Pentecostal spirituality proclaims deliverance from bondage to sickness, demonic oppression and evil spirits. Recent studies on the Holy Spirit therefore are timely as well as refreshing,[62]

---

59. Amos Yong, *Beyond the Impasse: Toward a Pneumatological Theology of Religions* (Grand Rapids: Baker Academic), 2003.
60. Ibid., 169.
61. Ibid., 175.
62. See, for example, Veli-Matti Kärkkäinen, *Pneumatology: The Holy Spirit in Ecumenical, International, and Contextual Perspective* (Grand Rapids: Baker Academic, 2002); Jeffrey P. Greenman and George Kalantzis, eds., *Life in the Spirit: Spiritual Formation in Theological Perspective* (Downers Grove, IL: InterVarsity Press, 2010); C. Douglas McConnell, ed., *The Holy Spirit and Mission Dynamics*, Evangelical Missiological Society Series Number 5 (Pasadena, CA: William Carey Library, 1997); Amos Yong, *The Missiological Spirit: Christian Mission Theology in the Third Millennium Global Context* (Eugene, OR: Cascade Books, 2014).

and hold great promise for engagement with the religions in the task of building a Christian foundation in a pluralistic world.

SOURCES FOR FURTHER REFERENCE

Anchukandam, Thomas. *Roberto de Nobili's Responsio (1610), A Vindication of Inculturation and Adaptation*. Bangalore, India: Kristu Jyoti Publications. 1996.

Baago, Kaj. *The Movement around Subba Rao: A Study of the Hindu-Christian Movement around K. Subba Rao in Andhra Pradesh*. Bangalore, India: CISRS, 1968.

Barrett, David B., ed., *World Christian Encyclopedia*. Nairobi: Oxford University Press, 1982.

Chandler, Paul-Gordon. *Pilgrims of Christ on the Muslim Road: Exploring a New Path between Two Faiths*. Lanham, MD: Rowman & Littlefield Publishers, 2007.

_____. "Mazhur Mallouhi: Gandhi's Living Christian Legacy in the Muslim World." *International Bulletin of Missionary Research* 27, no. 2 (April 2003).

Chandran, Emil. "A Response to Herbert Hoefer's Article, 'Jesus, My Master: Jesu Bhakta Hindu Christian Theology'." Nairobi, Kenya: Daystar University, May 2003.

Clooney, F. X. "Roberto de Nobili's Response to India and Hinduism, In Practice and Theory." *Third Millennium* 1 (1998): 4, 72–80.

Dupuis, James. *Who Do You Say I Am? Introduction to Christology*. Maryknoll, NY: Orbis, 1994.

Escobar, Samuel. "Evangelical Missiology: Peering into the Future at the Turn of the Century." In *Global Missiology for the 21st Century*, edited by William D. Taylor. Grand Rapids: Baker Academic, 2000.

Giles, Kevin. *What on Earth Is the Church? An Exploration in New Testament Theology*. Downers Grove, IL: InterVarsity, 1995.

Hedlund, Roger E. *God and the Nations: A Biblical Theology of Mission in the Asian Context*. Delhi: ISPCK, 1997.

_____. *Quest for Identity: India's Churches of Indigenous Origin.* Delhi: ISPCK, 2000.

Hoefer, Herbert E. *Churchless Christianity: A Report of Research among Non-baptised Believers in Christ in Rural and Urban Tamilnadu, India, with Practical and Theological Reflections.* Madras, India: Gurukul Lutheran Theological College and Research Institute, 1991.

_____. "Jesus, My Master: 'Jesu Bhakta' Hindu Christian Theology." Unpublished paper, Portland, OR, April 2002.

Jones, E. Stanley. *The Christ of the Indian Road.* New York: Abingdon Press, 1925.

_____. *Mahatma Gandhi: An Interpretation.* New York: Abingdon Press, 1948.

Kalapati, Joshua. *Radhakrishnan and Christianity: An Introduction to Hindu-Christian Apologetics.* Delhi: ISPCK, 2002.

Latourette, Kenneth Scott. *Three Centuries of Advance, AD 1500–AD 1800.* Vol. 3 of *A History of the Expansion of Christianity.* New York: Harper & Bros., 1939.

Mani, Braj Ranjan. *Knowledge and Power: A Discourse for Transformation.* New Delhi: Manohar Publishers, 2014.

Mathew, C. V. *The Saffron Mission: A Historical Analysis of Modern Hindu Missionary Ideologies and Practices.* Delhi: ISPCK, 2001 (1999).

Michael, S. M. "Catholic Mission in the Region of Tamilnadu." In *Integral Mission Dynamics: An Interdisciplinary Study of the Catholic Church in India*, edited by Augustine Kanjamala. New Delhi: Intercultural Publications, 1995.

Oden, Thomas C. *A Change of Heart: A Personal and Theological Memoir.* Downers Grove, IL: InterVarsity Press, 2014.

Pannenberg, Wolfhart. "Religious Pluralism and Conflicting Truth Claims: The Problem of a Theology of the World Religions." In *Christian Uniqueness Reconsidered: The Myth of a Pluralistic Theology of Religions*, edited by Gavin D'Costa. Maryknoll, NY: Orbis, 1990.

Rajamanickam, S. *Roberto de Nobili on Indian Customs.* Palayamkottai, India: De Nobili Research Institute, St. Zavier's College, 1989.

Ramachandra, Vinoth. *The Recovery of Mission: Beyond the Pluralist Paradigm.* Grand Rapids: Eerdmans, 1996.

Richard, H. L. "The Christ-Centred Healer of Andhra Pradesh." Unpublished, undated paper, ca. 1995.

Richardson, Cyril C., ed. *Early Church Fathers*. New York: Simon & Schuster Touchstone, 1996.

Sauliére, Augustin. *His Star in the East*. Revised and re-edited by S. Rajamanickam. Anand, Gujarat, India: Gujarat Sahitya Prakash, 1994.

Scott, David C., ed. *Keshub Chunder Sen*. Madras, India: 1979.

Staffner, Hans. *Jesus Christ and the Hindu Community: Is a Synthesis of Hinduism and Christianity Possible?* Anand, Gujarat, India: Gujarat Sahitya Prakash, 1988.

Tennent, Timothy C. *Christianity at the Religious Roundtable: Evangelicalism in Conversation with Hinduism, Buddhism, and Islam*. Grand Rapids: Baker, 2002.

_____. *Building Christianity on Indian Foundations: The Legacy of Brahmabandhav Upadhyay*. Delhi: ISPCK, 2000.

Thomas, M. M. "A Christ-Centered Humanist Approach to Other Religions in the Indian Pluralistic Context." In *Christian Uniqueness Reconsidered: The Myth of a Pluralistic Theology of Religions,* edited by Gavin D'Costa. Maryknoll: Orbis, 1990.

Tiwari, Ravi. *Yisu Das: Witness of a Convert*. Delhi: ISPCK, 2000.

Wingate, Andrew. "The Secret Christians of Sivakasi, Tamil Nadu: one pattern of Conversion in a South Indian Town." *Religion and Society, XXXIII*, 1, March 1986.

Wright, Chris. "Christ and the Mosaic of Pluralisms." In *Global Missiology for the 21st Century*, edited by William D. Taylor. Grand Rapids: Baker Academic, 2000.

Yong, Amos. *Beyond the Impasse: Toward a Pneumatological Theology of Religions*. Grand Rapids: Baker Academic, 2003.

11.

Poverty, Evangelisation, and Christian Identity

INTRODUCTION

The original assigned topic was "Mission and Evangelism among the Poor and Needy with Special Reference to Christian Identity."[1] I have modified the title slightly to focus on the question of Christian identity as it impinges upon the evangelisers as well as the evangelised. In preference to "mission and evangelism" the term "evangelisation" more fully comprehends all that is included in the mission of the Church. Evangelisation is a broad concept comprising a wide span of social and proclamation activities manifesting the Christian presence in the world.

The mission of the Church is not limited to the marginalised. Yet the overwhelming response to the gospel has been from the margins. The transformational power of the gospel has made possible a new identity of dignity and worth for oppressed peoples. Evangelisation of the poor and forgotten raises certain hermeneutical questions. It also challenges the evangelisers to a fuller appropriation of the gospel for their own ongoing conversion.

From these preliminary observations we turn to the topic before us. We begin with a short definition.

---

1. Originally a public lecture at Madras Theological Seminary on October 13, 2003.

DEFINITION: DEFINING THE POOR

Poverty in this paper has to do with impoverished human beings, those who lack the means to obtain basic needs. This paper does not directly address that "spiritual poverty" which is our common human lot. This paper accepts George Ninan's definition of India's poor as "the economically exploited and marginalized section of the society."[2]

Poverty is a complex problem. From a medical viewpoint, the economically deprived are those who have suffered most "from undernutrition, poor sanitation and exposure to infection."[3] Impoverishment cannot be isolated from the inter-related issues of landlessness, employment, income, caste and gender discrimination,[4] exploitation, globalisation and hunger.

Landless labourers earn a minimum wage of around 10 rupees per day, an annual income of about 3,000 rupees, which is totally inadequate for a small family.[5] The struggle for subsistence results in a vicious cycle of child labour and female exploitation together with other social evils.

Bonded labour, officially abolished, continues with an estimated forty million persons, including fifteen million children, as bonded labourers in India, according to a recent report.[6] Inevitably a majority of the victims are tribals and Dalits. It is these sections of the population who are forced into the most unpleasant and unhealthy occupations, such as carting away human feces from public latrines and scooping buckets of excrement from clogged sewers which they enter naked with no protective gear whatsoever.[7] Economic deprivation also encourages criminal activities and undesirable avenues such as the sex trade. In Kolkata an estimated one lakh (100,000) women engage in prostitution, and India is believed to have four lakhs (400,000) child prostitutes.[8]

---

2. A. George Ninan, "Defining the Poor in India Today," in *Good News to the Poor: The Challenge to the Church*, ed. Sebastian C. H. Kim and Krickwin C. Marak (Delhi: ISPCK, 1997), 80.

3. Chiranjivi J. Nirmal, *Madras Perspectives: Explorations in Social and Cultural History* (Madras, India: Institute of Indian and International Studies, 1992), 33.

4. For a discussion of the implications see Francis Nallappan, "*Hindutva* and the Minorities: Communalism and Discipleship," *Mission Today* 5 (July–September 2003): 197–214.

5. Ninan, "Defining the Poor," 94.

6. Meena Menon, "Escape from Bondage," *The Hindu*, Sunday, September 7, 2003.

7. Tom O'Neill, "Untouchables," *National Geographic*, June 2003, 2–31.

8. Gouri Salve, "A Glimmer of Hope." *The Hindu*, Sunday, September 7, 2003.

Rehabilitation is a crucial need for former bonded labourers as well as for sex workers, beggars, and other marginalised persons and groups to find human dignity and a productive place in society. Here is a great challenge and obligation for the Christian mission today.

Tragically, huge sections of the poor are caught in a web of deprivation and increasing poverty which is not alleviated by modernisation and globalisation. To the contrary, the suffering of the deprived has increased. Developmental studies reveal that the gap between rich and poor has widened. "Disparities in income distribution have risen sharply with the introduction of global market mechanisms."[9] India and other developing countries are unable to compete with subsidised goods and food products from the rich countries of the North Atlantic.[10]

The future is bleak for India's farmers and others. Despite advances in production, "it is estimated that 360 million people living in poverty now suffer from chronic hunger."[11] Although we do not undergo famine, multitudes experience malnutrition. Economic as well as demographic and ecological factors converge to impact the present crisis. "Poverty and population growth are linked to environmental degradation."[12] The poor would appear to have little hope for their future. Nevertheless, states Bishop George Ninan, "empowering of the powerless and the marginalized is the key to alleviating poverty and bringing about justice, peace and integrity."[13]

EVANGELISATION: BEING, DOING, AND SAYING

What, then, should be the Christian response to the injustices of the poor and marginalised? The good news of the gospel comes not only in words but also in affirmative action. Felix Wilfred calls for a

> rethinking of mission in relation to religious pluralism, massive poverty, oppression and injustice. There can be no true understanding of the nature of evangelisation in this country without bringing into focus these pressing issues.[14]

9. Ninan, "Defining the Poor," 88.
10. Ibid., 89.
11. Ibid.
12. R. L. Sarkar, *The Bible, Ecology and Environment* (Delhi: ISPCK, 2000), 309.
13. Ninan, "Defining the Poor," 103.
14. Felix Wilfred, *Beyond Settled Foundations* (Madras, India: Department of Christian Studies, 1993), 207.

Rehabilitation for bonded labourers, sex workers, and beggars; critiquing the structures in society that cause sex workers and bonded labourers, and providing alternatives; creating awareness of environmental degradation; challenging the dehumanising effects of globalisation; offering training for access to better options for the marginalised; providing information on HIV-AIDS, hygiene, substance abuse, and addiction; exposing corruption—these are some of the components of the church's mission in today's world.

The poorest of the poor generally lack the means to escape their poverty. Yet it can be done. How so? Offer them computer training! Indians excel in the computer field. But the poor never get the opportunity. The Tamil Brethren Church in Bangalore decided to offer that possibility to nearby slum residents. Would they respond? Some thirty-five young people turned up for summer classes and received training, most from non-Christian backgrounds. The same Church opened its doors to provide a study place for slum children who also receive free tuition from volunteers. The poor are being empowered to help themselves through education. A social project, done without preaching, yet the Name of Christ is honoured. Is not this too the mission of the church?

Evangelicals, it has been said, are strong on preaching but weak on doing. This ought not be. Words may be required, but doing is the essential expression of being in the household of faith. What good is religion devoid of compassion? According to St. James, true religion involves caring for human needs. Faith that is unaccompanied by action, James argues, is useless.[15] What, then, are the kinds of actions that are required?

Various solutions have been proposed to the problems of poverty, caste, untouchability and related issues. Sanskritisation is one possible consideration by which low status groups seek to achieve higher status through a process of change to Brahminical patterns including a new mythology of origins. Its chief exponent, eminent sociologist M. N. Srinivas, linked Sanskritisation with Westernisation. The latter meant mobility outside the framework of caste whereas the former was mobility within caste.[16] Srinivas provides several examples but admits that Sanskritisation does not help the Untouchables.[17] John

---

15. James 1:27; 2:14–26.
16. M. N. Srinivas, *Caste in Modern India and Other Essays* (Bombay: Media Promoters & Publishers, 1962), 9.
17. Srinivas, *Caste in Modern India*, 59.

Maliekal is of the opinion that Westernisation rather than Sanskritisation is more important in India's modernization.[18] Lynch, however, concluded that participation in the political process rather than either Sanskritisation or Westernisation was a stronger factor for the upward mobility of some castes.[19]

None of the above, however, are adequate choices for today. Sanskritisation serves the fundamentalist agenda for reinforcing caste hierarchy. Westernisation has become virtually synonymous with the negative impact of globalisation on the poor and marginalised. And in light of its propensity to corruption, it is simplistic to propose political participation as an effective alternative.

What are the implications for the Christian mission in India? A former judge of the Supreme Court of India charged that the ruling class do not want to abolish untouchability and thus be deprived of its socio-economic benefits![20] The venerable Justice A. Varadarajan appealed to the Scheduled Castes and Tribes to revolt against the evils of caste and untouchability.[21] Movements of protest have followed, accompanied by occasional conversion movements into other religions. Much more recently, as we know, a section of the excluded opted for Buddhism. Christians follow these developments with interest and compassion. Disciples of Jesus Christ must identify with the poor and downtrodden. In imitation of their Master they too offer cups of cold water to the thirsty and wash the feet of the wounded and weary. Hospitality[22] and service to the least of Jesus's brothers and sisters: that too belongs in the Christian mission.

---

18. John Maliekal, *Caste in India Today* (Bangalore, India: Centre for Social Action, 1980), 22–23.

19. Owen M. Lynch, *The Politics of Untouchability: Social Mobility and Social Change in a City of India* (Delhi, India: National Publishing House, 1974), 8.

20. A. Varadarajan, "Untouchability in Contemporary India Worse Than Apartheid: Call to Youth for Ending Discrimination," *Presidential Address of Justice A. Varadarajan*, December 10, 1988, New Delhi.

21. Ibid., 15.

22. Hospitality is an important missiological theme, as several recent publications attest. See an extensive treatment of aspects of hospitality in Amos Yong, *Hospitality and the Other: Pentecost, Christian Practices, and the Neighbor* (New York: Orbis Books, 2008). Also Scott W. Sunquist and Amos Yong, eds., *The Gospel and Pluralism Today: Reassessing Lesslie Newbigin in the 21st Century* (Downers Grove, IL: InterVarsity Press, 2015); Jayson Georges and Mark D. Baker, *Ministering in Honor-Shame Cultures* (Downers Grove, IL: InterVarsity Press, 2016); William A. Dyrness, *Insider Jesus: Theological Reflections on New Christian Movements* (Downers Grove, IL: InterVarsity Press, 2016); and others.

TRANSFORMATION: THE NEW IDENTITY

In a recent article, Kancha Ilaiah introduces the head of the IBM international marketing division who happens to be a Dalit from Maharashtra (the only Dalit among Brahmins in IBM) and a Christian.[23] This young man had lived with us for a short time while he was completing his computer engineering studies in Chennai (then Madras). A happy story. His father, a pastor, once experienced abduction by terrorists—another story, fortunately with a happy ending.

Writing about Evangelicals' recovery of social dimensions of the Gospel, Jacob Thomas (of the Union Biblical Seminary faculty in Pune) points to the emergence of World Vision International, Tear Fund, World Concern, EFICOR and other expressions of compassion. Then he notes that Evangelicals from India and the developing world have a far greater concern than relief services and the alleviation of suffering. The greater issue is to struggle with questions about the evil structures of society which have pushed masses of humanity to the periphery of history.[24] Integrity of the gospel demands that evangelicals grapple with the root causes of poverty.

REFLECTION: THEOLOGIZING AND INTERNALIZING THE GOSPEL

Jesus's invitation to discipleship is a call to conversion. It is unfortunate that in our day conversion has been politicized so that its essential meaning is lost.[25] Biblically understood conversion is a spiritual event initiated by the Spirit of God resulting in life transformation.[26]

---

23. Kancha Ilaiah, "Blacks, Science and National Pride," *Deccan Chronicle,* July 2, 2003.

24. Jacob Thomas, "The Church's Response to the Poor—Evangelical Tradition," in Kim and Marak, *Good News to the Poor,* 196.

25. By President George Bush, for example, in order to gain the support of a section of the American electorate. More recently by Prime Minister Modi in India. See *Dharma Deepika* 38, vol. 17, no. 2 (July–December 2013), the entire issue devoted to conversion. See especially the essay by Ram Puniyani, "Religious Conversion and Violence in India: A Secular Perspective," 26–36.

26. Conversion studies amplify this point. See William Barclay, *Turning to God: A Study of Conversion in the Book of Acts and Today* (Grand Rapids: Baker, 1962); E. D. Devadason, *A Study on Conversion and Its Aftermath* (Madras, India: Christian Literature Society, 1982); Cedric B. Johnson and H. Newton Malony, *Christian Conversion: Biblical and Psychological Perspectives* (Grand Rapids: Zondervan, 1982); V. Gnanasikhamani, *The Conversion Story of H. A. Krishna Pillai and His Family* (Madras, India: Bible Literature Service, 1977); S. M. Michael, *Anthropology of Conversion in India* (Mumbai, India: Institute of Indian Culture, 1998); Krickwin C.

Conversion is for everyone, rich as well as poor. The evangelisers themselves must first be converted! This is a call to internalise the gospel. "At root the struggle is not for the wealth that the rich have but for their heart."[27] The rich are called to leave everything and come follow the Master. Conversion is a call to a spirituality of discipleship.

Evangelical spokespersons tend to be activists rather than deep thinkers. Perhaps. Nevertheless the Christian mission requires theological reflection. It is rewarding and revealing to engage in theological dialogue from the perspective of the poor.[28] Dehumanising poverty is an affront to the image of God that is found in every human. The poor, in evangelical perspective, are not only the victims of evil structures and systems, but through no fault of their own they are also deprived of God's love and compassion. The root cause of poverty is human sinfulness, not infrequently manifested in acts of selfishness and greed which deprive the poor of their basic rights to an abundant life. Rich and poor alike are in need of Christ's redemption.[29]

A disturbing reality is the marred identity of sections of the poor traditionally assigned subordinate positions of perpetual exploitation. Generations of poverty produce a negative outlook. "Low identity sanctions all forms of oppression."[30] Theologically the poor are victims of cosmic principalities and powers which "belong to the kingdom of Satan and wield control over people, structures and systems."[31] The Christian mission involves rescuing humans from the power of Satan and bringing them under the influence of the realm

---

Marak and Plamthodathil S. Jacob, eds., *Conversion in a Pluralistic Context* (Delhi: ISPCK, 2000); Joseph Mattam and Sebastian Kim, eds., *Mission and Conversion: A Reappraisal* (Mumbai, India: St. Pauls, 1996); Julian Saldanha, "The Great Conversion Debate," (Mumbai: Roshan Graphics, 2000); A. R. Tippett, "Religious Group Conversion in Non-Western Society," Research in Progress Pamphlet 11 (Pasadena, CA: School of World Mission, 1967); Gauri Viswanathan, *Outside the Fold: Conversion, Modernity, and Belief* (Princeton, NJ: Princeton University Press, 1998); Samuel Jayakumar, *Dalit Consciousness and Christian Conversion* (Delhi: ISPCK, 1999); Joshua Iyadurai, "Psychology of Religious Conversion," *Journal of Asian Evangelical Theology* (2008); W. R. Burrows, "Conversion: Individual and Cultural," in *Understanding World Christianity: The Vision and Work of Andrew F. Walls* (Maryknoll, NY: Orbis Books, 2011); and others.

27. Dewi Hughes, "Good News to the Poor—and to the Rich" in Kim and Marak, *Good News to the Poor*, 76.

28. This is achieved by Jayakumar Christian in his landmark study, *God of the Empty-Handed: Poverty, Power and the Kingdom of God* (Monrovia, CA: MARC World Vision, 1999).

29. Ibid., 67–73.

30. Ibid., 140.

31. Ibid., 150.

of God's kingdom of justice and new life in Christ. Evangelisation is the multi-faceted process of bringing this about. For whole sections of society this has meant the beginning of a new identity in Christ. The evil powers which have marred the self-identity of the poor are to be displaced by the power of the Kingdom of God "affirming their humanity and the image of God in them."[32]

A distorted image of God is our common human lot. In the words of an old hymn, we all are "sinners, ruined by the Fall." The good news is about the possibility of a new beginning. Grinding poverty mars the image, but the image can be restored. A start can be made. "This shaping of humans into the image of God is accomplished in the context of the church (that is, community). Therefore, community is an essential corollary to belief that we are made in the image of God."[33]

Awareness of the role of the church in the struggles of the alienated for humanisation is growing. A new subaltern hermeneutic involves "the rediscovery, re-reading, and reinterpretation of their socio-political history, and religious and cultural resources and texts" by subaltern groups.[34] History writing generally is by the powerful. "The very process of history-making becomes a source of powerlessness for the poor, because the way history is written assigns an identity to the poor."[35] Their distorted history perpetuates the powerlessness of the poor.[36] A remedial alternative is to "reread history from God's viewpoint."[37] A further corrective is a possible re-writing of history from the underside. Becoming a voice for the voiceless—that too is part of the mission of the church.

God's identity with the poor and oppressed is seen in Scripture. "You are the sons and daughters of the Lord your God. . . . You are a people holy to the Lord your God, and the Lord has chosen you to be a people for his own possession, out of all the peoples that are on the face of the earth."[38] "Remember that you were a slave in the land of Egypt, and the Lord your God redeemed you."[39] God's reclamation

---

32. Ibid., 197.
33. Ibid., 128.
34. Anthoniraj Thumma, *Voices of the Victims* (Delhi: ISPCK, 1999), 18.
35. Christian, *God of the Empty-Handed*, 137.
36. Ibid., 182.
37. Ibid., 183.
38. Deut 14:1–2.
39. Deut 15:15.

of his Old Testament people from slavery and their priestly reinstallation is replicated in the New Testament declaration:

> But you are a chosen race, a royal priesthood, a holy nation, God's own people, that you may declare the wonderful deeds of him who called you out of darkness into his marvelous light. Once you were no people but now you are God's people; once you had not received mercy but now you have received mercy.[40]

CONCLUSION

That impoverished peoples have risen to claim their spiritual inheritance is a fact of history and a contemporary reality. Many have found new human dignity through a new identity in Christ. Evangelisation begins a process of spiritual recovery whereby those of no social status have discovered their true identity of equality and self-esteem as the children of God and full citizens of his Kingdom.

SOURCES FOR FURTHER REFERENCE

Burrows, William R., Mark R. Gornik, and Janice A. McLean, eds. *Understanding World Christianity: The Vision and Work of Andrews F. Walls*. Maryknoll, NY: Orbis Books, 2013.

Christian, Jayakumar. *God of the Empty-Handed: Poverty, Power and the Kingdom of God*. Monrovia, CA: MARC World Vision, 1999.

Hughes, Dewi. "Good News to the Poor—and to the Rich." In *Good News to the Poor: The Challenge to the Church,* edited by Sebastian C. H. Kim and Krickwin C. Marak. Delhi: ISPCK, 1997.

Ilaiah, Kancha. "Blacks, Science and National Pride." *Deccan Chronicle,* July 2, 2003.

Jones, E. Stanley. *Conversion*. Nashville: Abingdon Press, 1959.

Kim, Sebastian C. H. *In Search of Identity: Debates on Religious Conversion in India*. New Delhi: Oxford University Press, 2003.

---

40. 1 Pet 2:9–10.

_____, and Krickwin C. Marak, eds. *Good News to the Poor: The Challenge to the Church.* Delhi: ISPCK, 1997.

Lynch, Owen M. *The Politics of Untouchability: Social Mobility and Social Change in a City of India.* Delhi: National, 1974.

Maliekal, John. *Caste in India Today.* Bangalore, India: Centre for Social Action, 1980.

Menon, Meena. "Escape from Bondage." *The Hindu*, September 7, 2003.

Nallappan, F. E. "Hindutva and the Minorities: Communalism and Discipleship." *Mission Today* 5, no. 3 (July–September 2003): 197–214.

Ninan, George. "Defining the Poor in India Today." In *Good News to the Poor: The Challenge to the Church*, edited by Sebastian C. H. Kim and Krickwin C. Marak. Delhi: ISPCK, 1997.

Nirmal, Chiranjivi J. *Madras Perspectives: Explorations in Social and Cultural History.* Madras, India: Institute of Indian and International Studies, 1992.

O'Neill, Tom. "Untouchables." *National Geographic,* June 2003, 2–31.

Salve, Gouri. "A Glimmer of Hope." *The Hindu*, September 7, 2003.

Sarkar, R. L. *The Bible, Ecology and Environment.* Delhi: ISPCK, 2000.

Srinivas, M. N. *Caste in Modern India and Other Essays.* Bombay: Media Promoters and Publishers, 1962.

Thumma, Anthoniraj. *Voices of the Victims: Movements and Models of People's Theology.* Delhi: ISPCK, 1999.

Varadarajan, Justice A. "Untouchability in Contemporary India Worse Than Apartheid: Call to Youth for Ending Discrimination." *Presidential Address of Justice A. Varadarajan.* December 10, 1988, New Delhi.

Viswanathan, Gauri. *Outside the Fold: Conversion, Modernity, and Belief.* Princeton, NJ: Princeton University Press, 1998.

Wallis, Jim. *The Call to Conversion: Why Faith Is Always Personal, but Never Private.* Rev. ed. San Francisco: HarperSanFrancisco, 2005 (1981).

Wilfred, Felix. *Beyond Settled Foundations.* Madras, India: Department of Christian Studies, University of Madras, 1993.

12.

Creative Ministries of New Christian Movements

Indigenous Christianity is a relatively new field for academic research in India.[1] A project designed to highlight the existence of numbers of Little Tradition Churches resulted in the publication initially of three books[2] as well as several articles in academic journals.[3] The Little Tradition comprises Churches of Indigenous Origins (CIOs) also

---

[1]. Originally for the Fellowship of Indian Missiologists (FOIM) Workshop on Creative Ministries, Mount Abu, Rajasthan, August 14–18, 2002.

[2]. Roger E. Hedlund, *Quest For Identity: India's Churches of Indigenous Origin; The "Little Tradition" in Indian Christianity*; Hedlund, ed., *Christianity Is Indian: The Emergence of an Indigenous Community*; and O. L. Snaitang, ed., *Churches of Indigenous Origins in North East India*, all three published by ISPCK (Delhi, 2000).

[3]. Articles and essays include (1) "Subaltern Movements and Indian Churches of Indigenous Origins," *Journal of Dharma* 22, no. 1 (1998): 8–38; (2) "Indigenous Christian Movements in India," *Light of Life*, May 1998, 51–57; (3) "Indian Christians of Indigenous Origins and Their Solidarity with Original Groups," *Journal of Dharma* 24, no. 1 (1999): 13–27; (4) "Indian Instituted Churches: Indigenous Christianity, Indian-Style," *Mission Studies* 16-1, no. 31 (1999): 26–42; (5) "The Search for Indigenous Church Models in India," in *Mission and Missions: Essays in Honour of I. Ben Wati*, ed. J. Kanagaraj (Pune, India: Union Biblical Seminary, 1998) (6) three articles in the *New International Dictionary of Pentecostal/Charismatic Movements*, ed. Stanley M. Burgess (Grand Rapids: Zondervan, 2002); (7) an article in the *Dictionary of Asian Christianity*, ed. Scott Sunquist, John Chew, and David Wu (Grand Rapids: Eerdmans, 2001); (8) "Approaches to Indian Church History in Light of New Christian Movements," *Indian Church History Review*, December 2000, 153–70; (9) an entire issue of *Dharma Deepika* devoted to Indigenous Christianity, January–June 2002, viz., Daniel Jeyaraj, "Glimpses of Vedanayagam Sastriyar," 5–12; Grace Parimala Appasamy, "Christian Music of Tamil Nadu," 13–18; Roger E. Hedlund, "India's Quest for Indigenous Christianity," 19–29; Sudheer Merugumalla, "Christian Santhi Ashram," 31–36; P. Solomon Raj, "Songs of the Pilgrim Churches," 37–42; Samanta Naik, "Churches of Indigenous Origins in Orissa," 43–46; Ravi Tiwari, "Christ-Bhakta Yesu

designated as Indian Instituted Churches (IICs). In contrast to "missionary" Christianity—that is, Great Tradition Churches and institutions that are the product of foreign missionary effort, commonly known as "mainline" Churches—indigenous Indian Christianity has its own structures and cultural expressions that are frequently outside the orbit of the traditional Churches, hence overlooked by earlier studies which concentrated on Churches of the Great Tradition.[4] This phenomenon is believed to be more extensive and more influential than is generally realised.

A recent article describing thousands of non-baptised *Khrist Bhaktas* in the Diocese of Varanasi challenges us to derive new insights for the concept of evangelisation in the multir-eligious and multicultural context of India.[5] The purpose of this essay is to document some of the creative ministries which are characteristic of indigenous Indian Christianity. My method of research was very simple. No national or regional survey was attempted. A number of individuals and agencies were asked to tell their story. "Tell me about the creative ministries of . . . (your church or organization)." Additional information was gleaned from published sources. In no sense should this paper be considered definitive. The organisations may be representative of the larger movement of indigenous Christianity, but the stories they tell are unique to each Church or agency. In what follows, I have tried to let the spokespersons speak for themselves.

THE INHERITORS

The Inheritors is a registered charitable society located in Nagpur, Maharashtra. According to its mission statement, "The Inheritors exists to provide wholistic care for families and the first generation Christians through teaching, training and nurture to establish them in Christian love." The two-pronged mission of The Inheritors grows out of this statement.

Families today experience enormous pressures. To minister to the needs of families, The Inheritors has developed a team of experienced men and women with expertise in communication and counselling

---

Das," 47–60; Daniel Jeyaraj, "De Nobili Research Institute," 61–65; Jyothi Uday Kumar, "What Liberates a Woman? The Story of Pandita Ramabai," 66–70.

4. See Hedlund, "Approaches to Indian Church History."

5. Roque D'Costa, "Evangelization: New Modes and New Avenues," *Mission Today* 3, no. 1 (January–March 2002): 22–27.

who bring insights from their cultural and ethnic backgrounds to facilitate building strong families. Workshops and seminars are offered on parenting and on building and sustaining strong marriages. Programmes focused on living in relationship include seminars for couples, for young people, for professionals, for lay leaders and pastors, and for heads of organisations.

First Generation Christians (FGCs) are people with special needs. Having become disciples of Jesus Christ from various faith backgrounds, the transition is sometimes traumatic. The Inheritors is committed to assisting FGCs in the face of family rejection, suspicion and non-acceptance by the local church.

Help is provided in the form of mentoring and teaching to enable the FGCs to comprehend their relationship with the local church and society as well as to strengthen their ties with their original community. Simultaneously the local church is enabled to respond to the needs of the FGCs.[6] Two projects demonstrate The Inheritors' pro-active philosophy. One is an HIV-AIDS awareness programme offering information, counselling, guidance and help. A skill training centre is designed to enable the infected or affected to live and earn their livelihood with dignity.

The other project is a progressive school linked with home schooling to serve the needs of Indian missionary parents in North India. Griha Shiksha prepares and sends educational materials monthly thus providing home schooling for children up to the age of nine. A play school in Nagpur and summer camps for missionary children are also offered.

In summary, The Inheritors is a creative response to the contemporary Indian context as well as to needs in the Indian missionary community.

MAHARASHTRA VILLAGE MINISTRIES

Originally founded in 1981 by students of the Union Biblical Seminary while it was located at Yavatmal, Maharashtra Village Ministries (MVM) is focused on the spiritual and social needs of rural Maharashtra.[7] From its original base in Yavatmal District, MVM has expanded

---

6. Information is from a newsletter, *The Inheritor*, January–February 2002; *The Inheritors* brochure; and *Griha Shiksha* brochure.

7. Information provided by Mr. Sujit David, a missionary staff worker of MVM, in an interview at Union Biblical Seminary, Pune, February 16, 2002.

progressively into Wardha, Chandrapore, Nagpur, Amravati, and Thana, a total of six out of thirty-five districts in the state. At present MVM has eighty-five workers, including office staff as well as missionaries, and has started twenty-four congregations. Maharashtra Village Ministries is a holistic agency with a vision to proclaim the gospel by word and deed in remote villages through systematic church planting among unreached peoples in unreached villages.[8] The policy of the mission is to work in close relationship with existing Indian churches.

In Mumbai MVM partners with the Church of North India Bombay Diocese and the Mar Thoma Church by providing personnel and supervision for rural outreach. Church members from the urban CNI and Mar Thoma congregations are involved directly by providing expertise including medical assistance. A village church was started, and the tribal converts accepted into the Mar Thoma Church. For its part, the CNI Bombay Diocese has formed the Mumbai Diocese Missionary Movement under the patronage of the Bishop. Elsewhere, MVM entered into a Memorandum of Understanding with the South India Conference of the Free Methodist Church to serve the ecclesiastical needs of converts, that is, for sacraments, church discipline, marriage and funerals.

MVM has recognised the potential of resource-sharing through cooperation with specialist agencies. Thus Campus Crusade for Christ provides the Jesus film with equipment, World Cassette Outreach (WCO) offers the New Testament on cassette and Project Philip provides lessons for nurturing new converts. MVM aims for development of grass-roots leaders through a five to six year process. Local evangelists are trained in summer camps which serve as short-term Bible schools. This is followed by further in-house training. The Shalom Mela, conducted for three days during December, encourages the believers, provides opportunity to meet possible marriage partners and thus strengthens the developing church. Some 450 attended a recent mela where 50 percent of the cost was paid for locally.

Maharashtra Village Ministries is one example of an indigenous mission serving quietly, and with little publicity, making innovative use of local resources to serve human needs in neglected rural communities.

---

8. Maharashtra Village Ministries, *MVM at a Glance 2001* brochure.

EMMANUEL MINISTRIES, KOLKATA

A comprehensive mission to the city is found in Emmanuel Ministries[9] initiatives among addicted and afflicted sections of Kolkata society. The plight of fifty thousand (50,000) street children and the problems of slum dwellers as well as the suicidal depressions of sophisticated urbanites are some of the motivating factors behind the multiple projects of Emmanuel Ministries and the Jivan Jyoti Fellowship (church) it has fostered in the heart of the city.[10] A brief description follows of some of these creative answers to the city's challenges.

PAULINE BHAVAN

The railway platforms of Howrah Station and other train stations of Kolkata are "home" to hundreds of lost, abandoned or runaway children in the city. Exploited and abused, these children are deprived of childhood and destined to a life of anti-social behaviour and crime. Pauline Bhavan, with facilities for fifty children, seeks to rescue such children by providing a secure home environment complete with medical care, education, recreation, and cultural activities.

PAVEMENT CLUB

Surely a unique service is the Pavement Club conducted at the Emmanuel Ministries' Headquarter in Rippon Street for destitute children living with their parents in makeshift shelters on the streets. The pavement club caters to the needs of these children on a daily basis by providing nutritious food, hygiene and nonformal education. Minor ailments are treated and immunizations provided. The Pavement Club seeks to affirm the worth and dignity of street children, and prevent them from becoming victims of exploitation, substance abuse and AIDS.[11]

---

9. Founded in the 1970s by the late Vijayan Pavamani and his wife Premila Pavamani who originally had come to Kolkata in 1968 as YFC (Youth For Christ) workers.

10. Information is from personal observation during visits to various ministries over a period of several years as well as from the definitive article by Beena Nathan, "Emmanuel Ministries Calcutta: An Indian Urban Mission Response to the City," in Hedlund, *Christianity Is Indian*, 288–99.

11. Ibid., 292.

MIDWAY HOME

In order to facilitate the rehabilitation of recovering addicts and their reintegration into society, a halfway house was established. Arunoday Midway Home provides counseling and therapy in a disciplined environment and also offers detoxification camps, seminars and workshops on AIDS awareness and the dangers of substance abuse.

NEW MARKET COMMUNITY DEVELOPMENT PROJECT

The project aims at improving the quality of life of inhabitants of a slum area. Particular attention is given to children of prostitutes to affirm their human dignity, achieve their potential and lead productive lives.

SERAMPORE COMMUNITY DEVELOPMENT

In cooperation with the Theology Department of Serampore College, a non-formal education programme is conducted in the portico of St. Olaf's Church for children from the surrounding slums along with health, hygiene and drug and alcohol abuse awareness programmes.

CALCUTTA EMMANUEL SCHOOL

Originally an effort to get street children off the street, Calcutta Emmanuel School today is a recognized educational institution housed in a modern building providing formal education for two hundred and fifty (250) underprivileged children.

Other services provided by Emmanuel Ministries include an Extension Care Centre providing a residential training course to integrate recovering addicts and rehabilitated young adults into society as well as a Rickshaw Pullers Fellowship extending God's love to two hundred (200) members of a neglected community through awareness and empowerment. The liberating dynamism of the

Gospel is clearly manifested in the lives of individuals and groups discovering the truth which sets free.[12]

NEW TESTAMENT CHURCH OF INDIA

Creative ministries of the New Testament Church of India (NTCI), headquartered at Bheemunipatnam, Visakhapatnam, in Andhra Pradesh, address issues of poverty and the Indian brain drain to the West (Titus 2000).[13] The primary strategy of the NTCI is to use already available resources for the development of rural India. Church buildings, which represent a considerable cash investment, generally are utilised for but a few hours during the week, mainly for Sunday worship. In under-developed villages such buildings should be put to use to provide needed educational facilities. At present the NTCI operates fifteen (15) such primary schools in fifteen (15) villages, six each in Vizianagaram and Visakhapatnam Districts, one in Hyderabad District, and two in the Bastar District of Chhattisgarh. About five hundred (500) poor village children are being educated in these schools without any discrimination as to caste, creed, religion or race. The local NTCI pastor supervises each school and provides Christian and moral value education.

In many respects women may be the key to the modernisation of India. COTR Theological Seminary[14] offers seminars for Christian women, and a Vocational Training School offers basic computer training for poor and destitute women who are offered market placement upon successful completion of the course. In 1998, a Women's Vocational College was launched which has proven effective for socio-economic empowerment of the poor and destitute as well as outreach to lower and middle income group employees.

Information technology training for women has proven effective. It is part of a process of making Christians feel proud of their Indian culture and helping them to cherish their Indian heritage.

---

12. Ibid., 291.
13. Information about the creative ministries of the New Testament Church of India is provided by the late Apostle Dr. P. J. Titus, Founder-President of the COTR College of Ministries, Bheemunipatnam, Visakhapatnam, in a paper and letter dated January 30, 2002.
14. COTR houses not only a theological institution but also a residential school and has facilities for large conventions and other projects.

THE PENTECOSTAL MISSION

The exclusivistic Ceylon Pentecostal Mission, now also known as The Pentecostal Mission or The Pentecostal Church, is an indigenous movement originating in South India.[15] Its founder, Ramankutty, born in 1881 to Hindu parents in Trichur District, Kerala, was converted to Christianity in Ceylon (Sri Lanka) at the age of eighteen through a vision of Christ which caused him to begin secretly to pray and meditate on Jesus.[16] Then, in 1902, at the age of twenty-two, a third vision convinced Ramankutty that he could not remain a hidden follower of Jesus. Ramankutty openly confessed Jesus as Lord, was baptised, and given the Christian name "Paul."

His ministry developed gradually. It was reported that a leper over whom Paul prayed was cured, and a person declared dead was brought to life. People were attracted to his new fellowship called the Ceylon Pentecostal Mission, among them a college lecturer, Alwin R. de Alwis. Under the leadership of Pastor Paul and Bro. Alwin the CPM ministry spread beyond Colombo to Tamil Nadu and Kerala, then to other countries.[17]

Historian G. P. V. Somaratna states that Alwin R. de Alwis was the main instrument in the foundation of the CPM in 1923, as a break-away from the ministry of Walter Clifford who had come to the region as an independent Christian worker but was now forming links with the Assemblies of God (AOG) in America.[18] Full-time CPM workers were expected to practice an ascetic life-style including celibacy, obedience to the chief pastor, communal living (including disposal of private possessions) in faith homes, corporate prayers beginning at 4:00 a.m., and the wearing of white dress as a biblical principle—the latter particularly appropriate in Sri Lanka where white was worn by Buddhist devotees in visits to the temples.[19] Indigenous forms of worship were incorporated. Worshipers were seated on mats on the floor–similar to Buddhist and

---

15. Information about the Ceylon Pentecostal Mission was provided by one of its stalwart members, Bro. Paul C. Martin in a paper entitled "A Brief History of the Ceylon Pentecostal Mission," presented at the Hyderabad Conference on Indigenous Christian Movements in India, October 27–31, 1998.
16. Ibid.
17. Ibid., 8.
18. Somaratna, *Origins of the Pentecostal Mission in Sri Lanka* (Nugegoda, Sri Lanka: Margaya Fellowship, 1996), 30, 33.
19. Ibid., 34.

Hindu worship procedures. Domestic musical instruments for worship, singing of indigenous tunes and other local cultural practices gave the CPM an identity of its own, yet the main driving force was the healing ministry.[20]

The CPM laid the foundation for other Pentecostal ministries not only in Sri Lanka and India but beyond. Today, states Paul C. Martin, the CPM under various names, is one of the largest Pentecostal movements in the world with branches in several countries. While exact membership figures are not available, there are 848 branches worldwide (including 708 in India) and about 3,984 full-time ministers presided over by chief pastor C. K. Lazarus.[21] In addition there are numbers of independent assemblies and movements which have severed connections with the CPM.

A recent web site, Shalomindia, provides addresses in several cities in India and other countries for TPM, The Pentecostal Mission (formerly CPM). Information technology utilisation suggests a current vitality in this early Pentecostal movement.

NEW LIFE ASSEMBLY OF GOD, CHENNAI

The Assemblies of God history in India dates from the early part of the twentieth century, but is fairly recent in Chennai. New Life AOG at Saidapet is a "mega-church" of about eighteen thousand (18,000) worshipers where the rich as well as poor sit together and worship side by side irrespective of caste or social background. Apart from its multiple Tamil and English week-end worship services utilising contemporary music and drama, the church engages in a wide range of social activities. Eye camps and medical teams recruited from the congregation provide free services in needy rural areas. Creative ministries include a degree-level evening Bible college, deployment of bi-vocational missionary "tentmakers" to North India, and outreach ministries in slums. The latter innovation merits attention.

Participatory lay leadership training has been a hallmark of the Pentecostal movement. Lay people of all ages are recruited into ministry. Much of the local ministry centers in some two thousand (2,000) care cells meeting in homes. New Life AOG adapted the cell system, first introduced by the Rev. Paul Yongi Cho of the Yoido

20. Ibid., 40, 30.
21. Martin, "Brief History of the Ceylon Pentecostal Mission," 5, 12.

Full Gospel Central Church in Korea, to the Indian context. It will be instructive to take a closer look.

Mr. A. Gabriel is a care cell leader.[22] He is from an agricultural family. After the third standard he quit school and learned basket-weaving and cane work in order to earn, then came to Madras where he works as a cobbler. After several tragic events, he became an alcoholic. Meanwhile his younger brother's wife was converted in the Assembly of God Church. She urged him to come to the church for healing. He suffered from a serious leg infection and doctors threatened possible amputation. He went, but was not healed. The second time he was carried into the church, but came home walking. Then Gabriel went to a nearby temple where he vowed to stop drinking. At home, however, the vow was soon broken. For three days he was unable to get up from his bed until one day he felt as if he had been slapped—and got up healed! From that day onward he was no more an alcoholic. Two months later Gabriel joined a care cell. In six months he became the leader of a care cell in his own house. After one year he became a sectional leader, and now has five care cells under his supervision.

Gabriel's testimony of the social, economic and personal transformative power of the gospel is but one example. Modern Pentecostalism from its early origins was a multi-racial integrationist movement characterised by maximum participation of all its members.[23] New Life Assembly is a dynamic example.

GEMS HOUSE OF PRAYER

The story of the Gospel Echoing Missionary Society (GEMS) is a remarkable account of one local Church in mission. It is a record of the achievement of one local Church in South India, the GEMS House of Prayer at Chrompet, Chennai, whose concentrated missionary outreach has brought an entire new denomination into existence in an area of North India where previously there was no Church.

Today the GEMS Church is growing rapidly with 438 workers at

22. Interview with Mr. A. Gabriel at the residence of Mrs. Annie Valsarajan, Luz Avenue, Mylapore, March 14, 2002.

23. Walter J. Hollenweger, "The Black Roots of Pentecostalism," in *Pentecostals after a Century: Global Perspectives on a Movement in Transition*, ed. Allan H. Anderson and Walter J. Hollenweger (Sheffield, UK: Sheffield Academic Press, 1999).

142 centres in the different parts of Bihar as well as in bordering Uttar Pradesh and Madhya Pradesh. Some six thousand (6,000) believers attended the GEMS convention in Bihar during October 1998.

Many projects are carried out including three children's homes plus a home for one hundred children of stonecutters and a home for sixty polio-victim children. GEMS also operates seventy-seven middle schools and four English schools including a high school. Out of sixty-nine linguistic dialects in Bihar, GEMS concentrates mainly in three major Hindi dialects: Bhojpuri, Maitali, and Magai.[24] The Mission works mainly in neglected areas of North Bihar, Central Bihar, and West Bihar. With seven thousand (7,000) baptised and eight thousand (8,000) known believers, the GEMS Christian community in Bihar also includes some fifteen thousand (15,000) children cared for in schools.

The GEMS approach includes a balanced programme of medical ministry involving a hospital and clinics, free medical camps, education, and social services including emancipation of children from bonded labour. Because of this benevolent social dimension the Mission is well-accepted in Bihar, despite some opposition and persecution.[25] It is a significant achievement in North India through the concerted cross-cultural missionary effort of a single local congregation in South India.

FRIENDS MISSIONARY PRAYER BAND AMONG THE MALTOS

The experience of the Malto people in Jharkand is an impressive story of social and spiritual redemption. Decimated by malnutrition, tuberculosis, goiter, jaundice, cholera, malaria and various water-born diseases, the Malto people also were exploited by rapacious money lenders. Addiction to alcohol and other substances was a further degrading influence.[26] This dehumanized tribe had declined from one million to less than seventy thousand (70,000) during the past

---

24. Information provided by Mr. Goforth, son of the GEMS mission director in Bihar, Pastor Augustine Jebakumar, by telephone at Chennai-Chrompeth, on January 11, 1999.

25. Pastor Augustine Jebakumar, telephone interview, Chrompet-Chennai, on January 13, 1999.

26. Muthusami Raj, "Christianity and the Social Transformation of the Maltos People of Bihar, India" (MA diss., All Nations Christian College, Hertfordshire, England, 1997). Mr. Muthusami Raj is an FMPB missionary to the Maltos.

forty years and was moving toward extinction.[27] Religion, requiring expensive animal sacrifices to godlings and demons, was a costly affair.[28]

Into this context of human despair, missionaries of the Friends Missionary Prayer Band (FMPB) and other social development workers came to live and serve. Learning the Malto language and adopting the Malto culture, they identified with the people. Several Christian workers gave their lives, including the FMPB General Secretary's son who succumbed to a sudden attack of cerebral malaria.[29] In response to this outpouring of love the Maltos began to turn to Christ resulting in a growing people movement which has brought large numbers into the Church.

The Malto Christians have experienced radical change in their lifestyle bringing release from fear, from addictions and other costly practices. Self-help projects assisted by EFICOR have made it possible for the people to counteract their own poverty and to rid themselves of exploitation by money lenders and other oppressors. "The message of equality and liberty in Christ came as a great impetus to the Maltos social transformation."[30] Their health status improved through health camps conducted by Emmanuel Hospital Association in which basic health and hygiene are taught.[31] The Maltos are no longer a population in decline.

A large section of the Malto tribe have been baptised, and a new diocese of the Church of North India has been formed. As of January 31, 2002, the records showed 43,048 Malto Christian believers in 520 congregations.[32] In January 2000, the New Testament in the Malto language was dedicated, translated by FMPB missionaries, and published by the Bible Society of India.[33]

Christianity has brought social transformation to a demoralised and disintegrating society. Today the Malto people find their self-identity

---

27. According to the 1981 Census there were 100,177 speakers of the Malto language. See K. S. Singh and S. Manoharan, *Languages & Scripts*, People of India National Series vol. 9, Anthropological Survey of India (Oxford: Oxford University Press, 1997).
28. Raj, "Christianity and the Social Transformation of the Maltos," 9, 11, 14–16.
29. Ibid., 24.
30. Ibid., 34.
31. Ibid., 41.
32. S. John Berlin, "Malto Update," e-mail communication to Roger E. Hedlund, March 18, 2002.
33. Information provided by the Rev. Dr. J. T. K. Daniel, Tambaram, in a telephone conversation, February 26, 2002.

in Christianity, the incarnational witness of the FMPB missionaries having performed a vital catalytic function.

A NASCENT KORKU CHURCH IN CENTRAL INDIA

In his descriptions of tribes in central India, anthropologist Stephen Fuchs described the alienation of the tribes who are dispossessed of their lands and reduced to the status of daily labourers or forced to emigrate.[34] Governmental and other tribal social welfare efforts have been ineffective. Schools run by Christian missions are said to be more successful, however, and Christian tribals have a higher rate of literary.[35] This has led to "fears" that the tribals would convert in large numbers, despite the fact that this has never happened, nor are they likely. "If any mass conversions are taking place, they are to Hinduism alone."[36] Fuchs deplored the sad reality that "aboriginal religion and culture are doomed to disappear from India in the near future"—a likelihood particularly in central India where there is no strong tribal solidarity.[37]

A possible exception might be the Korku tribe of the highlands of central India, a tribe not in decline but struggling to improve their status. One possible path would be through conversion to Islam. However the Korkus exhibit an aversion to Islam and strive rather "to be accepted as a respected Hindu caste."[38] Probably for similar reasons conversions to Christianity have been few despite one hundred and twenty-five years of Protestant and Catholic missionary presence. Fuchs noted some seven hundred Catholics at Chikaldera and six hundred and fifty in Nimar District.[39] The Korkus have had a much longer period of contact with Hinduism resulting in a dual identity in which traditional tribal religion is combined with Hindusim, making conversion to Christianity difficult.[40]

Where conversions have taken place they tend to be along kinship lines and in response to human need. A study of sixty-seven converts

---

34. Stephen Fuchs, *The Aboriginal Tribes of India* (New York: St. Martin's Press, 1973), 136.
35. Ibid., 140.
36. Ibid., 143.
37. Ibid., 141, 143.
38. Stephen Fuchs, *The Korkus of the Vihdhya Hills* (New Delhi: Inter-India Publications, 1986), 391.
39. Ibid., 392.
40. Noel Kotian, "Neglected or Resistant: The Response of the Korku People to Christianity" (MA diss., All Nations Christian College, Hertfordshire, England, 2001), 47, 49.

has shown that 90 percent "believed in Jesus Christ through healing from diseases or release from demonic oppression. Healings have come through prayer and also by medicines."[41] Kinship lines can either help or hinder the spread of the gospel.

In 1982, the Indian Evangelical Mission (IEM) opened a missionary training centre at Chikaldara in Amravati District.[42] Missionaries trained in linguistics and translation principles carried on the Korku Bible translation work which had been started by their American and English missionary predecessors.[43] Portions of the Bible have been translated into Korku and published by the Bible Society. Translation continues primarily through the Indian Evangelical Mission.[44] Since the 1970s, literacy and translation projects, medical services and developmental efforts have been carried out by indigenous Catholic and Protestant missionary personnel.[45] One of the unique developments has been a working agreement between the local Baptist Christian Association (BCA), and indigenous mission agencies working for the evangelisation of the Korku and other peoples in Central India.[46]

DIN BANDHU MINISTRIES

Din Bandhu ("Friend of the Poor") has its roots in the campus of the Yavatmal College for Leadership Training (YCLT), at Yavatmal, Maharashtra.[47] Sunil Sardar, a well-known political activist for the farmers' cause in Yavatmal District, started the ministry in 1990 along with his American wife and several associates, including Friends Missionary Prayer Band (FMPB), partnered with Sunil for the redemption of the Kolami-speaking Kolawar people.

41. Ibid., 40.
42. Ibid., 38.
43. Miss Beryl Girard from America and Miss Lillian Merry from England, missionaries of the Conservative Baptist Foreign Mission Society (now WorldVenture), were pioneer translators among the Korkus.
44. See J. Ganesapandy, "Korkus of Chikaldara: A Study of Resistance and Response" (MA thesis, South Asia Institute for Advanced Christian Studies, Kothanur, Bangalore).
45. Protestant agencies include the Baptist Christian Association, Indian Evangelical Mission and Zoram Baptist Mission in addition to Catholic congregations and institutes.
46. Leonard Tuggy, "Case Study: Western/Indian Mission Cooperation to Reach Korku Tribals," a paper for the EFMA/IFMA Executives' Retreat, Kansas City, USA, September 29, 1981.
47. Information that follows is from "Creative Ways of Dinbandhu Ministries" by Sunil Sardar, 2002, and other miscellaneous papers in a communication to Roger E. Hedlund, February 2002.

A Kolawar Sanghatana (Kolam's Association) was formed. Films and a songbook in the Kolami language were utilised to present the gospel in more than one hundred fifty Kolawar villages. Starting with five Kolawar believers, their efforts resulted in forty-seven baptisms on the YCLT campus. News that the Kolawar were becoming Christians brought disruption and false propaganda. The campus was attacked. Sunil was arrested and jailed. The "conversion conspiracy" brought inquiries from former Farmer's Association activists and others who also began to convert. YCLT bid Sunil to leave the campus, and his former associates abandoned him.

"Dinbandhu Ministries" was formed and registered. Worship continued in the Sardar home. A couple from Youth With A Mission (YWAM) came to work with the Sardars and the ministry grew. Even the Banjara (Gormati) tribe responded. Space proved inadequate and a building was rented in Yavatmal for Wednesday fasting, prayer and teaching and for Sunday worship, which included open communion. Soon they were invited into the neighbouring Wardha District.

Inspired by Mahatma Jyotiba Phule's literature, Sunil began to address Jesus as "Baliraja" (the King who was sacrificed for his people). Baptism was given the Indian cultural name *Ganga Snan* (Holy Bath) to better communicate the idea of repentance and cleansing. "The ritual of dipping people in the River Ganges can be used as a bridge to bring people to Christ."[48] As Sunil explains, "Believers need only to come once, as Jesus Christ has done the cleansing for us by His work on the cross. The Lord revealed this bridge as a way to bring people to a full knowledge of who Jesus Christ is and what He has done for us."[49] The breaking of coconuts, familiar to Hindus in their rituals, became a meaningful spiritual Indian symbol in communion. Sunil explained the one-time sacrifice Jesus made for sin for all eternity is also symbolic of his body being broken and his blood shed for each of us thus making it easier for Hindus to better understand Christ's sacrificial act.[50]

Commenting on this contextual adaptation of the Eucharist, it is pointed out that "a coconut must be broken first, before its water can be drunk and the meat eaten. In communion, we are reminded

---

48. Sunil Sardar, "Redeeming the Hindu Culture for His Glory," unpublished paper, February 2000.
49. Ibid.
50. Ibid.

that the breaking of the bread symbolizes the breaking of the body."[51] New believers were encouraged to be able to worship according to their culture and in their homes.

Din Bandhu reaches out to OBCs (lower castes) and Dalits by providing affordable English medium education for the poor at Wardha through the Staines Memorial School, named in memory of the martyrdom of Graham Staines and his two young sons, who gave their lives for Christ among the Poor in Orissa.

Sunil continues to develop friendships among the Dalit and OBC leaders in an effort to promote personal and social reform.[52] He testifies that hurdles are being overcome. "We are looking forward to the church that will take place in each caste and home, where worship to Jesus Christ, the Baliraja, will be supreme."[53]

CONCLUSION

Creative ministries of new Christian movements take many forms and include empowerment activities among slum dwellers and street children, liberation of backward communities and tribals, encouragement of women's movements and Christ *Bhaktas*, use of indigenous communication media, employment of local proverbs and sayings, as well as more traditional roles of community development, Bible translation, village schools, and church planting. A few examples have been provided, but most stories remain untold.

---

51. Jan L. Beaderstadt, "The Theology of the Coconut," unpublished paper, n.d., provided by Sunil Sardar.

52. See various articles by Sunil Sardar, e.g., "Who Is the True Mahatma of India?," unpublished paper, February 2000; "Thoughts on Brahminism and Hinduism," unpublished paper, June 2001.

53. Sunil Sardar, "Creative Ways of Dinbandhu Ministries," unpublished paper, February 2002, 2.

SOURCES FOR FURTHER REFERENCE

D'Costa, Roque. "Evangelization: New Modes and New Avenues." *Mission Today* 3, no. 1 (January–March 2002): 22–27.

Fuchs, Stephen. *The Aboriginal Tribes of India*. New York: St. Martin's Press, 1973.

———. *The Korkus of the Vihdhya Hills*. New Delhi: Inter-India Publications, 1986.

Ganesapandy, J. "Korkus of Chikaldara: A Study of Resistance and Response." MA thesis, South Asia Institute for Advanced Christian Studies, Kothanur, Bangalore, 1998.

———. "The Advent of the Gospel to the Korkus." *Dharma Deepika* 27, vol. 12, no. 1 (January–June 2008): 54–65.

Hedlund, Roger E. "Approaches to Indian Church History in Light of New Christian Movements." *Indian Church History Review*, December 2000, 153–70.

———. *Quest For Identity: India's Churches of Indigenous Origin; The "Little Tradition" in Indian Christianity*. Delhi: ISPCK, 2000.

———, ed. *Christianity Is Indian: The Emergence of an Indigenous Community*. Delhi: ISPCK, 2004 (2000).

Hollenweger, Walter J. "The Black Roots of Pentecostalism." In *Pentecostals after a Century: Global Perspectives on a Movement in Transition*, edited by Allan H. Anderson and Walter J. Hollenweger. Sheffield, UK: Sheffield Academic Press, 1999.

Kotian, Noel. "Neglected or Resistant: The Response of the Korku People to Christianity." MA diss., All Nations Christian College, Hertfordshire, England, 2001.

Mihindukulasuriya, Prabo, Ivor Poobalann, and Ravin Caldera, eds. *A Cultured Faith: Essays in Honour of Prof. G. P. V. Somaratna on His Seventieth Birthday*. Colombo, Sri Lanka: Colombo Theological Seminary, 2011.

Martin, Paul C. "A Brief History of the Ceylon Pentecostal Mission." In *Christianity Is Indian: The Emergence of an Indigenous Community*, edited by Roger E. Hedlund. Delhi: ISPCK, 2004 (2000).

Nathan, Beena. "Emmanuel Ministries Calcutta: An Indian Urban Mission Response to the City." In *Christianity Is Indian: The Emergence of an Indigenous Community*, edited by Roger E. Hedlund, 288–99. Delhi: ISPCK, 2004 (2000).

Raj, Muthusami. "Christianity and the Social Transformation of the Maltos People of Bihar, India." MA diss., All Nations Christian College, Hertfordshire, England, 1997.

Singh, K. S., and S. Manoharan, eds. *Languages & Scripts.* People of India National Series vol. IX. Anthropological Survey of India. Oxford: Oxford University Press, 1997.

Snaitang, O. L., ed. *Churches of Indigenous Origins in North East India.* Delhi: ISPCK, 2000.

Somaratna, G. P. V. *Origins of the Pentecostal Mission in Sri Lanka.* Nugegoda, Sri Lanka: Margaya Fellowship, 1996.

_____. *Walter H. Clifford: Apostle of Pentecostalism in Sri Lanka.* Nugegoda, Sri Lanka: Margaya Fellowship, 1997.

13.

Living Water and the Holy Spirit

INTRODUCTION

I am grateful to the organizers for their kind invitation to present this paper on an important topic.[1] It is a privilege to participate in this significant conference. "Living Water and the Holy Spirit" is a profound theme, deserving serious biblical exegesis beyond the limited scope of this paper. The conference, as I understand it, is called to highlight the primacy of evangelism in the Baptist witness in Asia and specifically Sri Lanka. Paper topics and the messages presented bear this out. My assigned topic addresses a basic truth: authentic evangelism must center in Jesus Christ, the cross and resurrection, and is empowered by the Holy Spirit.

Our topic comes from a text of Scripture:

> "Whoever believes in me, as Scripture has said, rivers of living water will flow from within them." By this he meant the Spirit, whom those who believed in him were later to receive. Up to that time the Spirit had not been given, since Jesus had not yet been glorified. (John 7:38–39)

Together now let us explore this rich theme, in humility and gratitude, asking the Lord's enablement, for the blessing of his People and the evangelization of the world.

---

1. Originally presented as a paper at the Living Water Conference of the Asia Baptist World Alliance and the Sri Lanka Baptist Sangamaya at Colombo, Sri Lanka, November 13–16, 2008.

LIVING WATER—AND THE "I AM" SAYINGS OF JESUS

Jesus's "I Am" sayings are found throughout the Gospel of John. In this Conference two instances are addressed by Bro. Elmo de Mel (John 7:37) and by Rev. Kingsley Perera (John 4:10, 46), both texts concerning "Living Water" which is the theme of this conference. "I Am" declarations in John's Gospel include "Bread of Life" (6:35, 51), "Light of the World" (8:12), "Gate" or "Door" (10:7), "Good Shepherd" (10:11, 14), "Resurrection and Life" (11:25), "Way, Truth, Life" (14:6), "Vine" (15:1, 5) and others.

Pivotal to them all is Jesus's emphatic, "Before Abraham was, I am" (8:58), an exclusive statement of his claim to deity. Coupled with Jesus's further statement of oneness with God the Father, "The Father and I are one" (10:30), it provoked a charge of blasphemy and an attempt to kill Jesus (10:31–33). Jesus's "I Am" statements take us back to God's revelation of himself to Moses[2] in Exodus 3:13–15 as the God of Abraham, Isaac and Jacob. David M. Ball argues that the "I Am" sayings of Jesus in the fourth Gospel refer to similar sayings in Isaiah spoken in a pluralistic context and thus identify Jesus with the God of the Old Testament. The high density of "I Am" sayings of Jehovah found in chapters 40–55 of Isaiah match the high concentration of "I Am" sayings of Jesus in the Gospel of John. The theme of Isaiah 40–55 is the unique identity of Jehovah, and the theme of John is the distinct identity of Jesus. When Jesus echoes the sayings of Jehovah in Isaiah, he is clearly applying this "language of deity" to himself as a proof of his deity. Identifying himself with the forgiving action of God, and applying to himself language reserved for God, Jesus claims for himself the very nature of God. In John's Christology, "Jesus is unique not because of what God has done through him as a man but because he himself is divine."[3]

This incarnational Christology is challenging for dialogue with followers of other religions in the pluralistic environment of South

---

2. See Exodus 3 for the account of Moses at the burning bush and God's revelation of himself to Moses: "I am the God of your father, the God of Abraham, the God of Isaac, and the God of Jacob" (3:6). In response to Moses's inquiry as to God's name, God replied saying, "Thus you shall say to the Israelites, 'I am who I am'. . . . 'I am has sent me to you'" (3:14). This is repeated in more detail in God's instruction to Moses as to what to say to the Israelites: "The Lord, the God of your ancestors, the God of Abraham, the God of Isaac, and the God of Jacob, has sent me to you. This is my name for ever, and this is my title for all generations" (3:15).

3. David M. Ball, "'My Lord and My God': The Implications of 'I Am' Sayings for Religious Pluralism," in *One God One Lord in a World of Religious Pluralism*, ed. A. D. Clarke and B. W. Winter (Cambridge: Tyndale House, 1991), 64.

Asia. In a context of suffering, it is significant that God identifies with us in our humanity. As Peskett and Ramachandra state,

> The incarnation speaks of a God who is entangled with our world, who immerses himself in our tragic history, who embraces our humanity with all its vulnerability, pain and confusion, including our evil and our death. God is neither absent from nor irrelevant in our age. . . . Here is a God who comes to us not as master but as a servant, who stoops to wash the feet of his disciples, and to suffer brutalization and dehumanization at the hands of his creatures.[4]

The John 7:37–39 event took place on the final day of the Feast of Tabernacles in the Temple, during which water was ritually poured out at the altar while Isaiah 12:3 was recited: "With joy you will draw water from the wells of salvation." This was a familiar reminder of God's provision for thirsty Israel in the wilderness. In this context Jesus declares himself the source of this Living Water (7:38), then points ahead to the coming of the Holy Spirit (7:39). The offer of Living Water (7:38, cf 4:10) is activated following Pentecost. Acts 2 is a commentary on this passage! After the Holy Spirit came, the apostles became vehicles for offering Living Water to the multitudes.

The Water of Life is God's free gift of salvation (Rev 22:17) which is for all peoples. Jesus's encounter with the woman at the well (John 4) is a meaningful response to the spiritual thirst of a woman who was a despised outcaste Samaritan, a non-Israelite seeker for Truth and for God. How significant that this woman's testimony served to evangelise her fellow Samaritans (4:39–41). How important that to the Samaritans was given the revelation that "this is truly the Saviour of the world" (4:42).

Hunger and thirst are connected. Water of Life has affinity to the Bread of Life declaration (6:35, 51) which followed the feeding of the five thousand (5,000) (6:1–15). The setting was around the time of the Passover festival (6:4) with its Breaking of the Bread reference to the Passover meal commemorating the Exodus from Egypt. A discourse on bread is a reminder of food, of God's gracious provision in the wilderness of "daily bread" which was one aspect of their redemption. Bread points to God's provision of food, of life, of sustenance. Salvation is more than mere physical, material substance—yet that also is included! Food in the wilderness, our daily bread or rice,

---

4. Howard Peskett and Vinoth Ramachandra, *The Message of Mission* (Leicester, UK: Inter-Varsity Press; India reprint, Delhi: ISPCK, 2003), 86.

all from the hand of God. Hunger and thirst speak of human longing for God. Loaves and fishes? Our Father is concerned for human needs—food for the hungry, water for the thirsty, homes for the homeless, security for the defenseless, help for the helpless—and these should be our concerns too, but not to the exclusion of the spiritual dimension. That is the error of prosperity theology, the so-called health and wealth gospel. "Material blessings are in themselves tangible expressions of divine benevolence," states Chris Wright. Concern for justice is part of the biblical understanding of salvation. "Blessing is God's original intention for human life on earth," but prosperity theology distorts God's intention, panders to human lustful greed, but fails to address the causes of poverty or join the struggle for justice.[5] Bread (food) is no luxury, but sustains life. The Bread of Life is Jesus Christ. We are called to become partakers of life in Christ, to receive the benefits of his passion, death and resurrection. In evangelism we share with others what we have found in Christ. It was a Sri Lankan Methodist who defined evangelism this way: it's one beggar telling another beggar where to find bread.[6] In the South Asian context that involves a lot of doing and being as well as speaking. We present Christ in deed as well as in word.

Jesus's presentation as the Light of the World (8:12; cf 1:4–9), probably set in the Temple which was regarded as the centre of light, illuminated by a giant Menorah during the festival, provides a contrast to darkness and is to be distinguished from falsehood. Jesus as the source of light is the dispenser of a light which is genuine, not temporary, not to be extinguished at the conclusion of the festival. Our task in evangelism is to extend the Light of the Gospel in a world of need.

Witness must be sensitive to context. We are not called to propagate religion but to present Christ in word and deed. Religion does not save. As followers of Christ we have a story to tell of how God has acted in Christ. Other religions do not have this story.

> Salvation is to be found within the context of Christian faith and witness only because Christianity tells this story, whereas other religions do not. Salvation is contained not in Christianity as a religion . . . , but in the

---

5. Christopher J. H. Wright, *Salvation Belongs to Our God: Celebrating the Bible's Central Story* (Downers Grove, IL: InterVarsity Press, 2007), 64.

6. D. T. Niles, "Evangelism Is Just One Beggar Telling Another Beggar Where to Find Bread." *They That May Have Life* (New York: Harper & Brother, 1951, London: Lutterworth Press, 1962).

story that Christians tell—in bearing witness to the biblical God and what God has done in history for our salvation. Salvation is guaranteed by and because of what God has done, not by our religious beliefs or practices.[7]

Our witness is possible through the enablement of the Holy Spirit.

THE ROLE OF THE HOLY SPIRIT IN EVANGELISM

John relates the Holy Spirit to the mission of evangelism. The Spirit bears witness to Jesus (15:46), glorifies Jesus (16:14), speaks what Jesus spoke (16:13). Jesus's Upper Room discourse (John 13–16) focuses on the coming of the Holy Spirit. The main event between Advent and the Parousia is Pentecost. John's rendition of the Great Commission (20:21) joins the mission of Jesus to the mission of the Church, the latter to be empowered by the Holy Spirit. The Holy Spirit came on Pentecost in fulfilment of the promise of Jesus (John 14:26; 16:7; Acts 1:5) and the Prophets (Joel 2:28–29; Acts 2:16).

The mission of the Church was inaugurated by the Holy Spirit at Pentecost (Acts 2). The coming of the Holy Spirit enabled the Church to carry out its primary task of reconciling people from every nation, tribe and culture, drawing them together into one body in Christ. We live in the eschatological age of the Spirit.

> With Pentecost the last days have dawned, and they will not be finished until the gospel of the Kingdom is preached throughout the whole world as a testimony to all nations (Matt 24:14). This means that Jesus Christ has inaugurated this age of the Spirit and will consummate it.[8]

The Pentecost event was accompanied by signs. "The Church was born universal," declares Dupont.[9] At Pentecost the apostles spoke in foreign tongues, the languages of the nations (Acts 2:6–8). The assembled crowd represented "every nation under heaven" (Acts 2:5). Pentecost was prophetic and symbolic of the worldwide missionary spread of the gospel which began from that point.

---

7. Wright, *Salvation Belongs to Our God*, 110.
8. Arthur F. Glasser, *Announcing the Kingdom: The Story of God's Mission in the Bible* (Grand Rapids: Baker Academic, 2003), 263.
9. Jacque Dupont, *The Salvation of the Gentiles* (New York: Paulist, 1979), 58.

The phenomenon of tongues, equally intelligible to people of diverse languages, underscores the fact that it is of the essence of the church to bear witness "by [what] is said and done" (Rom 15:18). Deeds need words of explanation, and words need deeds of confirmation (John 5:36). The gospel is for the devout "from every nation under heaven" (Acts 2:5, 39). Therefore the manifestation of tongues was a confirmation of God's intention to reverse the scattering and hostility of the nations that followed the judgment at Babel (Gen 11:1–9) and unite in Christ his people from all nations.[10]

The outcome was the expansion of the Church, the Holy Spirit the key providing power for witness in the world. The history of the church began in Jerusalem but continues in the world of the nations.

Pentecost continues. As recorded in the Book of Acts, the historic events of Pentecost were repeated at least three times, each in a missionary context. One is in the ministry to the Samaritans (Acts 8:14–17). The second is in the case of the Gentile convert Cornelius (Acts 10:44–46). The third instance was at Ephesus (Acts 19:6). The repetition is a guarantee that the Spirit really came and abides. As theologian Bernard Ramm states, "He is here as a permanent gift to the Church, a resident of the world until the Saviour returns."[11]

All service to God is dependent upon the power of God for fruitfulness. The text with which we began, John 7:38–39, points to the Holy Spirit as the source of spiritual life and its reality. Jesus here reminds us of the necessity of spiritual regeneration as the basis for all further renewal, fullness and blessing. Only so are we channels of God's grace to the world. As a preacher from a previous generation stated, "It is our part to hold up Jesus Christ, and then look to the Holy Spirit to illumine His face or to take the truth about Him and make it clear to the hearts of our hearers."[12] Jesus promised the Holy Spirit: he told his disciples to wait for the coming of the Spirit to be "clothed with power from on high" (Luke 24:49; cf. Acts 1:4–5). Just before his ascension he repeated it, adding a significant outcome: "But you will receive power when the Holy Spirit has come upon you; and you will be my witnesses in Jerusalem, and in all Judea and Samaria, and to the ends of the earth" (Acts 1:8). Baptism in the Holy Spirit would bring power for witness. The coming of the Spirit

---

10. Glasser, *Announcing the Kingdom*, 264.
11. Bernard Ramm, *The Witness of the Spirit* (Grand Rapids: Eerdmans, 1959), 78.
12. R. A. Torrey, *The Person and Work of the Holy Spirit* (Grand Rapids: Zondervan, 1976 [1910]), 85.

would initiate worldwide missionary witness. And that is what happened. Since Pentecost we live in the age of the Spirit.

Unfortunately today there is a lot of controversy and confusion surrounding the Holy Spirit. The spectacular events at Pentecost were historic, clearly marking the beginning of a new era. But were the signs to be repeated? According to some experts these were one-time events, never to be repeated. As we have seen, the Pentecostal signs were repeated on at least three occasions recorded in the Book of Acts. But what is normative for believers today?

What about the so-called initial evidence doctrine which is common among Pentecostal-Charismatics? Should every believer speak in tongues? These are some of the controversial points. Arguments may get us nowhere. What we need is the reality of the Spirit's witness in our lives and ministry. Power for witness is needed in the church today. Controversies aside, I find myself in agreement with Sri Lankan biblical scholar-evangelist and social activist Ajith Fernando:

> For a Christian filling is the norm. It is commanded of us in Ephesians 5:18 where Paul says, "Be filled with the Spirit." If the baptism is initiatory, then filling is implied in that baptism, and the door is opened to pursue that filling through entrance into God's salvation. What is clear is that God intends all Christians to be filled with the Holy Spirit .... Our lives must be lived and our service accomplished by the power of the Spirit.[13]

In a highly-recommended book, *Jesus Driven Ministry*, Ajith elaborates what the Spirit's fullness should mean in the life of the church. First of all, fullness of the Holy Spirit should be the norm. "This is something we must seek in our lives and expect from all Christians."[14] Acts 6:3 indicates that being filled was a requirement for appointment to service in the church. But how do we determine that someone is indeed full of the Spirit? This is where we can turn to the teachings of Paul. "This subject is a major aspect of Paul's teaching about the Spirit. Paul lays great stress on the Spirit's work in the formation of Christian character."[15] According to Paul the lives of spiritual leaders will be marked by the fruit of the Spirit (Gal 5:22–23). Ajith is troubled at the high rate of moral and spiritual failure among Christian

13. Ajith Fernando, *Jesus Driven Ministry* (Wheaton, IL: Crossway Books, 2002), 31–32.
14. Ibid., 32.
15. Ibid.

leaders. In some circles today it is common to talk much about one's "power" in ministry, for example, "God uses me greatly." But it is not enough to focus on "power" alone. The Spirit must be seen to govern people's lives "so that his work is evident in both their behavior and ministry."[16]

Commenting on "what the Spirit says to the churches" (Rev 3:14–22), J. I. Packer observes that the Spirit always says what Christ thinks, and in the case of the Church at Laodicea this had to do with their spiritual stagnation: "The Spirit ought to be blowing like the wind and flowing like a stream of water through your lives (John 3:8; 7:38), and under his influence you should be growing in grace and showing the Spirit's fruit in ways one can see."[17] But there is hope. Renewal is possible. The church in every age is called to "Keep in Step with the Spirit," as Paul writes (Gal 5:25).

Spiritual awakenings have been part of the church's history through the ages. The eighteenth century evangelical awakening associated with John and Charles Wesley, George Whitfield, and Jonathan Edwards—as well as the Pietist movement of the seventeenth century which preceded it—are examples of the renewing work of the Spirit resulting in movements of evangelisation in Europe and North America and contributing to the birth of the modern missionary movement. Particular Baptists in England were touched by the fresh winds of the Spirit leading to William Carey's challenge to fellow Baptists and the formation of the Baptist Missionary Society (BMS) in 1792 and Carey's arrival in India in 1793.[18] The story of Carey is well-known and not to be repeated here, but Baptists in Sri Lanka are heirs of Carey and the BMS.

Fresh winds of the Holy Spirit continue to blow. In the mid-twentieth century the charismatic movement brought new life to sections of the Christian community. Whatever else may be said, "The charismatic movement celebrates the ministry of the Holy Spirit in Christian experience."[19] Not without controversy. Sometimes churches split: is the fresh wine too potent for old wineskins? The charismatic movement has been styled a "stepchild" of Pentecostalism, itself shar-

16. Ibid., 33.
17. J. I. Packer, *Keep in Step with the Spirit* (Tarrytown, NY: Fleming H. Revell, 1984), 259.
18. For further on William Carey, see chapter 5 above, "Carey and the Evangelical Experiment at Serampore." For any not acquainted with the Carey story, the following scholarly account is highly recommended: Timothy George, *Faithful Witness: The Life and Mission of William Carey* (Birmingham, AL: New Hope, 1991).
19. Packer, *Keep in Step with the Spirit*, 172.

ing an earlier Wesleyan and Holiness heritage, both having affinity to historic evangelicalism. Yet there are differences: "Evangelical theology is precise and sharp honed as a result of centuries of controversy. . . . Charismatic theology by comparison looks loose, erratic, and naïve."[20] Baptists have responded in different ways—depending upon location and doctrinal orientation as well as degree of spiritual fervor.

Leaving aside a worst case scenario where Baptist members (at the instigation of their pastor) went down the street to join the nearest Pentecostal Church (but this paper should not digress): despite abuses and excesses, the renewal has brought many welcome changes. Dying churches have come alive with new growth and increased giving. Packer notes that charismatic renewal brings a new joyfulness, expression of emotion in worship, prayerfulness, participation in ministry and a new missionary zeal.[21] Ajith Fernando observes that the experience of the Spirit in many places has brought a fresh vibrancy in worship.[22]

The great growth of the church today is in Africa, Asia, and Latin America, much of it having a Pentecostal-Charismatic quality as well as a Baptist-Evangelical thrust. Christianity's vibrant centre today is in the Global South, not in Europe or North America. A majority of the world's Christians today are Africans, Latinos, and Asians.

The Holy Spirit brings revival. This has happened at several points in history. A dramatic case took place in 1905 in India at Mukti Mission at Kedgoan near Pune in India. Under the direction of Pandita Ramabai[23] the Mission provided shelter for famine victims, lepers and women. By the turn of the century nearly two thousand (2,000) needy persons were being cared for by the staff. The 1905 Revival at Mukti was an important event. First of all was its impact in the spiritual formation of the residents. Many felt convicted of sin, then experienced pardon and cleansing and the fullness of the Spirit for life and service. A detailed account of the Revival given by Minnie Abrams describes sorrow for sin intermingled with joy. "Some who had been shaken violently under the power of conviction, now

20. Ibid., 173.
21. Ibid., 186–89.
22. Fernando, *Jesus Driven Ministry*, 37.
23. For more on Pandita Ramabai, see chapter 6 above, "Ramabai Dongre Medhavi: Change Agent in Modern Indian History." See also the book, *Indian and Christian: The Life and Legacy of Pandita Ramabai*, ed. R. E. Hedlund, Sebastian Kim and Rajkumar Boaz Johnson (Delhi: ISPCK, 2011).

sang, praised, danced for joy. Some had visions, others dreams."[24] Abrams discusses power for witness and mentions the bestowal of gifts such as faith, healing, tongues, prophecy and discernment of spirits. Abrams's interpretation is reminiscent of the Wesleyan theology of the Holiness Movement. Characterised by emotional phenomena, the impact of the awakening was long-lasting in terms of conversions and changed lives. Ramabai channeled the enthusiasm of the believing community into famine relief work as well as social rehabilitation. In this way the spiritual awakening had an enduring influence in Maharashtrian society.

Jesus began his Galilean ministry with a quotation from the Prophet Isaiah, now commonly known as the Nazareth Manifesto:

> The Spirit of the Lord is upon me,
> because he has anointed me
> to preach good news to the poor.
> He has sent me to proclaim release to the captives
> and recovery of sight for the blind,
> to let the oppressed go free,
> to proclaim the year of the Lord's favour. (Luke 4:18–19; cf. Isa 61:1, 2)

Today too the social ministries of the church need to be empowered by the Holy Spirit. May God the Holy Spirit guide and empower the People of God for social and spiritual witness and ministry which will draw others to the Saviour Jesus Christ.

CONCLUSION

In this paper we have endeavoured to summarise the biblical metaphor of Living Water as found in the "I Am" sayings of John's Gospel. Jesus himself related his work and the ministry of his disciples to the witness of the Holy Spirit. As Christian leaders today we are challenged to experience the reality of the Spirit's witness in our own lives and ministry, and to pray for the coming of the Spirit in revival and renewal of our congregations for mission in the world.

> The Spirit makes one person a teacher of divine truth, inspires another to prophesy, gives another the power of casting out devils, enables another

---

24. Minnie F. Abrams, *The Baptism of the Holy Ghost & Fire* (Kedgaon, India: Pandita Ramabai Mukti Mission, 2000 [1905]), 2.

to interpret holy Scripture. The Spirit strengthens one person's self-control, shows another how to help the poor, teaches another to fast and lead a life of asceticism, makes another oblivious to the need of the body, trains another for martyrdom. His action is different in different people, but the Spirit himself is always the same. In each person, Scripture says, the Spirit reveals his presence in a particular way for the common good. (From *The Living Water of the Holy Spirit*, by Cyril of Jerusalem, a 4th century catechetical instruction.)

It seems fitting to conclude with a hymn from Joseph Hart, cited by J. I. Packer, as a prayer to God the Holy Spirit:[25]

Come, Holy Spirit, come!
Let thy bright beams arise;
Dispel the sorrow from our minds,
The darkness from our eyes.

Convince us of our sin,
Then lead to Jesus' blood,
And to our wondering view reveal
The secret love of God.

Revive our drooping faith,
Our doubts and fears remove,
And kindle in our breasts the flame
Of never-dying love.

'Tis thine to cleanse the heart,
To sanctify the soul,
To pour fresh life in every part,
And new-create the whole.

Dwell, therefore, in our hearts,
Our minds from bondage free;
Then shall we know, and praise, and love,
The Father, Son, and Thee.

---

25. Packer, *Keep in Step with the Spirit*, 262.

SOURCES FOR FURTHER REFERENCE

Abrams, Minnie F. *The Baptism of the Holy Ghost & Fire*. Kedgaon, India: Pandita Ramabai Mukti Mission, 2000 (1905).

Ball, David M. "'My Lord and My God': The Implications of 'I Am' Sayings for Religious Pluralism." In *One God One Lord in a World of Religious Pluralism*, edited by A. D. Clarke and B. W. Winter. Cambridge: Tyndale House, 1991.

Dupont, Jacque. *The Salvation of the Gentiles*. New York: Paulist, 1979.

Fernando, Ajith. *Jesus Driven Ministry*. Wheaton, IL: Crossway Books, 2002.

Glasser, Arthur F. *Announcing the Kingdom: The Story of God's Mission in the Bible*. Grand Rapids: Baker Academic, 2003.

Hedlund, Roger E. *God and the Nations: A Biblical Theology of Mission in the Asian Context*. Delhi: ISPCK, 2001 (1997).

———. "Evangelical Christians and Social Transformation." In *Integral Mission the Way Forward: Essays in Honour of Dr. Saphir P. Athyal*, edited by C. V. Matthew. Tiruvalla, India: Christaya Sahitya Samithi, 2006.

Johnson, B. W. *New Testament Commentary*, vol 3, *John*. St. Louis: Christian Publishing Co., 1896.

Mathew, C. V., ed. *Integral Mission the Way Forward: Essays in Honour of Dr. Saphir P. Athyal*. Tiruvalla, India: Christaya Sahitya Samithi, 2006.

Niles, D. T. *That They May Have Life*. New York: Harper & Brother, 1951. London: Lutterworth Press, 1962.

Packer, J. I. *Keep in Step with the Spirit*. Tarrytown, NY: Fleming H. Revell, 1984.

Peskett, Howard, and Vinoth Ramachandra. *The Message of Mission*. Leicester, UK: Inter-Varsity, 2003.

Ramm, Bernard. *The Witness of the Spirit*. Grand Rapids: Eerdmans, 1959.

Tenney, Merril C. *The Gospel of John*. The Expositor's Bible Commentary, vol. 9. Grand Rapids: Zondervan, 1981.

Torrey, R. A. *The Person and Work of the Holy Spirit*. Grand Rapids: Zondervan, 1976 (1910).

Walvoord, John F. *The Holy Spirit*. Grand Rapids: Zondervan, 1978 (1954).

Wright, Christopher J. H. *Salvation Belongs to Our God: Celebrating the Bible's Central Story*. Downers Grove, IL: InterVarsity Press, 2007.

14.

Fourth Branch Christianity and the Historiography of New Christian Movements

INTRODUCTION

History is a vast field with a number of related areas such as contextualization and inculturation of Christian faith.[1] As Christianity encounters other religious traditions in the Asian context, new insights are discovered into the riches of God in Christ. Translation of the Gospel into new cultural settings results in new Christian movements deserving careful documentation, all of which has implications for dialogue and for historiography.

INDIGENEITY

In his study of Pentecostal origins in Sri Lanka, G. P. V. Somaratna observes that from its beginnings in 1923 the full-time workers of the Ceylon Pentecostal Mission (CPM) were expected to follow an

---

1. An earlier rendition of this essay appeared as "Fourth Branch Christianity: Indigeneity, Contextuality, Pentecostalism, and Independent Christian Movements," in *A Cultured Faith: Essays in Honour of Prof. G. P. V. Somaratna on His Seventieth Birthday*, ed. Prabo Mihindukulasuriya, Ivor Poobalan and Ravin Caldera (Colombo, Sri Lanka: Colombo Theological Seminary, 2011), and is used by permission.

ascetic life-style which included celibacy, obedience to the chief pastor, communal living in faith homes, early morning corporate prayers and the wearing of white clothing—practices reminiscent of Sri Lankan Buddhist spirituality and culture. Features of indigenous worship were incorporated. Worshipers seated on mats on the floor, use of domestic musical instruments, singing of indigenous tunes and other local cultural practices gave the CPM a distinctive Sri Lankan cultural identity and also set the Pentecostal believers apart from other Christian groups.[2] It is noteworthy that its doctrine and practices proved congenial in South India as well where the CPM took root in Tamil Nadu and Kerala and spread rapidly.[3] In the present paper we explore aspects of Christian indigeneity with particular attention to the historiography of new Christian movements, issues stirred by Professor Somaratna's seminal study. Questions arise as to what constitutes an indigenous Church and what qualifies as an indigenous movement.

Writing in *Lausanne World Pulse*, Bishop Hwa Yung of the Methodist Church in Malaysia addresses some of the complexities of life in Asia today.[4] Asian countries like Japan, Hong Kong and Singapore are in the forefront of technological and economic advance offset by grinding poverty in Bangladesh and rural areas of China, India, Indonesia and Philippines. Christian population also advanced from 2.3 percent in 1900 to 8.5 percent in 2000, in other words, more than 300 million Christians in Asia—highly Evangelical and Charismatic—with phenomenal growth in Korea and China and in parts of India and Nepal. Christian vitality in Singapore, Malaysia, Philippines and India gives promise that the twenty-first century will be a great century of advance especially in Asia. Korean Churches have sent out 18,000 missionaries. The India Missions Association represents more than 200 agencies with more than 30,000 cross-cultural missionaries. China's house Church movement aims to send 100,000 missionaries along ancient "Silk Road" trade routes "Back-to-Jerusalem" preaching the Gospel in the heartlands of Buddhism, Hinduism and Islam

2. G. P. V. Somaratna, *Origins of the Pentecostal Mission in Sri Lanka* (Nugegoda, Sri Lanka: Margaya Fellowship, 1996), 34, 40.

3. Paul C. Martin, "A Brief History of the Ceylon Pentecostal Church," in *Christianity Is Indian: The Emergence of an Indigenous Community*, ed. R. E. Hedlund, rev. ed. (Delhi: ISPCK, 2004), 432.

4. Hwa Yung, "Asian Missions in the Twenty-First Century—An Asian Perspective," in *Lausanne World Pulse* at http://tinyurl.com/y74dqsnq.

along the way. Evangelicals in the Philippines speak of sending out 200,000 tentmakers in the form of migrant workers. Hwa Yung goes on to posit two essential considerations without which there can be no real advance of the Gospel, namely dependence on God rather than mere human resources, and genuine commitment and sacrifice.

NEW CHRISTIAN MOVEMENTS

In the introduction to his edited volume *Christian Movements in Southeast Asia: A Theological Exploration*, Michael Poon[5] grapples with diverse understandings of the term "movement" in the title of the book. For Ralph Winter,[6] "movement" meant the worldwide impact of the Christian mission beyond the institutional Church. Andrew Walls[7] as well as Dale Irwin and Scott Sunquist[8] use the term to refer to the worldwide spread of Christianity. The Roman Catholic Church from Vatican II onward gives a theological framework for new Christian movements which are viewed as significant for the Church's work of evangelisation. It is this theological and ecclesial component—without the Roman connectivity of the Catholic Church—which Michael Poon seeks to capture as essential to new Christian movements. Poon, who regrets the neglect of Asian Church history and historical research, issues a call to ecclesial responsibility beginning with serious academic analysis of the legacy of the well-known Chinese evangelist John Sung (1901–1944).[9]

In an effort to move this agenda forward, the Centre for the Study of Christianity in Asia (CSCA) in 2009 convened a workshop on Primal Spirituality aiming to better understand the texture of Christianity in Southeast Asia in the twenty-first century, with particular focus on Malaysia, Singapore and Indonesia.[10] In a paper addressed to participants at the workshop, Simon Chan delineated "folk Christianity" as the "contextualization of the Gospel in primal religious contexts"

---

5. Michael Nai-Chiu Poon, ed., *Christian Movements in Southeast Asia: A Theological Exploration* (Singapore: Genesis Books & Trinity Theological College, 2010), x–xviii.
6. Ralph D. Winter and Steven C. Hawthorne, *Perspectives on the World Christian Movement: A Reader* (Pasadena, CA: William Carey Library, 1981), xiii–xiv.
7. Andrew F. Walls, *The Missionary Movement in Christian History: Studies in the Transmission of Faith* (Maryknoll, NY: Orbis Books, 1996).
8. Dale T. Irwin and Scott Sunquist, *History of the World Christian Movement*, vol. 1, *Earliest Christianity to 1453* (Maryknoll, NY: Orbis Books, 2001).
9. Poon, *Christian Movements*, xviii–xxvi.
10. Michael Poon, "CSCA Project Primal Spirituality," November 21, 2008.

and noted that the process is particularly evident in the spread of Pentecostalism.[11] The evident success of Pentecostal Christianity in Asia demonstrates its ability to adapt. Pentecostalism contextualises the Gospel.

But when does contextualisation become syncretism? Simon Chan defines contextualisation as the attempt to borrow language and concepts from a context in order to effectively communicate the Gospel message in terms meaningful in that context yet always consistent with the larger Christian tradition. Syncretism is similar but goes farther, and the result is that "instead of the Gospel challenging culture, it becomes a part of culture."[12] Creative use of modern media technology and effective response to social issues are examples of successful Pentecostal contextualisation. Prosperity theology and the modern health and wealth Gospel are instances of Pentecostal syncretism based on questionable theological premises which trivialise the Gospel.[13]

Organisers of the Workshop tended to rue popular expositions of present-day world Christianity by Jenkins and others as "generalized and inadequate."[14] The organisers seek instead for a more theological interpretation centred in the work of the Holy Spirit in Asia today. The earlier work of Harold Turner[15] as well as the insights of John V. Taylor[16] are recognised as foundational. Theological concerns not withstanding, the significant contribution of social scientists and anthropologists is acknowledged. This also has been my own experience in researching this field. In the case of Singapore, for example, I found myself enlightened by the findings of secular scholars. A significant sociological study of religious conversion in Singapore finds that conversion is on the increase especially among the Chinese, into Christianity as well as into Buddhism, and that an English education appears to predispose many towards Christianity whereas persons whose education is in Chinese tend to convert to

---

11. Simon Chan, "Folk Christianity and Primal Spirituality: Some Theological Reflections," Workshop on Primal Spirituality, Trinity Theological College, September 21–25, 2009.
12. Ibid., 3.
13. Ibid., 4.
14. Poon, "CSCA Project Primal Spirituality."
15. Harold W. Turner, *Bibliography of New Religious Movements in Primal Societies* (Boston: G K. Hall, 1977).
16. John V. Taylor, *The Primal Vision: Christian Presence amid African Religion* (London: SCM, 1963).

Buddhism.[17] Utilising the findings of the social sciences can help us to better understand the context which we seek to interpret. As Simon Chan states, "At present folk Christianity is still largely the preserve of social anthropologists, missiologists and historians. Theologians have yet to come to terms with it and address its rich implicit theologies."[18]

New movements are one part of the equation, another has to do with new Independent Churches. "Independent" in this construct has little to do with mega-Churches in North America and Europe who shun ecclesiastical identity and affiliation. Rather "the great new fact of our time," the simultaneous emergence of multiple new centres of vibrant faith neither Roman Catholic nor Protestant nor Orthodox, is described by Tim Tennent as a *fourth branch of Christianity* outside the territorial legacy of Christendom centred in Africa, Latin America and Asia:

> Many of these new Christians belong to various independent, Pentecostal-oriented movements. Others belong to independent, prophetic movements that are difficult to classify. Some of these movements are currently only quasi-Christian but are moving toward orthodoxy. Other quasi-Christian movements are emerging as independent movements outside the boundaries of historic orthodoxy. Still others claim to be following Christ from within the boundaries of Hinduism or Islam, a phenomenon known as "insider movements" which has received considerable attention in missiological literature over the last decade.[19]

Christians in many parts of Asia have come from marginalised and impoverished backgrounds. This is true in India where a majority of India's Christians are from the oppressed, the products of tribal and Dalit conversion movements (estimates vary from perhaps 70 percent to 80 percent or more). Conversion movements in India not infrequently have been movements of social protest, the response of Dalits and the poor to the call to a counter-culture, movements of affirmation in quest of dignity and equality. Numerous "Messianic" movements among tribal and other subaltern communities are examples of social protest movements which did not become explicitly

---

17. C. K. Tong, *Rationalizing Religion: Religious Conversion, Revivalism and Competition in Singapore Society* (Leiden: Brill, 2007), 1–12.
18. Simon Chan, "Folk Christianity and Primal Spirituality," 8.
19. Timothy C. Tennent, *Invitation to World Missions: A Trinitarian Missiology for the Twenty-First Century* (Grand Rapids: Kregel Publications, 2010), 39.

Christian.[20] In India today, however, in North as well as South, a number of subaltern movements are taking place in which oppressed peoiples are finding dignity in a new identity as disciples of Jesus Christ. For many, upward mobility resulted from conversion by which the downtrodden discovered new dignity and hope.[21] Not all conversions are among the oppressed, of course, nor are all the emerging Churches of indigenous origins to be so classed, but nevertheless subaltern categories are critical in the broad sweep of diversity among Asia's indigenous Christian movements. Many such new Churches represent an oral culture, which challenges historiographers to fresh approaches. Indigenous Christianity is a world phenomenon, yet a relatively new field for academic research and study in South Asia.[22] Sociological methodologies may prove productive.[23] Oral communities have oral traditions, songs and stories and symbols to be observed, collected and recorded, and archival deposits created.[24] For the most part, with a few notable exceptions, these new movements have not been studied and present ample scope for academic study, research, writing and publishing.[25] They are splendid examples of what Lamin Sanneh calls the "translatability" of the Gospel.[26]

PENTECOSTALISM

New movements comprise a major development in world Christianity. The modern Pentecostal movement, for instance, is a major factor in world Christianity today.[27] Within a century, from humble

20. Stephen Fuchs, *Rebellious Prophets: A Study of Messianic Movements in Indian Religions* (New York: Asia Publishing House, 1965).
21. Roger E. Hedlund, "Indian Christians of Indigenous Origins and Their Solidarity with Original Groups," *Journal of Dharma* 24, no. 1 (1999): 13–27.
22. The phenomenon is documented with examples from around the world in chapter 2 of my book *Quest For Identity: India's Churches of Indigenous Origin; The "Little Tradition" in Indian Christianity* (Delhi: ISPCK, 2000), 25–46.
23. See, for example, Rodney Stark, *Cities of God* (New York: HarperOne, 2007), especially chapter 1, "Missions and Methods," in which he explains his use of sociological methodology.
24. Roger E. Hedlund, "Approaches to Indian Church History in the Light of New Christian Movements," *Indian Church History Review* 34 (2000): 153–70.
25. Ibid., 156, 165.
26. Lamin Sanneh, *Translating the Message: The Missionary Impact on Culture* (Maryknoll, NY: Orbis Books, 1991).
27. Pentecostalism today is producing a corps of young international scholars, but much of the foundational research was done by Walter J. Hollenweger at Birmingham University, UK. See his *Pentecostalism: Origins and Developments Worldwide* (Peabody, MA: Hendrickson Pub-

origins at Azusa Street in Los Angeles in 1906, Pentecostalism has grown to become a major global Christian tradition, second in number only to the Roman Catholics.[28] Today a quarter of all full-time Christian workers worldwide are said to be Pentecostal- Charismatics![29] Pentecostalism, from its beginning, has been a missionary religion.[30] It is not surprising, then, that Pentecostal missionaries appeared in India almost immediately following the Azusa Street experience. It is to be noted, however, that tongue speaking and other Charismatic phenomena were reported in India at Mukti Mission in Kedgaon in 1905, a year earlier than the Azusa Street Revival of 1906.[31] Today Pentecostal and other independent movements comprise the fastest growing sectors of the Church in several areas of India.[32] Hollenweger, who notes the Black oral roots of the modern Pentecostal movement, observes that it is strongest in areas of the

lishers, 1997). Hollenweger's successor at Birmingham is Allan Anderson, *An Introduction to Pentecostalism: Global Charismatic Christianity* (New York: Cambridge University Press, 2004). Other important research scholars include the late Ogbu U. Kalu, *African Pentecostalism: An Introduction* (New York: Oxford University Press, 2008); Veli-Matti Kärkkäinen, *The Spirit in the World: Emerging Pentecostal Theologies in Global Contexts* (Grand Rapids: Eerdmans, 2009); Gary B. McGee, *Miracles, Missions, & American Pentecostalism* (Maryknoll, NY: Orbis Books, 2010); Cecil M. Robeck Jr., *The Azusa Street Mission and Revival: The Birth of the Global Pentecostal Movement*, Nashville: Thomas Nelson, 2006); Vinson Synan, *The Century of the Holy Spirit: 100 Years of Pentecostal and Charismatic Renewal, 1901–2001* (Nashville: Thomas Nelson, 2001); Grant Wacker, *Heaven Below: Early Pentecostals and American Culture* (Cambridge, MA: Harvard University Press, 2001). For South Asia the most important reference is Michael Bergunder, *The South Indian Pentecostal Movement in the Twentieth Century* (Grand Rapids: Eerdmans, 2008).

28. Russell P. Spittler, "Foreword," in *The Globalization of Pentecostalism*, ed. Murray W. Dempster, Byron D. Klaus and Douglas Petersen (Oxford: Regnum Books, 1999).

29. Vinson Synan, *The Spirit Said "Grow": The Astounding Worldwide Expansion of Pentecostal and Charismatic Churches* (Monrovia, CA: MARC World Vision, 1992), 13.

30. This point is documented in several recent studies. See, for example, L. Grant McClung, *Azusa Street and beyond: Pentecostal Missions and Church Growth in the Twentieth Century* (South Plainfield, NJ: Bridge Publishing, 1986); Gary B. McGee, *"This Gospel Shall Be Preached": A History and Theology of Assemblies of God Foreign Mission to 1959* (Springfield, MO: Gospel Publishing House, 1986); Murray A. Dempster, Byron D. Klaus and Douglas Petersen, eds., *Called and Empowered: Global Mission in Pentecostal Perspective* (Peabody, MA: Hendrickson Publishers, 1991); Allan Anderson, Michael Bergunder, André Droogers and Cornelis van der Laan, eds., *Studying Global Pentecostalism: Theories and Methods* (Berkeley: University of California Press, 2010).

31. See essays in the compendium, Roger E. Hedlund, Sebastian Kim, and Rajkumar Boaz Johnson, eds. *Indian and Christian: The Life and Legacy of Pandita Ramabai* (Delhi: ISPCK, 2011).

32. See, for example, findings in fifteen cities of Tamil Nadu, in Roger E. Hedlund, *Evangelization and Church Growth: Issues from the Asian Context* (Madras, India: Church Growth Research Centre, 1992), 202–11.

world where oral communication predominates.[33] This fact has serious implications for historiography and the study of Church history in South Asia and especially India.

The first major scholarly study of South Indian Pentecostalism[34] touches the history of all known Pentecostal bodies in South India and lists a total of 71 Pentecostal bodies in the four southern states. Andhra Pradesh has 14 Pentecostal denominations, Karnataka has seven, Kerala eleven, but Tamil Nadu has the greatest number with 33 Pentecostal bodies of which 27 appear to be of indigenous origins. This is not an exhaustive listing of South Indian Pentecostals. New groups frequently appear, other groups inadvertently are overlooked by researchers and compilers. A similar investigation in North India would reveal parallel developments of new indigenous Pentecostal and Charismatic movements in Mumbai, in Punjab, Uttar Pradesh, West Bengal and in Delhi. A common thread running through these Pentecostal Churches is a conscious expression of their Indian identity and character. Their Pentecostal faith binds them to fellow-believers worldwide. Yet their life and witness at home and in the diaspora are indelibly marked by an Indian identity and character. This is true as well of "international" bodies represented in India such as the Assemblies of God and the Church of God. Their expression of Indian Christian nationalism deserves commendation and respect.

The new so-called small Churches do not necessarily remain small. In Chennai, for example, the mother Church of the Apostolic Christian Assembly, a notable movement of indigenous origin, attracts more than 13,000 worshipers to its Sunday morning bi-lingual service.[35] Also in Chennai, the New Life Assembly of God at Tenempet attracts more than 33,000 worshipers to its multiple weekend services every Saturday and Sunday. These and other mega-Churches call for documentation and further analysis. In Mumbai the New Life Fellowship is an indigenous urban movement which has grown to several thousand members found in more than 300 house Churches and 500 house groups plus 140 prayer cells and 122 composite celebration centres in rented facilities throughout the city.[36]

33. Hollenweger, *Pentecostalism*, 20. Also see Estrelda Y. Alexander, *Black Fire: One Hundred Years of African American Pentecostalism* (Downers Grove, IL: IVP Academic, 2011).
34. Bergunder, *South Indian Pentecostal Movement*.
35. This was observed during visits on February 13 and April 1, 2000, and confirmed in interviews with Pastor Sam Sundaram on March 30 and Pastor Kumar on April 1, 2000, at Chennai.
36. Information was provided by the lead pastors who were interviewed at the home of the founder, Pastor S. Joseph, at Mahim, Mumbai, on February 26, 1998. Growth has continued.

Indian Christianity is incarnate in a diversity of cultures as the new movements demonstrate. Indigenous Christianity is vigorous. India in 1995 observed the twenty-fifth anniversary of the founding of the Church of North India, and in 1997, celebrated the fiftieth anniversary of the merger which created the Church of South India. CSI and CNI are significant ecumenical milestones, rightly celebrated as creative achievements in indigenization. Simultaneously have arisen hundreds (perhaps thousands) of new entities arising spontaneously from the Indian soil. These diversified independent Churches and structures should not be overlooked.[37] Diversity not withstanding, Indian Christianity has in common with Churches in other sections of the non-Western world "an indigenous, grassroots leadership; embeddedness in local cultures; and reliance on a vernacular Bible."[38]

THEOLOGICAL IMPLICATIONS

Response to the Gospel took various forms some of which carried important theological implications. In Bengal India's great social reformer Raja Ram Mohan Roy (1772–1833), inspired by Christianity and hostile to Vedanta, established the Brahmo Samaj as a theistic society which solidified into a new religious movement, monotheistic yet "Hindu" rather than Christian.[39] M. M. Thomas provides a perceptive analysis of Ram Mohan Roy's controversy with Joshua Marshman (1768–1837) of Serampore showing that the central issue concerned Christology. "Rammohan Roy was a Protestant Hindu moving away from the amoral and monistic/polytheistic tendencies of traditional Hinduism under the influence of Western liberalism."[40] Marshman defended the orthodox doctrine of Jesus Christ.

At this early stage of the encounter Roy was not prepared to embrace the full historic Christological and Trinitarian creed which Marshman wanted to impose. This tragic insensitivity pushed Roy into a premature definition of his understanding of Christ. Marshman's rigidity did not permit sufficient latitude for an Indian

---

37. See David B. Barrett and Todd M. Johnson, "Annual Statistical Table on Global Mission: 2000," *International Bulletin of Missionary Research* (January 2000): 24–25.
38. Dana Robert, "Shifting Southward: Global Christianity since 1945," *International Bulletin of Missionary Research* (April 2000): 50–58, at 56.
39. Nicol Macnicol, *The Living Religions of the Indian People* (London: SCM, 1934).
40. M. M. Thomas, *The Acknowledged Christ of the Indian Renaissance* (London: SCM, 1969), 9.

approach to the mystery of Christ, and forced Roy into an Unitarian stance. The Church in South Asia thereby was deprived of a potentially innovative theologian and a distincively Indian theological perception. Roy rejected the Indian belief in multiple incarnations (and with that the Christian doctrine of incarnation) "because he cannot see it except as idolatry, doing violence to the unity of the Godhead."[41]

In contrast to Roy, Keshub Chunder Sen (1838–1884) had no difficulty accepting belief in Christ's incarnation. Sen's devotion to Christ, his passion for fellow Indians to appropriate and follow Christ according to an Indian pattern, are important for indigenous Christianity. Sen is a key figure in the Hindu dialogue with Christianity and a pioneer in the development of Indian Christian theology.

Keshub was devoted to Christ, sometimes calling himself the slave of Jesus. Many Hindus regarded him as a Christian, and Christ truly became the centre of his life, although he never converted to Christianity. There is no denying the reality of his experience of Christ and the genuineness of his effort to express his experience and knowledge in terms of his own well-loved Indian tradition. Keshub's lectures on Jesus bear witness of his love for Jesus Christ.[42]

Among early Bengali converts, Brahmabandhab Upadhyay sought to utilise Advaita as a platform for Christianity.[43] His proposal was "to win over Hindu philosophy to the service of Christianity as Greek philosophy was won over in the middle ages."[44] In similar fashion Upadhyay sought to communicate Christian beliefs through Vedantic terminology.[45] This approach is not without its critics, not least that Christ's teachings contradicted a number of Hindu doctrines, but more recently that its Brahminical sources fail to resonate with the realities of oppressed and marginalised peoples.

By way of contrast another more recent convert, Pandita Ramabai, also of Brahmin heritage, was careful to avoid use of Hindu terminology which made the narration of Biblical theology more complicated, and she rejected terminology intended to subject women and

41. Ibid., 22; cf. 14, 35.
42. David C. Scott, *Keshub Chunder Sen* (Madras, India: CLS, 1979).
43. Julius J. Lipner, "Introduction," in *The Writings of Brahmabandhab Upadhyay*, ed. Julius Lipner and George Gispert-Sauch (Bangalore, India: United Theological College, 2002), xxxvi, xxxvii.
44. Lipner and Gispert-Sauch, *Writings of Brahmabandhab Upadhyay*, 18.
45. Timothy C. Tennent, *Building Christianity on Indian Foundations: The Legacy of Brahmabandhav Upadhyay* (Delhi: ISPCK, 2000), 45, 138, 228.

Dalits to Brahmanic oppression.[46] She also avoided Western philosophical models. She used vernacular terminology that is pre-Vedic, nonracial and nonsubversive.

> Ramabai's work was influenced greatly by her biblical and theological formulations. Her understanding for the transformation of Indian society was influenced by her interpretation of the Bible and its application to the context of India. Her words and works are a stellar example of how the Bible and Christ confront and transform culture.[47]

Ramabai is an outstanding figure in modern Indian history. An articulate spokesperson on behalf of suppressed Hindu women, her advocacy earned her a place of honour in modern Indian history.[48] Rajkumar Boaz Johnson considers Ramabai the first authentic Indian Christian feminist theologian as well as a genuine Dalit theologian.[49]

Like Ramabai, Narayan Vaman Tilak (1862–1919), was of Brahmin Maharashtrian ancestry. Dissatisfied with orthodox Hinduism, convinced of the truth of Christianity following a long period of mental conflict, Tilak was baptized in 1895—but insisted that the ceremony be performed by an Indian.[50] In a recent study, Gauri Viswanathan hypothesises that although Tilak assimilated Christian beliefs and norms, he "sought to indigenise Christianity and make it compatible with Hinduism"[51]—a proposition not without likely objection. As P. S. Jacob has pointed out, when Tilak joined the Christian Church he found that Christians in Maharashtra, due to their predominantly outcaste backgrounds, remained isolated from national life. This deficiency he set about to counteract using the instrumentality of his poetic works to instill love for India.[52] "Tilak was strongly convinced that India's spiritual heritage is of great importance for expressing Indian Christianity."[53] For Tilak there was no conflict between nationalism and his Christian faith. A recognized Marathi literary figure, Tilak brought his poetic gifts to the service

---

46. Rajkumar Boaz Johnson, "Pandita Ramabai's Biblical Theological Contribution as a Christian Feminist Theologian," in Hedlund, Kim, and Johnson, *Indian and Christian*, 133.
47. Ibid., 116.
48. S. M. Adhav, *Pandita Ramabai* (Madras: CLS, 1979), 18, 238–41.
49. Boaz Johnson, "Pandita Ramabai's Biblical Theological Contribution," 135.
50. Eric J. Sharpe, "Tilak, Narayan Vama," in *Biographical Dictionary of Christian Missions*, ed. G. H. Anderson (New York: Simon & Schuster Macmillan, 1998), 671.
51. G. Viswanathan, *Outside the Fold: Conversion, Modernity, and Belief* (Delhi: Oxford University Press, 1998), 40.
52. P. S. Jacob, *The Experiential Response of N. V. Tilak* (Madras, India: CLS, 1979), 44.
53. Ibid., 45.

of Christ and the Church. Some 254 of his hymns are found in the Marathi Christian hymnal.[54] In place of translated Western hymns, Tilak introduced the singing of bhajans and brought the use of kirtan into the Marathi Church, thus enriching its devotional life through familiar art forms—perhaps his greatest gift to the Christian Church. Tilak never gave up his Indian cultural birthright. He declared that he had come to Christ over the bridge of Tukaram, the Hindu poet-saint of Maharashtra. He brought the riches of his Hindu heritage into the Church. His devotional poetry, lyrics and hymns represent "a permanent treasury of devotion and theology for the Indian Church."[55] Later in life Tilak embraced the Indian sanyasa ideal as a channel for communicating the meaning of Christ, and his home became a prototype for later Christian ashrams.[56] His practice of sanyasa was a renunciation of alien trappings in order to present Christ in familiar Eastern garb.

CONTEXTUALITY

Implicit in the preceeding discussion is a drive toward indigenous cultural affirmation. Failure to inculturate results in alienation. An example is seen in the ambivalent attitudes of Sri Lanka Protestant Christians toward the traditional puberty ritual. It appears that "Protestant Christianity has long failed to take Sinhalese culture seriously and to respond appropriately to it."[57] In this connection, Prof. Somaratna noted that converts were taught to reject the traditional culture of their people and to accept Western forms which, not surprisingly, "led to an alienation of the converts from the main body of the population in South Asia."[58] Sri Lankan Protestants thereby are deprived of a significant opportunity for interacting theologically and culturally with the customs of the majority population.

In a lucid chapter on "Disentangling the Gospel from Empire and

54. Sharpe, "Tilak," 671.
55. Robin Boyd, *Introduction to Indian Christian Theology* (Madras, India: CLS, 1975), 117.
56. H. L. Richard, *Christ Bhakti: Narayan Vaman Tilak and Christian Work among Hindus* (Secunderabad, India: OM Books, 1998), 61.
57. Mantae Kim, "A Comparative Missiological Study of Sinhalese Buddhist and Sinhalese Christian Attitudes toward the Puberty Ritual," *Missiology: An International Review* 38, no. 4 (October 2010), 418.
58. G. P. V. Somaratna, "The British Expansion and Church Growth in Asia," in *Western Colonialism in Asia and Christianity*, ed. M. D. David (Bombay: Himalaya Publishing House, 1988), 96–97. Cited by Mantae Kim, "Comparative Missiological Study," 2010.

Colonialism," Robert Hunt argues that indigenous Christian movements constitute a way forward. Hunt provides examples from Java where a local evangelist named Sadrach effectively "Christianised" typical Javanese customs and communication patterns so that some entire villages embraced Christianity.[59] Likewise in Africa, indigenous leaders sometimes broke away from established "mission" Churches to form "African" Independent (Instituted or Indigenous) Churches. William Wadé Harris was one such who encouraged indigenous forms of worship, prophecies, healings and exorcism, and permitted polygamy—and sparked a movement into Protestant Christianity in West Africa.[60]

At around 1914 Harris carried out an eighteen-month, three hundred-mile preaching tour from southern Liberia through Côte d'Ivoire into Ghana. Eighty prior years of Catholic and Protestant missionary work had produced only a few hundred converts in Côte d'Ivoire. "Ten years after Harris's momentous journey, with little intervening mission effort, estimates of Christians in that area ranged between two and three hundred thousand."[61]

A considerable amount is written about the southward tilt of the World Christian community. World Christianity today is "the movement of Christianity as it takes form and shape in societies that previously were not Christian," as Lamin Sanneh explains.[62] "The new world situation for the Christian religion demands a new history of Christianity," states historian Mark Noll.[63] More believers gathered for Sunday worship in Nagaland than in Norway, as many practicing Christians in China as in the USA, India now home to the world's largest chapter of the Jesuit order—these are some of the facts.[64] Africa is becoming a Christian continent, while the West becomes a

---

59. Robert A. Hunt, *The Gospel among the Nations: A Documentary History of Inculturation* (Maryknoll, NY: Orbis Books, 2010), 23.

60. Ibid., 24.

61. Mark A. Noll and Carolyn Nystrom, *Clouds of Witnesses: Christian Voices from Africa and Asia* (Downers Grove, IL: InterVarsity Press, 2011), 66.

62. Lamin Sanneh, *Whose Religion Is Christianity? The Gospel beyond the West* (Grand Rapids: Eerdmans, 2003), 22.

63. Mark A. Noll, *The New Shape of World Christianity* (Downers Grove, IL: IVP Academic, 2009), 9.

64. Ibid., 10.

post-Christian society.⁶⁵ "Global revivals," states Mark Shaw, "are at the heart of the global resurgence of Christianity."⁶⁶

The case for the new paradigm promoted by Philip Jenkins and others ought not be over-stated. As Robert Wuthnow reminds us, with the exception of Pentecostalism, "much of the apparent growth of Christianity in certain parts of the world is simply the result of high fertility."⁶⁷ Nevertheless the vitality of Christianity in Africa, Asia, Latin America and the Pacific is cause for joyful hope and gratitude to Almighty God. The new situation also provides fresh possibilities for theologising together and for creative new partnerships in leadership training,⁶⁸ in providing humanitarian aid, for growth in mutual understanding and acceptance.

RELIGIOUS PLURALITY

As Christianity encounters other religious traditions in the South Asian context, new insights are discovered into the riches of God in Christ. Translation of the Gospel into new cultural settings has been the primary avenue to discover new aspects of grace. "Historically it has been the diverse religious-cultural complexes Christianity has encountered, that have been the primary contexts for theological development."⁶⁹ Christian theology arising from a Hindu context will bear distinctive marks of its context. The same is to be said of Christianity arising from a Buddhist setting as in Sri Lanka, or an Islamic background as in Bangladesh. Antony Kaliath points out that before Christian theologians began to think about Indian Christology, Hindus like Vivekananda, Ramakrishna, Keshub Chunder Sen and Mahatma Gandhi had already owned Jesus and developed a Christological spirituality—an experiential Christology and a vibrant Christophany among non-Christians!⁷⁰ "Asian Christology rises out

---

65. Sanneh, *Whose Religion Is Christianity?*, 36.
66. Mark Shaw, *Global Awakening: How 20th-Century Revivals Triggered a Christian Revolution* (Downers Grove, IL: IVP Academic, 2010), 12.
67. Robert Wuthnow, *Boundless Faith: The Global Outreach of American Churches* (Berkeley: University of California Press, 2009), 44, 59.
68. Leon P. Spencer, "Not Yet There: Seminaries and the Challenge of Partnership," *International Bulletin of Missionary Research* 34, no. 3 (July 2010): 150–54.
69. S. Mark Heim, "Witness to Difference: Mission and the Religions in Post-Pluralist Perspective" in *News of Boundless Riches: Interrogating, Comparing, and Reconstructing Mission in a Global Era*, vol. 1, ed. Max L. Stackhouse and Lalsangkima Pachuau (Delhi: ISPCK, 2007), 103.
70. Antony Kalliath, "Liberative Dialogue towards Harmony of Life: Interrogating Catholic

of a situation in which millions of poor struggle with the basic issues of life."[71] The uniqueness of the cross distinguishes Jesus from Buddha or Krishna, and identifies Jesus with the multitudes of poor and suffering. This is the reality in which a large number of Hindus as unbaptised *Jesu Bhaktas* (devotees of Jesus) accept Jesus as Lord and *Guru*.[72]

Christianity in Asia has always existed alongside other religious traditions. Not only does this enrich the form and substance of Christian theology, but Christianity has made an imprint upon other world faiths. In various ways "Hinduism and Buddhism have undergone renewal as a result of being confronted with a missionary Christianity."[73] Christian theology in Asia is molded in a variety of differing contexts. The result is a diversity of theological expression. Sebastian Kim traces five strands of Korean theology: Bible Christianity concerned with translation and dissemination of the Bible, Revival Christianity which seeks for holistic blessing, Liberation Christianity struggling for justice, Folk Christianity assimilating Korean shamanistic culture and Reconciling Christianity concerned for Korea's unification.[74] Each strand emerges from particular moments in Korea's turbulant history. Thomas Thangaraj offers an overview of seven models of Christian encounter in Asia with other religions: the Other as enemy of God, as potential convert, as primitive superstition, as unfulfilled seeker, as storehouse of culture, as companion in struggle, as partner in dialogue.[75] From these encounters Thangaraj highlights four theological themes: the place of the Bible, God among gods, Christ among other saviours, the Church among other religious communities.[76]

Whatever else may be said, the Churches of Asia inculturate in a variety of ways including adaptation of local customs and rites

---

Missiology in a Futuristic Perspective" in Stackhouse and Pachau, *News of Boundless Riches*, 83–84.

71. Ibid., 85.
72. Ibid., 71.
73. David M. Thompson, "Introduction: Mapping Asian Christianity in the Context of World Christianity," in *Christian Theology in Asia*, ed. Sebastian C. H. Kim (Cambridge: Cambridge University Press, 2008), 13.
74. Sebastian C. H. Kim, "The Word and the Spirit: Overcoming Poverty, Injustice and Division in Korea," in Kim, *Christian Theology in Asia*, 130–50.
75. M. Thomas Thangaraj, "Religious Pluralism, Dialogue and Asian Christian Responses," in Kim, *Christian Theology in Asia*, 159–63.
76. Ibid., 163–75.

deemed suitable for Christian worship, communication and life.[77] Whatever else we may do, dialogue seems inescapable in Asia and essential for building an authentic Asian Christian theology and apologetic. Preaching in an Asian mode can utilize poetry, drama, short story, apocalyptic and word play which are rich in Asian cultures; yet this is where many fall short and hence fail to reach an impoverished oral audience in which video games and TV have replaced reading.[78]

CONCLUSION

In correspondence prior to the September 2009 CSCA Workshop on Primal Spirituality and Southeast Asian Christianity, John Roxborogh mentioned the need for a non-Western integrative historiography and that Asia has much to offer in this regard. Not least is the longevity of Christian history in Asia from the earliest time, but also that alternative models of Christianity in society are developing in Southeast Asia which deserve a place in discourse on global historiography of Christianity.

Aspects of indigeneity, contextuality and plurality together with Pentecostalism and theological implications as they pertain to new Christian movements have been touched upon in this paper. Hopefully these reflections may contribute to further dialogue in which South Asia also has much to offer. To return to the earlier question by Bishop Hwa Yung, God is doing a new thing in Asia today and it is important that we not repeat the mistakes of the past. Imperative then it is that we learn the lessons of history.

In conclusion, a word from John Roxborogh seems appropriate,

> Awareness of the history and expression of the faith in their own and other contexts provides a language which enables people to talk about what is going on, and to explore in every generation what it means to be true to the Gospel of Jesus Christ and relevant to the societies where God has placed us.[79]

---

77. Ibid., 174.
78. See Adonis Abelard O. Gorospe, ed., *Naming the Unknown God* (Manila: OMF Literature, 2006).
79. W. John Roxborogh, "Situating Southeast Asian Christian Movements in the History of World Christianity," in Poon, *Christian Movements in Southeast Asia*, 36.

"For the Kingdom is His,
and the Power is His,
and the Glory forever. Amen."

SOURCES FOR FURTHER REFERENCE

Anderson, Allan, and Edmond Tang, eds. *Asian and Pentecostal: The Charismatic Face of Christianity in Asia*. Oxford: Regnum, 2005.

Bergunder, Michael. *The South Indian Pentecostal Movement in the Twentieth Century*. Grand Rapids: Eerdmans, 2008.

Brown, Judith M., and Robert Eric Frykenberg, eds. *Christians, Cultural Interactions, and India's Religious Traditions*. Grand Rapids: Eerdmans, 2002.

Daniel, J. T. K., and R. E. Hedlund, eds. *Carey's Obligation and India's Renaissance*. Serampore, India: Serampore College, 1993.

Frykenberg, Robert Eric. *Christianity in India: From Beginnings to the Present*. New York: Oxford University Press, 2008.

_____, ed. *Christians and Missionaries in India: Cross-Cultural Communication since 1500*. Grand Rapids: Eerdmans, 2003.

Glaser, Ida. *The Bible and Other Faiths: Christian Responsibility in a World of Religions*. Downers Grove, IL: IVP Academic, 2005.

Gorospe, Adonis Abelard O., ed. *Naming the Unknown God*. Manila: OMF Literature, 2006.

Hanciles, Jehu J. *Beyond Christendom: Globalization, African Migration, and the Transformation of the West*. Maryknoll, NY: Orbis Books, 2008.

Harper, S. Billington. *In the Shadow of the Mahatma: Bishop V. S. Azariah and the Travails of Christianity in British India*. Grand Rapids: Eerdmans, 2000.

Hedlund, Roger E. "Approaches to Indian Church History in Light of New Christian Movements." *Indian Church History Review*, December 2000, 153–70.

_____. "The Church in Mission Contextualizes the Gospel." *Evangelical Fellowship of India: All India Congress on the Church in Mission*. Hyderabad, India, 13–16 October, 2009.

_____. *Quest for Identity: India's Churches of Indigenous Origin*. Delhi: ISPCK, 2000.

_____, ed. *Christianity Is Indian: The Emergence of an Indigenous Community*. Delhi: ISPCK, 2004 (2000).

_____, and Paul Joshua Bhakiaraj, eds. *Missiology for the 21st Century: South Asian Perspectives*. Delhi: ISPCK, 2004.

Hunt, Robert A. *The Gospel among the Nations: A Documentary History of Inculturation*. Maryknoll, NY: Orbis Books, 2010.

Irwin, Dale T., and Scott Sunquist. *History of the World Christian Movement*. Vol. 1, *Earliest Christianity to 1453*. Maryknoll, NY: Orbis Books, 2001.

Jenkins, Philip. *The New Faces of Christianity: Believing the Bible in the Global South*. New York: Oxford University Press, 2006.

_____. *The Next Christendom: The Coming of Global Christianity*. New York: Oxford University Press, 2002.

Kim, Sebastian C. H. "The Word and the Spirit: Overcoming Poverty, Injustice and Division in Korea." In *Christian Theology in Asia*, edited by Sebastian C. H. Kim, 130–50. Cambridge: Cambridge University Press, 2008.

Lewis, Donald, ed. *Christianity Reborn: The Global Expansion of Evangelicalism in the Twentieth Century*. Grand Rapids: Eerdmans, 2004.

Mani, Braj Ranjan. *Debrahmanising History: Dominance and Resistance in Indian Society*. New Delhi: Manohar, 2007.

_____, and Pamela Sardar. *A Forgotten Liberator: The Life and Struggle of Savitribai Phule*. New Delhi: Mountain Peak, 2008.

Massey, James. *Dalits in India: Religion as a Source of Bondage or Liberation*. Delhi: Manohar, 1995.

McPhee, Arthur. *The Road to Delhi: J. Wascom Pickett Remembered*. Bangalore: SAIACS Press, 2005.

Muck, Terry, and Frances S. Adeney. *Christianity Encountering World Religions: The Practice of Mission in the Twenty-First Century*. Grand Rapids: Baker Academic, 2009.

Noll, Mark A. *The New Shape of World Christianity*. Downers Grove, IL: IVP Academic, 2009.

O'Mahony, Anthony, and Michael Kirwan. *World Christianity: Politics, Theology, Dialogues.* London: Melisende, 2004.

Phule, Jotirao. *Cultivator's Whipcord.* Vol. 3 of *Collected Works of Mahatma Jotirao Phule.* Translated by Asha Mundlay. Bombay: Education Department, Government of Maharashtra, 2002.

———. *Selections.* Vol 2 of *Collected Works of Mahatma Jotirao Phule.* Translated by P. G. Patil. Bombay: Education Department, Government of Maharashtra, 1991.

Poon, Michael Nai-Chiu, ed. *Christian Movements in Southeast Asia: A Theological Exploration.* Singapore: Genesis Books and Trinity Theological College, 2010.

Ramabai, Pandita. *A Testimony of Our Inexhaustible Treasure.* Kedgaon, India: Pandita Ramabai Mukti Mission, reprint 1977.

Robert, Dana L. *Converting Colonialism: Visions and Realities in Mission History, 1706–1914.* Grand Rapids: Eerdmans, 2008.

Sanneh, Lamin, *Disciples of All Nations: Pillars of World Christianity.* New York: Oxford University Press, 2008.

———. *Translating the Message: The Missionary Impact on Culture,* Maryknoll: Orbis Books, 1991.

———. *Whose Religion Is Christianity? The Gospel beyond the West.* Grand Rapids: Eerdmans, 2003.

Shaw, Mark. *Global Awakening: How 20th-Century Revivals Triggered a Christian Revolution.* Downers Grove, IL: IVP Academic, 2010.

Somaratna, G. P. V. *Origins of the Pentecostal Mission in Sri Lanka.* Nugegoda, Sri Lanka: Margaya Fellowship, 1996.

Taylor, John V. *The Primal Vision: Christian Presence amid African Religion.* London: SCM, 1963.

Tennent, Timothy C. *Christianity at the Religious Roundtable: Evangelicalism in Conversation with Hinduism, Buddhism, and Islam.* Grand Rapids: Baker Academic, 2002.

———. *Invitation to World Missions: A Trinitarian Missiology for the Twenty-First Century.* Grand Rapids: Kregel Publications, 2010.

Thangaraj, M. Thomas. "Religious Pluralism, Dialogue and Asian Christian Responses." In *Christian Theology in Asia,* edited by Sebastian C. H. Kim, 159–63. Cambridge: Cambridge University Press, 2008.

Turner, Harold W. *Bibliography of New Religious Movements in Primal Societies.* Boston: G.K. Hall, 1977.

Walls, Andrew F. *The Missionary Movement in Christian History: Studies in the Transmission of Faith.* Maryknoll: Orbis Books, 1996.
Wilfred, Felix and Jose D. Maliekal. *The Struggle for the Past: Historiography Today.* Chennai, India: University of Madras, 2002.
Young, Richard Fox. "God of a Thousand Heads." *Dharma Deepika* (January–June 2009): 3–10.

15.

Christian Identity in a Pluralistic World

INTRODUCTION

Religious pluralism is a fact in the world in which we live. Today's globalisation has brought major world religions into the marketplace of all the inhabited continents. Migration, trade, world travel, world politics and media give wide exposure to the religious cultures of the world. In today's world, Eastern religions are engaged in a vigorous six-continent missionary propaganda. The call of the minaret is heard in the cities of Europe and America as well as in Africa and Asia. Hindu and Buddhist temples are found in Australia, Oceania, Africa and the West as the adherents of Asia's ethnic religions travel the globe in search of employment, education, recreation, social and economic opportunity.

This twenty-first century phenomenon has demolished the myth of Western Christendom. Christian theologians, missiologists, and Church leaders find themselves confronted with "new" questions. What about the Christian claim: Is Christianity unique? In what does Christian distinctiveness consist? Is Christ the unique and only Saviour? In what sense is the Christian Gospel exclusive? These and other seemingly "new" questions—though they have been faced before—must be confronted anew in the present pluralistic context.

INDIAN IDENTITY

In his brilliant book, *The Argumentative Indian*, Nobel Prize winner Amartya Sen includes an essay on "The Indian Identity" in which he discusses differing interpretations but rejects the thesis of a religious definition. Professor Sen reminds us that "India has been a multi-religious country for a very long time, with Jews, Christians, Parsees, and Muslim traders arriving and settling in India over the first millennium."[1] Nor is it correct to see pre-Muslim India as mainly Hindu since "Buddhism was the dominant religion in India for many hundreds of years and Jainism has had an equally long history."[2] India has a "rich tradition of heterodoxy," and hundreds of millions who are defined as "Hindu" do not in fact hold central Hindu beliefs.[3] Professor Sen laments a "narrowly Hinduised view of India's past" in which "the justifiable pride Indians can take in the achievements of non-Hindu as well as Hindu accomplishments in India is drowned in the sectarianism of seeing India as mainly a vehicle for Hindu thought and practice" which means a denial of much in Indian history "that Indians have reason to remember and to celebrate."[4]

A Christian identity therefore is not in conflict with one's patriotism and nationalism. Christians in India in fact have been ardent nationalists who participated in the Freedom struggle and have contributed to nation building. During nearly two thousand years of history in India, Christianity has had considerable impact on the cultures of the peoples in various regions of the Indian sub-continent. The local cultures in turn have modified and influenced the forms and expressions of Christianity. It has been a mutual enrichment process including the development of an indigenous Christianity. There has been significant Christian presence and influence in such diverse cultural centres as Bengal and Maharashtra, in Kerala and Tamil Nadu, in Punjab, and in North East India as well as among India's aboriginal peoples.

---

1. Amartya Sen, *The Argumentative Indian* (New York: Penguin Books, 2005), 353.
2. Ibid.
3. Ibid., 354.
4. Ibid., 83.

CHRISTIAN CONTRIBUTIONS

In North East India, Christianity has been an effective catalyst for cultural renewal and social integration especially through education and developmental work. The Church, as seen by Christians, has been both an agent of change and a means of enforcing traditional values as well as filling voids, as is pointed out by several scholars. But there is a flipside: the alleged Christian exploitation of tribes and the erosion of culture, religion and traditions. Critics tend to repeat this charge, which is conceded by local Christians to be at best a partial truth, at worst a gross distortion. In point of fact Christianity has been a major source of moral, social and cultural transformation among the peoples of North East India.

Conversion among the Kachin of upper Burma likewise provides an example of inculturation of Christian beliefs into the local Kachin Tribal culture.[5] "Adoption of Christianity allowed the Kachin to involve themselves in a wider social world, and at the same time to be able to reformulate their distinctive ethnic identity vis á vis the Burmans" while retaining traditional kinship patterns and social structure. The Kachin found Christianity compatible with aspects of their traditional belief about God and so were able to identify themselves both as Kachin Christians and as Christian Kachin. "Kachinness is intertwined with distinctive socio-political and religio-cultural systems and the strong group consciousness they engender." Education played a positive role in turning the Kachin toward Christianity,[6] much as it had among the Naga tribes in Nagaland.

Apart from the dominant Christianised peoples of the North East, India's marginalised adivasis (aboriginal tribes) present quite a different picture. These exploited peoples regarded the land and its forests and resources as the gifts of God to the original inhabitants of Central India's Tribal belt. Against the devastating effects of deprivation of Tribal rights, Christianity gave the Tribals a new identity and sense of dignity. Christian missionaries gave a written form to Tribal languages, provided modern education, and helped the Tribals fight legal battles to preserve their land rights.[7] Christianity has been a

---

5. La Seng Dingrin, "Conversion to Mission Christianity among the Kachin of Upper Burma 1877–1972," in *Asia in the Making of Christianity: Conversion, Agency, and Indigeneity, 1600s to the Present*, ed. Richard Fox Young & Jonathan A. Seitz (Boston: Brill, 2013), 109–34.

6. Ibid., 131, 129.

7. Nirmal Minz, "Religion, Culture and Education in the Context of Tribal Aspirations in

major sustaining force for India's original inhabitants in their struggle against cultural attacks and empowering them for social-economic liberation.

In several social and cultural spheres in various contexts Christianity has contributed to the revitalisation of India's cultures. Through it all a remarkable "Indianness" is evident.

RELIGIOUS NATIONALISM

South Asia is the region of "Indian civilization" consisting of eight nation-states, each of which has a number of different religions but one dominant religion: Hindu (India and Nepal), Muslim (Pakistan and Bangladesh) and Buddhist (Bhutan, Burma, and Sri Lanka).[8] Maldives is not included in this definition, Asia's smallest country with a population of 314,000, but a founding member of the South Asian Association for Regional Cooperation (SAARC), with Islam the official religion of the entire population.[9] Pakistan and Bangladesh likewise clearly distinguish insiders (Muslims) from outsiders on the basis of religion. In Sri Lanka, contending Sinhala Buddhists, Tamil Hindus and Tamil Muslims all are migrants from India.[10] Buddhism is the official religion of Bhutan, and was declared the state religion of Burma in 1961 although a principle of "equal respect for all religions" was adopted as the state policy in 1962.[11] Post-colonial Sri Lanka, without an explicit official recognition, tends to identify Sinhala Buddhism as the "national" religion.[12] In contrast, India, with no established state religion, professes respect for all religions, yet religious nationalism is alive and active.[13] In actuality Hindu nationalism expresses hostility to other religions.

India," in *Little Traditions and National Culture*, ed. Thomas Kadankavil (Bangalore, India: Dharmaram Publications, 2000), 128.

8. T. K. Oommen, "Religious Nationalism in South Asia," in *Missiology for the 21st Century: South Asian Perspectives*, ed. Roger E. Hedlund and Paul Joshua Bhakiaraj (Delhi: ISPCK, 2004), 618.

9. Simon Fuller, "Maldives," in *Oxford Encyclopaedia of South Asian Christianity*, ed. R. E. Hedlund, Jesudas Athyal, Joshua Kalapati, and Jessica Richard (New Delhi: Oxford University Press, 2012), 420–21.

10. Oommen, "Religious Nationalism in South Asia," 619.

11. Ibid., 622.

12. Ibid.

13. Ibid., 623.

Hinduism, although not proselytizing, is migratory. At least twenty million Hindus live outside the Indian subcontinent, the traditional sacred land of Hinduism. In some of the countries (e.g., Fiji, Surinam, Mauritius) they constitute majorities. Would it be correct to say that those Hindus who have settled outside the Indian subcontinent cease to be Hindus because they do not live in their ancestral homeland? The absurdity of the question is patent, but it emanates from the assumptions made by Hindu nationalists.[14]

Finally, as T. K. Oommmen concludes, the religious nationalism project is bound to fail because of the institutionalised inequality of the Hindutva ideology which has failed to gain the confidence of the majority of Indian population, such as the Dravidians, the OBCs, the Scheduled Castes and Scheduled Tribes.[15]

HISTORY FROM BELOW

In a trenchant essay addressing Christian history "from below," Chandra Mallampalli contends that a low tradition is both suitable and necessary to account for the "indigenous discovery" of Christianity by the Indians including Dalits and Tribals, and the implications thereof.[16] Take, for example, the question of inheritance: the Indian Succession Act of 1865 subjected native Christians to an English law of inheritance whereby the property of a deceased father would pass to his surviving spouse and children. The problem, however, was that many Christian families "continued to abide by the inheritance practices of their original castes."[17] Call it dual identity. The Christian movement was subject to the "initiatives, adaptations, and creativity of Indian converts."[18] This is but one example of ways in which Indian Christians retain their distinct cultural identities.[19]

Nevertheless misperceptions persist "that Christianity is essentially

---

14. Ibid., 626.
15. Ibid., 632.
16. Chandra Mallampalli, "Caste, Catholicism, and History 'from Below' 1863–1917," in *India and the Indianness of Christianity: Essays on Understanding—Historical, Theological, and Bibliographical—in Honor of Robert Eric Frykenberg*, ed. Richard Fox Young (Grand Rapids: Eerdmans, 2009), 147.
17. Ibid., 149.
18. Ibid., 154.
19. Robert Eric Frykenberg, "Introduction," in *Christians and Missionaries in India: Cross-Cultural Communication since 1500*, ed. Robert Eric Frykenberg (Grand Rapids: Eerdmans, 2003), 2.

European and that European religion has traditionally been Christian"[20]—neither of which is true.[21] Mass conversion movements into Christianity in the late eighteenth and nineteenth centuries, in which entire villages became Christian, became a focus of opposition in the twentieth century and were "severely criticized by higher-caste Hindus" such as M. K. Gandhi.[22] Gandhi denounced Anglican Bishop V. S. Azariah for leading mass conversions in Dornakal where Untouchables were living in sub-human conditions hitherto deprived of use of public wells, roads and other facilities. "Azariah and others like him represented an ongoing process of evangelization and Indianisation that would continue to grow among India's Christians and their leaders."[23]

QUESTIONS ARISING: WHAT IS TRUTH?

Bishop Lesslie Newbigin identified the central issue in the debate on religious pluralism and the uniqueness of Christ as abandonment of the belief that it is possible to know the truth.[24] Western society in particular has lost its belief in absolutes. If it is not possible to know, then it follows that it is quite plausible and acceptable to worship at any altar—or no altar—according to one's preference. Newbigin challenged this assumption. To claim complete possession of the truth is arrogance, but to believe and profess to have found access to trust is part of human responsibility.[25] Newbigin points out that Christian belief is not an individualistic affair but one which involves a community. "We do not know God . . . except as part of a community. . . . God's action for the salvation of the whole human family."[26] Truth can only be communicated which is embodied. According to Christian understanding, a true understanding of history is given to

---

20. Ibid., 5.
21. Christianity had an extensive vitality and development in Africa between 50 and 500 CE. See the scholarly findings of Thom C. Oden in *How Africa Shaped the Christian Mind: Rediscovering the African Seedbed of Western Christianity* (Downers Grove, IL: InterVarsity Press, 2008). "Decisive intellectual achievements of Christianity were explored and understood first in Africa before they were recognized in Europe, and a millennium before they found their way to North America," 10.
22. Frykenberg, "Introduction," 23.
23. Ibid., 24.
24. Lesslie Newbigin, "Religious Pluralism and the Uniqueness of Jesus Christ," *Internatioal Bulletin of Missionary Research* (April 1989): 50–54.
25. Ibid., 54.
26. Ibid.

a particular community which bears the name of Jesus and in which the Spirit of God is actively at work.[27] This gives logic to election. The Church, his Disciples, embody his mission for all families of earth.[28] The indispensable role of the believing community is overlooked by the advocates of a theocentric (non-Christocentric) theology of religious pluralism. The Bible is universal history, though communicated through one people, Israel. The Bible tells a unique story which has universal application.

Domestication of Jesus into the Hindu worldview therefore is neither helpful nor desirable. The Christian affirmation of Christ does not claim we know all truth, but it means we are committed. Our affirmation rests on a faith commitment.[29] Here is the basis for the clash with a philosophy of pluralism which assumes there is no absolute truth, only different perceptions of truth. The Christian affirmation holds that this is no mere question of preference, but that here are issues of truth and falsehood.[30] In our contemporary world, ultimate reality is considered unknowable; therefore all confident statements of belief are regarded arrogant. But Newbigin raises a "critique of doubt," and calls for an act of faith. Modern society, however, is not willing to make such commitments—for which reason Western culture is falling apart.[31] If there are no absolutes, Christian propositions are rejected in favour of spiritual experience of whatever kind. To affirm beliefs as factual truth is out of vogue and is labeled "fundamentalist," and to seek conversion of Atheists, Hindus, Buddhists, Sikhs and Muslims is considered "arrogant."[32] Secularism, Mary Poplin finds, has created a new political age in which "political power trumps truth claims." In democratic as well as totalitarian regimes, "decisions are made on the basis of who has the most power," and religion is suppressed because "the political state can stand no competitors."[33]

This the context in which followers of Christ announce the unique story of God's redemption which is the substance of the Christian

---

27. Lesslie Newbigin, *The Gospel in a Pluralistic Society* (Geneva: WCC Publications, 1990), 78.
28. Ibid., 86.
29. Ibid., 13.
30. Ibid., 14.
31. Ibid., 23.
32. Ibid., 25.
33. Mary Poplin, *Is Reality Secular? Testing the Assumptions of Four Global Worldviews* (Downers Grove, IL: InterVarsity Press, 2014), 42.

message and mission. The Church to be loyal to her Lord must challenge the powers, make the Kingdom present and cause people to ask the questions which the Gospel answers.[34] The logic of mission is that it discloses the true meaning of the human story. The role of the Christian community is to authenticate the Gospel. This obligation of the Christian mission extends to all nations.[35]

Secular society is a myth! Asian, African and Latina Christians take their evangelistic mission seriously. There is hope perhaps also for the re-conversion of the West.

QUESTIONS ARISING: THE ONE OR THE MANY

The Christological necessity is raised by Kenneth Cragg's question, "Is Christ Multiplied?" The question of plural Christologies is especially significant in India. Christian Christology, Cragg points out, is committed to history, whereas Hinduism's capacity to absorb is quite ready to dispense with the historical. Wider Christologies may well dissolve into myth or fantasy. Moreover, "plural Christologies suggest plural contexts of salvation, whereas Christianity is traditionally conversionist."[36]

Here, then, is a basic divide. How, then, to proceed? Dialogue tends to stress similarities but also must not overlook the differences. Nor must one ignore the "travail about the old in the very appeal of the new" brought about by the Gospel's encounter with ancient systems and ways of life. Confronted by the exclusive yet universal claims of Christ, people rightly ask, "Why did God leave us so long in the dark?" Christian advocates must feel troubled, must "share the perplexities that beset the Hindu mind at the otherness, the exclusivity, the privacy—as they see it—of truth which characterizes the Christian tradition."[37] The Gospel is universal, but its arrival appears wholly foreign: what does this say as to India's place in the "preparation of the Gospel?"[38] The question about the ancestors is a legitimate one. Various thinkers have sought to resolve the difficulty: C. F. Andrews (the seeds of Christian teaching were sown in India

---

34. Newbigin, *The Gospel in a Pluralistic Society*, 119.
35. Ibid., 124.
36. Kenneth Cragg, *The Christ and the Faiths* (Philadelphia: The Westminster Press, 1986), 178.
37. Ibid., 182.
38. Ibid., 181.

by *Bhakti*), A. G. Hogg (the theme of *karma* is never satisfactorily resolved in Hinduism which is crippled because the Hindu concept of God is never moralized, hence the need of Christ), and several contemporaries such as Raimundo Panikkar, M. M. Thomas and others.

Panikkar's multiple Christology distinguishes between the identification of Christ in Jesus (made by Christians) and a larger identity of Christhood wider than the historical particularity that is Jesus. But Cragg objects that this usage of "Christ" ceases to connote the Christ of the Christians.[39] Panikkar is trying to reconstruct Christology from within Hinduism, cut free from historicity. "Panikkar takes the Christ of history as only one construct for a mystery hidden otherwise elsewhere."[40] Christian Christologies are inseparable from Jesus and the cross, whereas Hindu Christologies require no concrete definition.[41] This is a basic, continental divide. Jesus, Cragg states, "is only available as a historical figure."[42] Christ is not a principle! The Christhood of Jesus is real and actual. It is set in history and generates history.

Moreover, there is a dynamic in the Christ-event not found in any mere myth or philosophical theory. "The actuality of the cross faces the rawness and realness of human evil with more authority than mythical figures could ever do."[43] The Biblical message of God's redemptive work in Christ has always formed the basis for the Christian mission. But it is precisely this purpose that is questioned today, as the late Prof. Myklebust pointed out, by a radical re-definition of Christian beliefs which asserts that Jesus Christ is not the only Saviour.[44] But, as Kenneth Cragg states, "The Jesus of history is crucial to the Christ of experience."[45] This understanding and realism is vital to the struggle for social justice. A notable example in India was that of Gandhiji whose deeds of service, expressions of the Christ-principle, were inspired by the Christ-event. India's Christologies may be many, Cragg concludes, but ultimately there is the one, tethered to the historical Messiah.

39. Ibid., 185.
40. Ibid., 187.
41. Ibid., 194.
42. Ibid., 197.
43. Ibid., 204.
44. Olav Guttorm Myklebust, "Missiology in Contemporary Theological Education: A Factual Survey," *Mission Studies: Journal of the International Association for Mission Studies* 6, no. 2 (1989): 87–107, at 100.
45. Cragg, *The Christ and the Faiths*, 214.

A QUESTION OF TRUE PLURALISM

"In a pluralistic world, is Christ the Only Way? If so, how so?" asks Professor S. Mark Heim. Pluraliam means that we live with real differences, with conflicting answers, which is not the same as mere toleration. The different religions and ideologies give distinctive answers, have different presuppositions: they are not merely differing ways of expressing the same thing. The central issue is the absoluteness of Jesus Christ: "Christianity makes a universal claim for a particular person."[46] The Christian affirmation is that the ultimate truth is not a proposition but a person. This "dogmatic" assertion does not deny the presence of truth in other religions, philosophies and ideologies. It does announce that something distinctive and unique has happened in Jesus Christ.

> The Christian confession is that in Jesus we find the particular which is healing and saving for the whole of our common humanity. . . . All our differences, apparent and real, cannot block the transfusion of divine gifts of grace which come from relationship with this single, particular Jesus.[47]

What, then, are the options in a pluralistic world?

Heim calls for a true pluralism. As Christians we confess Christ as the only Way. "The Christian affirmation is that all who come to what Christians mean by salvation—reconciliation with the personal, living God who made us and loves us—do come by Christ."[48] This does not mean there is no truth outside of Christ. We believe that we know God by knowing Christ. But it does not follow that we therefore know everything there is to know! Full knowledge rests with the Infinite. We remain finite. Knowing God in Christ is primarily a salvation issue. What does this imply for those outside the Christian tradition? "God is present to every seeking heart," states Heim, but, if the clearest knowledge of God is available in Christ, we must conclude that "God is not known save in the most fragmentary way in most other faiths."[49] The truth that comes from God is made known in Christ, and that truth is accessible to humanity. The fragments are

---

46. S. Mark Heim, *Is Christ the Only Way? Christian Faith in a Pluralistic World* (Valley Forge, PA: Judson Press, 1985), 84.
47. Ibid., 66.
48. Ibid., 131.
49. Ibid., 132.

true fragments, for all truth comes from God, though quite distinct from Christian faith. "To know Christ is to know God in a way not available in any other revelation. It is to know all that we need to know of God."[50]

We do not therefore consider other faiths as Christian variations or second-class Christians. "They are not to be made or remade into anonymous forms of Christianity."[51] We must take them seriously, but not treat them as Christian deviations: they are not trying to be "Christian." Their presuppositions differ from ours. The questions raised and the answers given are not the same as Christian ones. "None of these faiths is trying to solve the human problem as Christianity understands it."[52] The Christian claim is a narrow one, that Christ alone is the mediator of salvation. At the same time we dare not deny the values found in other faiths. The proper attitude therefore is one of true cordiality expressed through an honest pluralism which respects the basic differences and virtues.[53] Christianity affirms true pluralism, does not compromise it through a false unification.

God does not force anyone to choose a particular way against one's will. "God allows, and has even established, what we might call ultimate pluralism, the eternal right of choice and interpretation. No one is compelled to give up her or his view of reality."[54] In a pluralistic world, let every human creature have the possibility to exercise the human right to decide for his or herself.

CONCLUSION

Any number of questions arise concerning ecumenism, conversion and related issues beyond the scope of this essay. The truths found in other religions can be utilised "as points of contact and stepping-stones in preaching the Gospel."[55] We can learn from them: glimpses of truth are there. The Christian Scriptures contain all that is necessary for a complete life, yet our perceptions may be incomplete or faulty so that other cultures and faiths may shed some light, like the

---

50. Ibid., 134.
51. Ibid., 137.
52. Ibid., 138.
53. Ibid., 139.
54. Ibid.
55. Ajith Fernando, "Truth in Other Religions," *Evangelical Review of Theology* 11, no. 4 (October 1987): 299.

values of reverence and contemplation.[56] But the systems themselves are flawed, therefore unacceptable, and may lead people away from the truth of God.[57]

The question of conversion incites extremist reactions, particularly in the Hindu world. Perhaps against this background Samartha[58] argued for commitment to Christ without conversion—as more viable in the Hindu context. Noble as this sounds, the idea will not be attractive to many Evangelicals who desire a more visible obedience to Christ. While one can sympathise with secret followers of Christ, one cannot ignore the fact of remarkable response to the Gospel in our day in which many in Asia and Africa are being added to the Church. The Church is a crucial factor in the resolution of the debate on pluralism, as Newbigin stated.

Indian Christians in various spheres have contributed to the development of modern India: in literature and literacy, education and developmental work. Those of depressed and backward origins derive a new identity in Christ and a royal dignity as the People of God leading to a revitalisation of India's cultures. Thereby Christianity itself is enriched and marked by a distinctive Indian essence.

SOURCES FOR FURTHER REFERENCE

Arangaden, Christopher. "Carey's Legacy of Bible Translation." In *Carey's Obligation and India's Renaissance*, edited by J. T. K. Daniel and R. E. Hedlund, 176–86. Serampore, India: Council of Serampore College, 1993.

Chatterjee, S. K. "William Carey and the Linguistic Renaissance in India." In *Carey's Obligation and India's Renaissance*, edited by J. T. K. Daniel and R. E. Hedlund, 157–75. Serampore, India: Council of Serampore College, 1993.

Cragg, Kenneth. *The Christ and the Faiths*. Philadelphia: The Westminster Press, 1986.

---

56. Ibid., 297.
57. Ibid., 300.
58. Stanley J. Samartha, *One Christ—Many Religions: Toward A Revised Christology* (Maryknoll, NY: Orbis Books, 1991).

Daniel, J. T. K., and Roger E. Hedlund, eds. *Carey's Obligation and India's Renaissance*. Serampore, India: Council of Serampore College, 1993.
Fernando, Ajith. "Truth in Other Religions." *Evangelical Review of Theology* 11, no. 4 (October 1987): 292–301.
Hedlund, Roger E. "The Literary and Social Contribution of William Carey and the Serampore Mission to Modern India." Paper presented at the Seminar on Christian Literature and Its Social Contribution. Tamil University School of Philosophy, Thanjavur, November 22–23, 1999.
———. "Missiological Issues in the Study of Christianity in Tribal Areas." Paper presented at the Seminar on Christian Faith and Tribal Cultures in Eastern and North East India, Serampore College, August 21–24, 1996.
———. "William Carey's American Connections: Implications for the Serampore Mission, Indigenous Christianity and India's Renaissance." PhD thesis, University of Madras, Chennai, India, January 2003.
Heim, Mark S. *Is Christ the Only Way? Christian Faith in a Pluralistic World*. Valley Forge, PA: Judson Press, 1985.
Kadankavil, Thomas, ed. *Little Traditions and National Culture*. Bangalore, India: Dharmaram Publications, 2000.
Knitter, Paul. *No Other Name? A Critical Survey of Christian Attitudes toward the World Religions*. Maryknoll, NY: Orbis, 1985.
Minz, Nirmal. "Religion, Culture and Education in the Context of Tribal Aspirations in India." In *Little Traditions and National Culture*, edited by Thomas Kadankavil. Bangalore, India: Dharmaram Publications, 2000.
Myklebust, Olav Guttorm. "Missiology in Contemporary Theological Education: A Factual Survey." *Mission Studies: Journal of the International Association for Mission Studies* 6, no. 2 (1989): 87–107.
Newbigin, Lesslie. *The Gospel in a Pluralistic Society*. Geneva: WCC Publications, 1990.
———. "Religious Pluralism and the Uniqueness of Jesus Christ." *International Bulletin of Missionary Research* (April 1989): 50–54.
Oden, Thomas C. *How Africa Shaped the Christian Mind: Rediscovering the African Seedbed of Western Christianity*. Downers Grove, IL: InterVarsity Press, 2008.

Oommen, T. K. "Religious Nationalism in South Asia." In *Missiology for the 21st Century: South Asian Perspectives*, edited by Roger E. Hedlund and Paul Joshua Bhakiaraj. Delhi: ISPCK, 2004.

Panikkar, R. *The Unknown Christ of Hinduism*. London: Darton, Longman & Todd, 1968.

Poplin, Mary. *Is Reality Secular? Testing the Assumptions of Four Global Worldviews*. Downers Grove, IL: InterVarsity Press, 2014.

Samartha, Stanley J. *One Christ—Many Religions: Toward A Revised Christology*. Maryknoll, NY: Orbis Books, 1991.

Sen, Amartya. *The Argumentative Indian*. New York: Penguin Books, 2005.

Thomas, M. M. *Risking Christ for Christ's Sake: Toward an Ecumenical Theology of Pluralism*. Geneva: World Council of Churches, 1987.

16.

Hindus and Christians Together for Two Thousand Years

Christians and Hindus have interacted for two thousand years in the Indian sub-continent.[1] Two major assumptions underlie that bold assertion.

First, it assumes one accepts the Thomas tradition as to the origins of Christianity in South Asia. It is widely accepted in India that the Apostle Thomas came to India in 52 CE, and preached and established Churches during the first century.[2] The Thomas tradition cannot be proven, but neither can it be disproven, and the evidence indicates that the Gospel came and that Christianity has existed in India since the earliest times. If true, it seems surprising that there is no early record of a Hindu speaking about Christ.[3] Nevertheless a robust Indian Christian community adhering to the message of Christ, which they claimed had been handed down by St. Thomas, was discovered in the fourth century by Syrian Christians fleeing from Persian persecution. The existence of this venerable community, living

---

1. Published as a "Featured Article" at www.globalmissiology.org, January 2008. Originally presented as a paper at a Seminar on Hinduism at the Concordia Institute for World Religion and Evangelism, Concordia College, Bronxville, New York, June 23–27, 2008.

2. A. M. Mundadan, *From the Beginning up to the Middle of the Sixteenth Century*, History of Christianity in India, vol. 1 (Bangalore: Church History Association of India, 1989).

3. Anand Amaladass, "Indian Image of Christ," in *Co-worker for Your Joy: Festschrift in Honour of George Gispert-Sauch S.J.*, ed. S. Painadath and L. Fernando (Delhi: Vidyajyoti College & ISPCK, 2006), 61.

in peaceful co-existence with the majority community with whom it shared common roots, customs and values, is itself a remarkable historical instance of cordial relationships during the early centuries. The Thomas Christians no doubt came to terms with many of the practices of the larger community, as is reflected in customs continuing in the Syrian Christian community today. The opposite may also be observed: Hindu practices modified by Christian influence.

The second assumption concerns the antiquity of Hinduism. Contrary to popular opinion, what is known today as "Hinduism" is not the most ancient of religions. The terms "Hindu" and "Hinduism" are of recent origins, "categories invented by outsiders in an attempt to interpret and explain the complexities they found in Indian religious and social life."[4] Hinduism accordingly is reckoned the creation of colonialists, Orientalists, missionaries or a combination thereof. More to the point, Hinduism as a single entity does not exist. Rather the term is a convenient catch-all for a vast variety of religious cults and sects, regional and local deities and devotees, differing philosophies, spiritual disciplines, religious practices, guru cults and more. "Hinduism is an acceptable abbreviation for a family of culturally similar traditions."[5] Hinduism as we know it is a recent creation but with complex cultural traditions of three thousand years or more.

CHRISTIANITY AND VEDIC RELIGIONS IN SOUTH ASIA

Christianity thus has a long history of relating to Vedic religions in South Asia. It is only in the modern period that explicit Hindu-Christian interactions can be documented. It is of interest to note a number of Hindu responses to Christianity as well as specific Christian responses to Hinduism, then finally to consider the possibility of Hindu-Christian approaches to theology and witness, beginning with the earliest Christian response.

CHRISTIAN RESPONSE TO HINDUISM

Historically, Christians have interacted with Hindus from the earliest

---

4. Geoffrey A. Oddie, "Constructing 'Hinduism': The Impact of the Protestant Missionary Movement on Hindu Self-Understanding," in *Christians and Missionaries in India: Cross-Cultural Communication since 1500*, ed. R.E. Frykenberg (Grand Rapids: Eerdmans, 2003), 156.
5. Julius Lipner, *Hindus: Their Religious Beliefs and Practices* (New York: Routledge, 1994), 6.

advent of Christianity in India. According to local mythology original converts of St. Thomas included some from the Brahmin community in Kerala. Claiming descent from Namboodiri Brahmin converts has conferred high caste status upon the Thomas Christians. This respectable social status "enabled them to be in harmony with their predominantly Hindu neighbors."[6] Tensions between the Hindu caste system and the Christian value of equality became evident in the modern period, but must be understood in light of the historic context.[7] Caste-related practices, customs regarding food and occupation, modes of dress, faith in horoscopes, ceremonial bathing, rituals, and festivals developed in largely Hindu categories. Church architecture borrows simultaneously from Jewish synagogue and Hindu temples—"the cultural elements of Hinduism, Christianity and the Syrian tradition are clearly in juxtaposition."[8] Christian rites of passage likewise reveal use of ritual substances such as coconuts, oil lamps and rice (commonly used by Hindus) but with a distinct Christian imprint.[9] Death rituals for instance point to Christian belief in the afterlife and the second coming of Christ.

Moving to the modern period, and a context quite dissimilar to Kerala, a remarkable example of cultural interaction can be seen in Andhra Pradesh. There under the indigenous leadership of Bishop V. S. Azariah (1874–1945), the Dornakal Diocese became the fastest growing Anglican diocese in South Asia, demonstrating that "the Church has succeeded best when fully inculturated."[10] Through its schools the Church influenced Brahmin and other upper-caste students, but its greatest role was for social uplift among so-called lower castes accomplished through various means including not least the empowerment of village women. Conversion movements were an aspect of socio-economic and cultural change extending beyond the Church. "The arrival of Christianity may have set a process of

---

6. Anand Amaladass, "Dialogue between Hindus and the St. Thomas Christians" in *Hindu-Christian Dialogue: Perspectives and Encounters*, ed. H. Coward (Delhi: Motilal Banarsidass Publishers, 1993), 16.

7. Ibid., 19.

8. Susan Visvanathan, *The Christians of Kerala: History, Belief and Ritual among the Yakoba* (New Delhi: Oxford University Press, 1993), 9.

9. Ibid., 102.

10. Susan Billington Harper, "The Dornakal Church on the Cultural Frontier," in *Christians, Cultural Interactions, and India's Religious Traditions*, ed. J. M. Brown and R. E. Frykenberg (Grand Rapids: Eerdmans, 2002), 184.

catalytic cultural change into motion, but, once begun, even the Church could not control the outcome."[11]

Caste practices were condemned by Azariah as incompatible with Christianity. Some progress was made but many caste-based practices continued. Nevertheless something new had begun.

> In attempting to build a new community with a new identity that replaced and transcended old caste identities, the church almost inadvertently created new social organizations, rituals, and customs that bore remarkable similarities to the old ones they replaced.[12]

Azariah devised new indigenous Christian liturgies, festivals and art forms borrowed from Hindu and other sources. An example of the new synthesis was in the construction of the Dornakal Cathedral which incorporated aspects of Hindu temple and Muslim mosque architecture. "This cathedral, entirely hand-carved and hand-built by local people, was the bishop's most dramatic statement of Christianity's potential as the fulfillment of Indian faith and culture."[13]

Oppressed and backward peoples through conversion sought relief from the discrimination and stigma of untouchability as well as to improve their status in society.

> Evidence from the Dornakal diocese therefore supports the view that the conversion movements to Christianity were less a means of rejecting Hinduism and the prevailing caste system than a means by which subordinate groups tried to elevate their rank in the social hierarchy by accommodating and, sometimes, transforming the values of dominant non-Christian groups.[14]

Dornakal is but one example of Christian response which took various shapes in other settings.

The missionary approach to Hinduism not infrequently has been in terms of criticism and confrontation. To William Ward (1769–1823) of the Serampore Mission, Hinduism was an enemy to be opposed and exposed. That at least appears to have been one of the objectives in his publication of *History, Literature and Mythology of the*

---

11. Ibid., 193.
12. Ibid.
13. Ibid., 196.
14. Ibid., 210.

Hindoos.[15] Largely descriptive, the four volumes also contain translations and extracts from philosophers and religious writings.

Quite a different response is found in Orientalists such as F. Max Müller (1823–1900), William Jones (1746–1794) and Monier-Williams (1819–1899) who promoted Sanskit studies and the dissemination of India's sacred texts. These early Indologists held that Hinduism has much to teach the West. This proposition was in fact taken up by a re-invigorated Neo-Hinduism in its Vedantic mission to the West.[16] In the assumptions of the Orientalists we come closer to a Hindu response to Christianity.

Rather than confrontation, encounter today is more likely in terms of dialogue. Inter-religious dialogue is for mutual enlightenment and to dispel misunderstanding. Through dialogue Christians and Hindus can get to know each other better. The Round Table conferences conducted at Sat Tal Ashram in North India by Methodist evangelist E. Stanley Jones (1884–1973) were a forerunner of today's dialogue events. Jones sought an interpretation of Christ and the Christian *dharma* in keeping with the Indian ethos. At the Round Table, Hindus and Christians and others were able to share their views in a non-threatening environment. As a result Hindus and others came face to face with Christ.

Reflecting on the impact on Christian participants, Jones wrote, "The East now knows what it means to be a Christian and is demanding that we be Christian."[17] Jones found the Indian ashram a suitable indigenous forum for reflection, and utilized Hindu philosophy and culture for presenting the Gospel. For years Jones's disciple and successor, Acharya Daya Prakash (Rev. D. P. Titus), continued to present Christ and the Christian message in the form of a modified Vedanta fulfilment theology through *satsangs* in various religious settings.

Dialogue with Hinduism challenges the Church to examine the role of Christianity in a pluralistic society. In India this motivates the search for an authentic Indian Christianity and a contextual Indian theology.[18] Dialogue raises questions as to how far the Indian Church

---

15. William Ward, *History, Literature and Mythology of the Hindoos*, 4 vols. (Serampore, Bengal: first published 1817–1820 [Delhi: Low Price Publication, reprint 1990]).

16. Swami Tathagatananda, *Journey of the Upanishads to the West* (Kolkata, India: Advaita Ashrama, 2005), xv–xvi.

17. E. Stanley Jones, *The Christ of Every Road* (New York: Abingdon, 1930), 267.

18. Bob Robinson, *Christians Meeting Hindus: An Analysis and Theological Critique of Hindu-Christian Encounter in India* (Oxford: Regnum Books, 2004).

can go in Hinduising its theological identity. Is there danger that Church and theology may lose their way? Issues of language must be considered such as the implications of terms such as *avatara* and the use of Brahmanical versus Dalit categories for an Indian Christology. Hindu-Christian dialogue where Hindu populations have settled in Europe has proven fruitful in fostering good relationships and understanding.[19]

Since Vatican Council II, dialogue has emerged as a major component of the mission theology and practice of the Catholic Church. Ashrams and other centers for inter-religious dialogue have been established in India and Sri Lanka where Catholics, more than Protestants, are officially engaged in dialogue with Hindus. In this connection the work of Raimundo Panikkar might be mentioned, particularly his 900-page anthology, *The Vedic Experience Mantramanjari: An Anthology of the Vedas for Modern Man and Contemporary Celebration.*[20]

HINDU RESPONSES TO CHRISTIANITY

As a result of India's encounter with the West, various Hindu revitalization movements emerged to help identify Indians with Hinduism.[21] Some such as the *Hindu Mahasabha*, the *Rastriya Swayamsevak Sangh* (RSS) and the *Bharatiya Janata Party* (BJP) became overtly political. Others associated with the *Vishwa Hindu Parishad* (VHP, the World Council of Hindus) have remained distinctly religious in nature and include gurus with large followings, popular festival, shrine and pilgrimage movements as well as Neo-Hindu organizations.

Other Hindu reform movements tried to accommodate and adapt Christian concepts, particularly to oppose idolatry and caste practices. Hindu response to Christianity is exemplified in the Hindu Renaissance of the nineteenth century. The *Brahmo Samaj* was the most influential new movement, founded in 1828 at Calcutta by Raja Ram Mohan Roy (1772–1833), pioneer Hindu social reformer, as a

---

19. Freek L. Bakker, "The Hindu-Christian Dialogue in Europe: The Case of the Netherlands," *Dharma Deepika* 24, 10, no. 2, (2006): 35.

20. Raimundo Panikkar, *The Vedic Experience Mantramanjari: An Anthology of the Vedas for Modern Man and Contemporary Celebration* (Delhi: Motilal Banarsidass Publishers, 1977).

21. Paul G. Hiebert, "The Christian Response to Hinduism," in *Missiology for the 21st Century: South Asian Perspectives*, ed. R. E. Hedlund and Paul Joshua Bhakiaraj (Delhi: ISPCK, 2004), 331.

theistic society intended to precipitate a renewal movement in Bengal. Inspired by Christianity, yet derived from the Upanishads and the Gita, theistic and hostile to the Vedanta of Sankaracharya, the *Brahmo Samaj* may be considered a Hindu revival movement. The *Precepts of Jesus*, compiled by Roy, reveal a theistic, rational interpretation of the New Testament. Roy had considerable interaction with the Serampore missionaries with whom he initially collaborated, then entered into controversy over the issue of Christology. At this early stage of encounter, Roy was not prepared to embrace the full-orbed Christological and Trinitarian creed defended by Joshua Marshman (1768–1837) whose rigidity did not permit latitude for an Indian approach to the mystery of Christ. The Church was deprived of a potentially innovative theologian and a distinctly Indian theological perception. Roy rejected the Hindu concept of *avatar* (multiple incarnations) which he regarded as idolatry and with it the Christian doctrine of incarnation which he thought violated the Oneness of God.[22]

In contrast to Roy, Keshub Chandra Sen (1836–1910) had no difficulty accepting belief in incarnation. Sen is a key figure in the Hindu dialogue with Christianity and is a pioneer in the development of Indian Christian theology, although he never became a Christian. Dissatisfied with Hinduism, he began to study the Bible and Christian theology. In 1857, Keshub joined the *Brahmo Samaj*, and soon became its leader. Keshub was devoted to Christ, and called himself the slave of Jesus. Many Hindus regarded him a Christian. Christ became the centre of his life. There is no denying the reality of his experience of Christ and the genuineness of his effort to express his experience and understanding of Christ in terms of his own familiar Indian tradition. Keshub's lectures bear witness of his love for Jesus.[23]

The "*Brahmo*" movements were strongly theistic, cordial to Christianity and stand in contrast to movements marked by hostility such as the *Arya Samaj* founded by Dayananda Saraswati (1824–1883) as a missionary movement for the propagation of the Aryan religion and the reconversion of converts to Islam and Christianity back to the Vedic faith. The stance of the *Arya Samaj* is decidedly anti-Christian. Christians are considered deluded, all non-Vedic religions false.

---

22. M. M. Thomas, *The Acknowledged Christ of the Indian Renaissance* (London: SCM, 1969), 9.

23. David C. Scott, *Keshub Chunder Sen* (Madras, India: CLS, 1979), 106.

The Vedas alone are inspired, the Vedic religion true. Despite its apologetic and polemical tone, the *Arya Samaj* expressed belief in a personal God and concern for justice and compassion, ideas possibly derived from the Bible and the teachings of the missionaries.[24]

Less vitriolic than the *Arya Samaj*, the Ramakrishna Mission founded by Swami Vivekananda (1863–1902) established Neo-Hinduism as a modern missionary religion. Vivekananda rejected the Christian concept of sin and a fallen humanity in need of saving grace, and opted instead for a mystical Christ and the mystic's experience of the Ultimate. The vast system of educational and social institutions of the Ramakrishna Mission resemble the institutional expressions of the Christian mission prominent in Bengal at that time. In many respects the Mission founded by Vivekananda appeared a Hindu replica of the Society of Jesus. Vivekananda's participation in the World Parliament of Religions at Chicago in 1893 launched a missionary career dedicated to the advance of Vedantic Hinduism. Critical of Christianity, Vivekananda nevertheless recognized Christianity as a legitimate religion, and he had a great admiration for Christ. But his was a Vedantic Christ, interpreted according to Vedanta.[25]

Other new religious movements also arose, sometimes in reaction to the Christian message, more often due to inappropriate methods and approaches of insensitive messengers. A case is documented in Jaffna, Sri Lanka, wherein one Arumuga Navalar (1822–1879) appropriated Methodist circuit preaching methodology to propagate *Saiva Siddhanta* as a monotheistic religion. An interesting feature is Navalar's use of the Bible to demonstrate similarity between the temple worship of Siva and the worship of Yahweh in the Old Testament in order to prove that *Siva linga* worship was "Biblical" and thus to counter the missionary attack. From the Saiva viewpoint not the Saivites but the Christians are the heathen "because they do not know the true God, Siva."[26]

Religious movements aside, a number of key individuals interacted

---

24. Ronald Neufeldt, "The Response of the Hindu Renaissance to Christianity" in *Coward, Hindu-Christian Dialogue*, 39.

25. C. V. Mathew, *The Saffron Mission: A Historical Analysis of Modern Hindu Missionary Ideologies and Practices* (Delhi: ISPCK, 1999), 127.

26. Dennis Hudson, "Winning Souls for Siva: Arumuga Navalar's Transmission of the Saiva Religion" in *A Sacred Thread: Modern Transmission of Hindu Traditions in India and Abroad*, ed. Raymond Brady Williams (Chambersburg, PA: Anima Publications, 1992), 29.

significantly with Christianity. Mohandas Karamchand Gandhi (1869–1948), *mahatma* and nationalist, during the 1920s and '30s carried on an active dialogue with Christians in India. Initially repelled by missionary denunciations of Hinduism as superstition, Gandhi later came to an appreciation of the New Testament and especially the Sermon on the Mount. He interacted with several Christian friends. Among them were C. F. Andrews, whom he regarded as a model Christian, and E. Stanley Jones with whom Gandhi exchanged views concerning conversion and other vital issues. Gandhi objected to the Europeanising of Indian converts to Christianity. Untouchability however was an issue over which they disagreed. Although Gandhi remained a Hindu, eventually there emerged a "Gandhian Christianity" in which Gandhi was interpreted as putting Christian ideals into practice.[27]

Quite a different approach is that of Sarvepalli Radhakrishnan (1888–1975), late President of India, brilliant philosopher, and Hindu apologist, whose disagreement with his Christian teachers led him to a radical re-interpretation of Christianity according to a Vedantic hermeneutic. Radhakrishnan rejects the uniqueness of Christ, and affirms the superiority of Vedanta. To Radhakrishnan, "Hinduism is not just another religion but the very essence of all religious thinking" leading to monism and Advaita Vedanta.[28] Radhakrishnan presupposes a Christianity indebted to Eastern sources, a thesis not supported by historical evidences, and draws a distinction between the Jesus of history and the Christ of Faith—the latter resembling his Vedantic Christ. The resurrection, in this interpretation, is not historical and physical but symbolic and metaphysical, and true religion is measured not by doctrine but by religious experience. Despite deviations, Radhakrishnan borrows values from Christianity.[29]

From these explicitly Hindu responses we turn to examples of distinctly Hindu-Christian approaches to theology and witness.

---

27. John C. B. Webster, "Gandhi and the Christians: Dialogue in the Nationalist Era" in Coward, *Hindu-Christian Dialogue*, 94–95.
28. Joshua Kalapati, *Radhakrishnan and Christianity: An Introduction to Hindu-Christian Apologetics* (Delhi: ISPCK, 2002), 27.
29. Ibid., 169.

HINDU CHRISTIAN APPROACHES TO THEOLOGY AND WITNESS

One of the most interesting contextual experiments in mission history took place in the early seventeenth century in India. Early missionaries in India included scholars who made important contributions to the understanding of Indian cultures. The brilliant but controversial Jesuit scholar, Roberto de Nobili (1577–1656), is one example, whose radical cultural adaptations were viewed as a threat by the Portuguese ecclesiastical authorities, but who stands as a model of adaptation. His purpose was "to show that the Christian faith could be thought and lived in a truly Indian way."[30] Nobili demonstrated that one could be Indian without being Hindu, and Christian without being European. A remarkable scholar and critical thinker, Nobili wrote theological treaties in Tamil and insisted that religion can be separated from culture.

De Nobili's approach was through the traditions of Hinduism. Some strictly Hindu religious practices were removed, but other traditional practices were Christianised. Roberto de Nobili is a rare example of inculturation far in advance of his time. His adaptation was not superficial—it was not confined to dress and symbols, but represented a profound appreciation and appropriation of Tamil culture as a vehicle for Christian faith. In S. M. Michael's opinion, de Nobili so Tamilised Christianity that he touched the heart of Tamil culture. His adaptations enabled the Christians to retain their Tamil cultural identity. "As a result, the converted Christians were not culturally alienated from the other non-Christian Tamilians."[31]

Nobili's career at Madurai was marked by controversy. Still today the persistence of caste in the Tamil Church has been blamed on Nobili's accommodation policy. But according to historian Sauliére, "it is not correct to say that Nobili brought the caste system into the Church; rather he brought the Church into caste-ridden society, and Christianised it."[32] De Nobili is castigated by modern critics for

---

30. F. X. Clooney, "Roberto de Nobili's Response to India and Hinduism, in Practice and Theory," *Third Millennium* 1 (1998): 73.

31. S. M. Michael, "Catholic Mission in the Region of Tamilnadu," in *Integral Mission Dynamics: An Interdisciplinary Study of the Catholic Church in India*, ed. Augustine Kanjamala (New Delhi: Intercultural Publications, 1995), 63.

32. Augustine Sauliére, *His Star in the East,* rev. S. Rajamanickam (Anand, Gujarat, India: Gujarat Sahitya Prakash, 1994), 497.

methods designed to appeal exclusively to the Brahmins and other "twice-born" castes. It should be noted however that most converts were from the lower castes who were not excluded by his ingenious approach.

De Nobili's greatest contribution was through his scholarship. The author of more than twenty books in the Tamil language, he is regarded the father of Tamil prose, and has been honoured for his contribution to Tamil culture. His accurate knowledge of the people, and fluency in speech and writing opened an approach to the Tamil people, the fruits of which still continue. Nobili gave a terminology for Christian theology, a vehicle for conveying Christian ideas. Till today, the Tamil Church—Protestant, Pentecostal and Independent as well as Catholic—builds upon the foundation laid by de Nobili and other missionary scholars.

India has produced a number of thinkers and leaders presenting an "Indian" perception of the Christian Church and theology, for example Brahmobandhav Upadhyaya (1861–1907), Nehemiah Goreh (1825–1885), Pandita Ramabai (1858–1922), Sadhu Sundar Singh (1889–1929), P. Chenchiah (1886–1959), V. Chakkarai (1880–1958) and M. M. Thomas (1916–1996).

Among them, the famous Marathi poet Narayan Vaman Tilak (1862–1919), from a *bhakti* tradition, was drawn to Christ. Dissatisfied with orthodox Hinduism, through reading the New Testament Tilak became convinced of the truth of Christianity following a protracted period of mental conflict. Conversion brought alienation and persecution from his family and the Chitpavan Brahmin community. Eventually his wife Lakshmibai returned, believed, was baptised and became Tilak's greatest supporter and encourager. An acknowledged Marathi literary figure, Tilak brought his poetic gifts to the service of Christ and the Church. He utilised forms of Marathi spiritual literature to communicate the teachings of Christ. Some 250 of his hymns are found in the Marathi hymnal. In place of translated Western hymns, Tilak introduced the singing of *bhajans* and brought the use of *kirtan* into the Marathi Church, thus enriching its devotional life through familiar art forms. Tilak never gave up his Indian cultural birthright, but brought the riches of his Hindu heritage into the Church.

Of all Indian Christians, the best known is said to have been *Sadhu Sundar Singh (1889–1929)*. Born in Punjab of devout Sikh parents who also read the Gita and followed Hindu teaching, Sundar Singh was nourished on the Hindu scriptures. His mother, he claimed, instilled in him the love and fear of God which prepared him to work for the Lord as a *Sadhu*.[33] Prejudiced against Christianity, distraught and in despair, he prayed for God to reveal himself, failing which he determined to take his own life. In his own words,

> I remained till about half past four praying and waiting and expecting to see Krishna or Buddha, or some other *avatar* of the Hindu religion; they appeared not, but a light was shining in the room . . . and in this light there appeared, not the form I expected, but the living Christ whom I had counted as dead.[34]

This encounter was Sundar Singh's conversion. From that point in time he became an ardent disciple of Christ. In Sundar Singh we meet an Evangelical Indian mystic. In Singh's thought, meditation along with dreams and visions were possible vehicles for receiving Divine messages. Sundar Singh's mystical theology is Christocentric. He affirmed the uniqueness of the incarnation. Salvation is a work of the Holy Spirit for those who repent and believe in Christ.

A more recent Punjabi Sikh follower of Christ, Bakht Singh (1902–2000), converted in 1923 while an engineering student in Canada, returned for a ministry of faith and preaching all over India. The sermons of Bro. Bakht Singh were simple Bible expositions. His theology as revealed in the sermons is Biblicist, Christocentric in content, devotional in character. Bible teaching is a hallmark of the Assemblies (Movement) with which he was associated.

Weaknesses not withstanding, the ministry of Bro. Bakht Singh and the Assemblies is a remarkable indigenous Christian witness.[35] What is not often recognized is the Punjabi nature of the Movement with worship patterns borrowed from the *Gurdwara*. Cultural practices have been Biblicised, and North Indian cultural forms adapted and followed throughout a Movement which is largely South Indian in composition.

---

33. A. J. Appasamy, *Sundar Singh: A Biography* (Madras, India: CLS, 1996), 18.
34. Sundar Singh, *With and without Christ* (Madras, India: ELS, 1974), 55.
35. T. E. Koshy, *Brother Bakht Singh of India: An Account of 20th Century Apostolic Revival* (Secunderabad, India: OM Books, 2003).

A distinctly Hindu-Christian theological response is exemplified in the *logos* theology of Brahmabandhav Upadhyay (1861–1907). Committed to the uniqueness and finality of Jesus Christ, Upadhyay was equally convinced that God's revelation in Christ should be expressed in Indian categories. For example, the classical Christian doctrine of the Trinity should be re-stated in Sanskritic terms as *Sat-Chit-Ananda*. This gave rise to Upadhyay's Canticle to the Trinity, "*Saccidananda*," a Christian hymn indigenous to the soil of India expressing the doctrine in a contextual lyrical format appropriate to the culture.[36] More recent Christian-Hindu theological dialogue focusing on the doctrines of God and creation have had the objective of understanding each others beliefs, clearing misunderstandings and answering objections.[37]

CONCLUSION

Hindu-Christian followers of Christ are many and extend far beyond the borders of the Church. Expressions are found in art forms adapted and utilised in architecture, poetry, music, dance, painting and more—which are beyond the scope of this paper. The impact of Hindu-Christian interaction upon theology and Christian history is considerable.

SOURCES FOR FURTHER REFERENCE

Amaladass, Anand. "Dialogue between Hindus and the St. Thomas Christians." In *Hindu-Christian Dialogue: Perspectives and Encounters*, edited by H. Coward, 13–27. Delhi: Motilal Banarsidass Publishers, 1993.

_____. "Indian Image of Christ." In *Co-worker for Your Joy: Festschrift in Honour of George Gispert-Sauch S.J.*, ed. S. Painadath and L. Fernando, 61–85. Delhi: Vidyajyoti College & ISPCK, 2006.

---

36. Timothy C. Tennent, *Building Christianity on Indian Foundations: The Legacy of Brahmabandhav Upadhyay* (Delhi: ISPCK, 2000), 255.

37. Timothy C. Tennent, *Christianity at the Religious Roundtable: Evangelicalism in Conversation with Hinduism, Buddhism, and Islam* (Grand Rapids: Baker Academic, 2002).

Appasamy, A. J. *Sundar Singh: A Biography*. Madras, India: CLS, 1996.

Bakker, Freek L. "The Hindu-Christian Dialogue in Europe: the Case of the Netherlands." *Dharma Deepika* 24, 10, no. 2 (2006): 23–37.

Brown, Judith M., and Robert Eric Frykenberg, eds. *Christians, Cultural Interactions, and India's Religious Traditions*. Grand Rapids: Eerdmans, 2002.

Clooney, F. X. "Roberto de Nobili's Response to India and Hinduism, in Practice and Theory." *Third Millennium* 1 (1998): 72–80.

Coward, Harold, ed. *Hindu-Christian Dialogue: Perspectives and Encounters*. Delhi, India: Motilal Banarsidass Publishers, 1993.

Frykenberg, Robert Eric, ed. *Christians and Missionaries in India: Cross-Cultural Communication since 1500*. Grand Rapids: Eerdmans, 2003.

Harper, Susan Billington. "The Dornakal Church on the Cultural Frontier." In *Christians, Cultural Interactions, and India's Religious Traditions*, edited by J. M. Brown and R. E. Frykenberg. Grand Rapids: Eerdmans, 183–211.

Hiebert, Paul G. "The Christian Response to Hinduism." In *Missiology for the 21st Century: South Asian Perspectives*, edited by R. E. Hedlund and Paul Joshua Bhakiaraj, 324–35. Delhi: ISPCK, 2004.

Hudson, Dennis. "Winning Souls for Siva: Arumuga Navalar's Transmission of the Saiva Religion." In *A Sacred Thread: Modern Transmission of Hindu Traditions in India and Abroad*, edited by Raymond Brady Williams, 23–51. Chambersburg, PA: Anima Publications, 1992.

Jones, E. Stanley. *The Christ of Every Road*. New York: Abingdon, 1930.

Kalapati, Joshua. *Dr. Radhakrishnan and Christianity: An Introduction to Hindu-Christian Apologetics*. Delhi: ISPCK, 2002.

Koshy, T. E. *Brother Bakht Singh of India: An Account of 20th Century Apostolic Revival*. Secunderabad, India: OM Books, 2003.

Lipner, Julius. *Hindus: Their Religious Beliefs and Practices*. New York: Routledge, 1994.

Mathew, C. V. *The Saffron Mission: A Historical Analysis of Modern Hindu Missionary Ideologies and Practices*. Delhi: ISPCK, 1999.

Michael, S. M. "Catholic Mission in the Region of Tamilnadu." In *Integral Mission Dynamics: An Interdisciplinary Study of the Catholic Church in India*, edited by Augustine Kanjamala. New Delhi: Intercultural Publications, 1995.

Mundadan, A. M. *From the Beginning up to the Middle of the Sixteenth Century*. History of Christianity in India, vol. 1. Bangalore, India: Church History Association of India, 1989.

Neufeldt, Ronald. "The Response of the Hindu Renaissance to Christianity." In *Hindu-Christian Dialogue: Perspectives and Encounters*, edited by H. Coward, 28–46. Delhi: Motilal Banarsidass Publishers, 1993.

Oddie, Geoffrey A. "Constructing 'Hinduism': The Impact of the Protestant Missionary Movement on Hindu Self-Understanding." In *Christians and Missionaries in India: Cross-Cultural Communication since 1500*, edited by R. E. Frykenberg, 155–82. Grand Rapids: Eerdmans, 2003.

Painadath, S., and Leonard Fernando, eds. *Co-worker for Your Joy: Festschrift in Honour of George Gispert-Sauch S.J.* Delhi, India: Vidyajyoti College & ISPCK, 2006.

Panikkar, Raimundo. *The Vedic Experience Mantramanjari: An Anthology of the Vedas for Modern Man and Contemporary Celebration*. Delhi: Motilal Banarsidass Publishers, 1977.

Rajamanickam, S. *Roberto de Nobili on Indian Customs*. Palayamkottai, India: De Nobili Research Institute, St. Zavier's College, 1989.

Ramabai, Pandita. *Pandita Ramabai's America: Conditions of Life in the United States*. Edited by Robert E. Frykenberg. Grand Rapids: Eerdmans, 2003.

———. *Pandita Ramabai through Her Own Words: Selected Works*. Edited by Meera Kosambi. New Delhi: Oxford University Press, 2000.

Robinson, Bob. *Christians Meeting Hindus: An Analysis and Theological Critique of Hindu-Christian Encounter in India*. Oxford: Regnum Books, 2004.

Sauliére, Augustine. *His Star in the East*. Revised by S. Rajamanickam. Anand, Gujarat, India: Gujarat Sahitya Prakash, 1994.

Scott, David C. *Keshub Chunder Sen*. Madras, India: CLS, 1979.

Singh, Sundar. *With and without Christ*. Madras, India: ELS, 1974.

Tathagatananda, Swami. *Journey of the Upanishads to the West.* Kolkata, India: Advaita Ashrama, 2005.

Tennent, Timothy C. *Building Christianity on Indian Foundations: The Legacy of Brahmabandhav Upadhyay.* Delhi: ISPCK, 2000.

———. *Christianity at the Religious Roundtable: Evangelicalism in Conversation with Hinduism, Buddhism, and Islam.* Grand Rapids: Baker Academic, 2002.

Thomas, M. M. *The Acknowledged Christ of the Indian Renaissance.* London: SCM, 1969.

Visvanathan, Susan. *The Christians of Kerala: History, Belief and Ritual among the Yakoba.* New Delhi, India: Oxford University Press, 1993.

Ward, William. *History, Literature and Mythology of the Hindoos: Including a Minute Description of Their Manners and Customs.* 4 vols. Serampore, Bengal: first published 1817–1820; Delhi, India: Low Price Publication, reprint 1990.

Webster, John C. B. "Gandhi and the Christians: Dialogue in the Nationalist Era." In *Hindu-Christian Dialogue: Perspectives and Encounters*, edited by H. Coward, 80–99. Delhi: Motilal Banarsidass Publishers, 1993.

Williams, Raymond Brady, ed. *A Sacred Thread: Modern Transmission of Hindu Traditions in India and Abroad.* Chambersburg, PA: Anima Publications, 1992.

17.

Conclusion

"To the Ends of the Earth"

The story of the making of Christianity in India has been told in various segments from the earliest until the present. The following vignettes provide a summary of some of the highlights.

THOMAS CHRISTIANS

The Thomas Christians in Malabar (Kerala) South India from the earliest appear to have come to terms with the majority "Hindu" population. "The assimilation of the community to its environment is certainly one of the reasons for its survival through the centuries."[1] This ancient Christian community was augmented by migrating "Syrian" Christians fleeing persecution in Persia in the fourth century. Unmistakably Christian in faith, worship and ethic, Thomas Christians were distinctly Indian in culture and practices including caste by which they maintained existence as a separate closed community.[2] It is extremely unlikely that these earliest Indian Christians engaged in evangelism, as "a means of adding to one's own community," which would not have been tolerated by the Hindu majority. However "the very high moral standard" of the Thomas Christians in business dealings and family life is attested by various sources.[3]

---

1. Leslie W. Brown, *The Indian Christians of St. Thomas* (Cambridge: Cambridge University Press, 1982 [1956]), 3.
2. Ibid., 4.
3. Ibid., 5.

ROMAN CATHOLICS

An explicitly missionary expression of Indian Christianity is found following the arrival of the Portuguese (Vasco da Gama, 1498, in Malabar) and the beginning of Roman Catholicism in India. Francis Xavier (1542) and Roberto de Nobili (1605) are among the first of a series of Jesuits and other Catholic missionaries making significant contributions to the development of the Roman Catholic Church in India.

PROTESTANT PIETISTS

The first Protestant mission to India began 100 years later with the arrival in 1706 of Lutheran Pietists from Halle University in Germany, Bartholomäus Ziegenbalg and Heinrich Plütchau, under the royal Danish-Halle Mission. This was the beginning of the Tranquebar Mission.

SERAMPORE

Nearly ninety years later in 1793 William Carey and John Thomas arrived at Calcutta, the first missionaries of the Baptist Missionary Society (BMS) from England, followed shortly by Joshua and Hannah Marshman and William Ward. Together, in 1800, they launched the Serampore Mission, the beginning of a vast project of Bible translation and publishing, vernacular schools, women's education and much more. In 1818 they (the "Serampore Trio") began Serampore College, an arts and science college with a Department of Theology. In 1827, King Frederick of Denmark awarded a charter with the right to confer degrees,[4] which continues today as a basis for conferral of advanced theological degrees through the Serampore Senate.

FROM GOA

Indigenous South Asian missionary agencies are an important part of

---

4. M. K. Kuriakose, ed., *History of Christianity in India: Source Materials* (Delhi: ISPCK, 2003), 109–10. Cited by D. Arthur Jeyakumar, *History of Christianity in India: Selected Themes* rev. ed. (Madurai, India: Tamilnadu Theological Seminary, 2007), 42.

the story. An early example comes from Goa in the person of Joseph Vaz (1651–1711) a Goanese Brahman convert and Oratorian missionary to Ceylon (Sri Lanka), ca. 1685, which he entered incognito, disguised as a beggar. It was a time of severe persecution by the colonial Dutch. Vaz is credited with having saved the Catholic Church from extinction. Vaz trained underground local missionaries and lay leaders, fostered an indigenous Ceylonese (Sri Lankan) liturgy, literature and Church. The "Apostle of Ceylon/Sri Lanka" was canonized by Pope Francis on January 14, 2015.

MAR THOMA EVANGELISTIC ASSOCIATION

In India the Mar Thoma Syrian Evangelistic Association (MTSEA) is probably the earliest indigenous mission agency, organized in 1888, as part of the newly formed (Reformed) Malankara Mar Thoma Syrian Church of Malabar. The well-known Maramon Convention, considered the largest such Christian gathering in Asia, is conducted annually by the MTSEA. In 1924, a Mar Thoma Voluntary Evangelists Association (MTVEA) was started to equip Church members in evangelism.[5]

IMS AND NMS

Other early indigenous examples include the Indian Missionary Society (IMS) founded in 1903 by the first Indian bishop of the Anglican communion, Bishop V. S. Azariah of Tirunelveli Diocese (now Church of South India), patterned after the Church Missionary Society. Dornakal its first field among the Lambadies is now a diocese of the Church of South India. IMS continues its holistic mission in twenty states of India and beyond with some five hundred missionaries today.

V. S. Azariah also was instrumental in formation in 1905 of the National Missionary Society of India, founded on Christmas Day in the Library of Serampore College in Bengal, an expression of Christian nationalism of the Indian Christian community, also an early "ecumenical" voice representing all denominations. NMS today

---

5. E. Kuruvilla, "Mar Thoma Church and Its Educational Endeavour," available at http://tinyurl.com/ya6uoglk.

is active with more than 500 missionaries in 21 states plus Nepal, Bhutan, and Myanmar.

RAPID GROWTH

Following India's Independence in 1947, indigenous missions have experienced rapid growth. By 1978 there were 75 known indigenous mission agencies having a total of 1,270 missionaries.[6] By 1987 some 94 indigenous mission agencies had been identified with a total of more than 3,000 missionaries reported in 1983.[7] A brief description of three prominent agencies may serve as examples.

THREE EXAMPLES

The Indian Evangelical Mission (IEM) is a non-denominational agency founded in 1965 by the late Rev. Dr. Theodore Williams. IEM today has 580 missionaries trained at its Outreach Training Institute at Hosur near Bangalore, engaged in Church planting, healthcare, hostels, disaster relief, translation, literacy and educational work in 16 states of India plus six overseas partnerships.

The Friends Missionary Prayer Band (FMPB) evolved from a Tamil youth revival movement in South India. Its first mission opened in 1967 at Periyamalai near Hosur. Missionaries are trained at Bethel Bible Institute, Danishpet, Tamil Nadu. Wholistic ministries include child care and vocational training for more than 7,000 children, as well as Church planting and leadership training in partnership with Church and other organizations in eleven states across India.

The Indian Evangelical Team is a charismatic Church planting movement begun in 1972 by Bro. P. G. Vargis and his wife Lily at the popular Hindu pilgrimage centre, Katra, in the lower Himalayas. From there IET has spread across North India with more than 2,300 missionaries today. Missionaries are trained at South East Asia Leadership Training and Development Centre (SALTDC) and regional Bible schools.

---

6. R. E. Hedlund and F. Hrangkhuma, eds., *Indigenous Missions of India* (Madras, India: Church Growth Research Centre, 1980).

7. L. Joshi Jayaprakash, *Evaluation of Indigenous Missions of India* (Madras, India: Church Growth Research Centre, 1987).

MISSION EXPLOSION

Today India is experiencing a mission explosion. The India Missions Association (IMA) was formed in 1977 as an "umbrella" to connect and represent the issues and needs of the indigenous missions of India. Begun by four mission agencies, IMA today represents 243 Indian mission organizations with about 60,000 Christian workers. In addition to these IMA members, there are also others not members of IMA whose statistics are not included.

Finally, not to be forgotten are Mother Teresa's Missionaries of Charity, founded at Kolkata in 1950, today consisting of more than 4,500 religious sisters serving among the Poor all around the world.

WORLD CHRISTIANITY

Through these and many others bearing witness to Jesus Christ, South Asia makes its contributions to World Christianity "to the ends of the earth" until time shall be no more. Even so, come, Lord Jesus.

SOURCES FOR FURTHER REFERENCE

Amaladass, Anand. "Dialogue between Hindus and the St. Thomas Christians." In *Hindu-Christian Dialogue: Perspectives and Encounters*, edited by Harold Coward. Delhi: Motilal Banarsidass, 1993.

———. *Jesuit Presence in Indian History*. Anand, India: Gujarat Sahitya Prakash, 1988.

Brown, Judith M., and Robert Eric Frykenberg, eds. *Christians, Cultural Interactions, and India's Religious Traditions*. Grand Rapids: Eerdmans, 2002.

Brown, Leslie W. *The Indian Christians of St. Thomas*. New York: Cambridge University Press, 1982 (1956). An Indian edition, published by permission of Cambridge University Press, is available at St. Thomas Service & Community Centre and at B. I. Publications, Chennai.

Duerksen, Darren Todd. *Ecclesial Identities in a Multi-Faith Context: Jesus Truth-Gatherings (Yeshu Satsangs) among Hindus and Sikhs in Northwest India*. Eugene, OR: Pickwick, 2015.

Fernando, Leonard, and G. Gispert-Sauch. *Christianity in India: Two Thousand Years of Faith*. New Delhi: Viking Penguin, 2004.

Frykenberg, Robert Eric. *Christianity in India: From Beginnings to the Present*. New York: Oxford University Press, 2008.

———, ed. *Christians and Missionaries in India: Cross-Cultural Communication since 1500*. Studies in the History of Christian Missions. Grand Rapids: Eerdmans, 2003.

Gilliland, Dean S., ed. *The Word among Us: Contextualizing Theology for Mission Today*. Dallas: Word, 1989.

Hedlund, Roger E., ed. *Christianity Is Indian: The Emergence of an Indigenous Community*. Revised ed. Delhi: ISPCK, 2004 (2000).

Hedlund, R. E., and F. Hrangkhuma, eds. *Indigenous Missions of India*. Madras, India: Church Growth Research Centre, 1980.

Hedlund, R. E., J. M. Athyal, J. Kalapati, and Jessica Richard, eds. *Oxford Encyclopaedia of South Asian Christianity*. New Delhi: Oxford University Press, 2012.

James, Jonathan D. *McDonaldisation, Masala McGospel and Om Economics: Televangelism in Contemporary India*. Los Angeles: SAGE Publications, 2010.

Jayaprakash, L. Joshi. *Evaluation of Indigenous Missions of India*. Madras, India: Church Growth Research Centre, 1987.

Jenkins, Philip. *The Lost History of Christianity: The Thousand-Year Golden Age of the Church in the Middle East, Africa, and Asia—and How It Died*. New York: HarperOne, 2008.

Jeyakumar, D. Arthur. *History of Christianity in India: Selected Themes*. Revised ed. Madurai, India: Tamilnadu Theological Seminary, 2007.

Jeyaraj, Daniel. "Mission Reports from South India and Their Impact on the Western Mind: The Tranquebar Mission of the Eighteenth Century." In *Converting Colonialism*, edited by Dana L. Robert. Grand Rapids: Eerdmans Publishing Co., 2008.

Kalapati, Joshua. *Dr. Radhakrishnan and Christianity: An Introduction to Hindu-Christian Apologetics*. Delhi: ISPCK, 2002.

Kim, Sebastian C. H. *In Search of Identity: Debates on Religious Conversion in India*. New Delhi: Oxford University Press, 2003.

Kumaradoss, Y. Vincent. *Robert Caldwell: A Scholar-Missionary in Colonial South India*. Delhi: ISPCK, 2008.

Kuriakose, M. K., ed. *History of Christianity in India: Source Materials*. Delhi: ISPCK, 2003.

Mallampalli, Chandra. "Caste, Catholicism, and History 'from Below', 1863–1917." In *India and the Indianness of Christianity*, edited by Richard Fox Young. Grand Rapids: Eerdmans, 2009.

Mihindukulasuriya, Prabo, Ivor Poobalan, and Ravin Caldera, eds. *A Cultured Faith: Essays in Honour of Prof. G. P. V. Somaratna*. Colombo, Sri Lanka: Colombo Theological Seminary, 2011.

Rajendran, K. *Which Way Forward Indian Missions? A Critique of 25 Years 1972–1997*. Bangalore, India: SAIACS Press, 1998.

Ramachandra, Vinoth. *Church and Mission in the New Asia: New Gods, New Identities*. Singapore: Trinity Theological College, 2009.

Sanneh, Lamin. *Translating the Message: The Missionary Impact on Culture*. Maryknoll, NY: Orbis Books, 1989.

Solomon Raj, P. *The New Wine-skins: The Story of the Indigenous Missions in Coastal Andhra Pradesh*. India, Delhi: ISPCK, 2004.

Thomas, Pradip Ninan. *Strong Religion, Zealous Media: Christian Fundamentalism and Communication in India*. Los Angeles: SAGE Publications, 2008.

Walls, Andrew F. *The Missionary Movement in Christian History: Studies in the Transmission of Faith*. Maryknoll, NY: Orbis Books, 1996.

Wong, James, Peter Larson, and Edward Pentecost. *Missions from the Third World*. Singapore: Church Growth Study Centre, 1973.

Woodberry, J. Dudley. "Contextualization among Muslims: Reusing Common Pillars." In *The Word among Us: Contextualizing Theology for Mission Today*, edited by Dean S. Gilliland. Dallas: Word, 1989.

Yong, Amos. *The Future of Evangelical Theology: Soundings from the Asian American Diaspora*. Downers Grove, IL: InterVarsity Press, 2014.

Young, Richard Fox, ed. *India and the Indianness of Christianity: Essays on Understanding*. Grand Rapids: Eerdmans, 2009.

Young, Richard Fox, and Jonathan A. Seitz, eds. *Asia in the Making of Christianity: Conversion, Agency, and Indigeneity, 1600s to the Present*. Boston: Koninklijke Brill NV, 2013.

Glossary of Indian Terms

acharya	spiritual teacher
adivasi	Tribals, aboriginals
advaita/advaitic	non-dualism, monism
ahimsa	non-violence
Arya Samaj	militant Hindu sect propagating Aryan religion and infallibility of the Vedas
ashram	spiritual retreat centre, hermitage/monastery
atman	the soul, or self
avarna	outcaste
avatar	descent of a god/goddess in temporary forms
Bhagavad Gita	a well-known Hindu scripture: The Song of God
bhajan	devotional song
Bhakta	devotee
bhakti	devotion, devotional

bhakti marga	path of devotion
Brahma	Creator, first deity of the Hindu Trimurthi
Brahmin	priests, highest Hindu caste
Brahmo Samaj	monotheistic "Hindu" sect: new religious movement
caste	hereditary system for division of society
chela	disciple
Christbhakta	devotee of Christ
Dalit	Untouchables: 17 million, many sub-castes
darsana	auspicious seeing of a deity or holy person
Devadasi	dancing girls dedicated to the temple deity
dharma/dhamma	Sanskrit/Pali term, key concept with multiple meanings in Hinduism, Buddhism, Sikhism and Jainism; no single word translation in English, sometimes as religion, duty, righteousness
Din Bandhu	Friend of the Poor
Durga	female goddess, divine Sakti, the Divine Mother
dukkha	suffering (the problem of life, in Buddhism)
Ganga Snan	Holy Bath: Baptism
gnana marga	path of knowledge
Gorkha	a district of Nepal, an Indian Army regiment
Gurdwara	Sikh temple

guru	spiritual guide, teacher
harijan	"children of God": Gandhi's term for Untouchables
Hindu Mahasabha	Hindu militant organization
Hindutva	politicised Hinduism, Hinduness: Indian is Hindu
ishta devata	personal god
jagannath	ancient Jagannath temple and car festival at Puri
Jesubhakta	devotee of Jesus
Kabir	Muslim mystic, poet and song writer
Kali	four-armed Hindu goddess of power and destruction, a consort of Shiva
karma	effects of past actions on one's present life or future incarnations
karma marga	path of works
Khrist Bhaktas	devotees of Christ (non-baptised)
kirtan	devotional love song
Krishna	a Hindu deity, an avatar of Vishnu
Kshatriya	rulers and warriors, second of four Hindu castes
Lakshmi	Hindu goddess of Prosperity, consort of Shiva Mahabharata Hindu epic
Mahabharata	Hindu epic
mahatma	great soul, great one (a conferred title)

mandir	Hindu temple
mantra	sacred formula, holy words used in meditation
marga	path, way to salvation (three)
maya	illusion, causes ignorance
mela	festival, religious fair
moksha	salvation, enlightenment, liberation of atman from the cycle of births
mosque	Muslim place of worship
Nanak	founder of the Sikh religion
Nirguna Brahman	impersonal God without attributes
nirvana	bliss, extinction of suffering through annihilation of the self (in Buddhism) or merging of the self into Brahma (in Hinduism)
OBCs	Other Backward Castes: lower caste Hindus (shudras)
Padroado	patronage extended by the Pope to the King of Portugal over three Indian episcopal sees
Propaganda Fide	Department for Evangelization founded in 1622 by Pope Gregory XV
puja	Hindu devotional ritual, worship
Puranas	ancient texts: Hindu mythology
Qurbana	Eucharist
Ramakrishna Mission	Neo-Hindu missionary organisation founded by Swami Vivekananda

Ramanuja	exponent of qualified monism philosophy
Ramayana	Hindu epic by Valmiki
Rastriya Swayamsevak Sangh	religious nationalist organisation
Rig-Veda	first of four Vedas (Hindu Scriptures)
Rishi	Hindu sage: Seer of God
Sadhana dharma	Hindu spiritual duties: religion
sadhanas	asceticism, spiritual exercises, "yogas"
sadhu	holy man, ascetic, monk
Saiva Siddhanta	a monotheistic Hindu sect in Sri Lanka
samaj dharma	Hindu social duties: culture
samsara	endless cycle of birth, death, rebirth
sanatana dharma	eternal religion, Brahmanical Hinduism
Sangh Parivar	Hindu fundamentalists: India for Hindus only
Sankara	greatest exponent of Advaita philosophy
Sannyasi	Hindu holy man, renunciate seeking God-experience
Sanyasa	renunciation: mark of spirituality (Hinduism)
Sarasvati	Hindu goddess of learning, wisdom and song, a consort of Brahma
sati (suttee)	sacrifice of a Hindu widow on her husband's funeral pyre (banned since 19th century)

satsang	truth-gathering religious fellowship
satya	truth
Shaivites	worshipers of Shiva
Shakti	Mother Goddess, female creative power
Shalom	peace
Shanti	peace
shari'ah	sacred law (in Muslim countries)
Shiva/Siva	Destroyer, third deity of the Hindu Trimurti
Shruti	revealed scriptures: the Vedas
shuddhi	reconversion back into Hinduism
Shudra	lower Hindu caste, subservient to three upper castes
Smriti	remembered scriptures: any other than the Vedas
Sufi/Sufism	Islamic mystic/mysticism
swami	initiated member of a religious order: a monk
transmigration	reincarnation
Tantra	texts presenting God as Shiva and Shakti
Upanishads	canonical texts of Vedanta, Hindu philosophy
Vaishnavites	worshipers of Vishnu
Vaisyas	merchant/business caste, third in Hindu caste system

varna/s	caste, four classes of Hindu society subdivided into innumerable sub-castes
varnashrama dharma	caste-related religious duties
Veda/Vedic	primary Hindu scriptures
Vedanta	Hindu religious philosophy
Vishnu	Preserver, second deity of the Hindu Trimurti
Vishwa Hindu Parishad	Hindu World Council: Neo-Hinduism
Zamindar	official tax collector in precolonial India; landholder in British and Moghal India
zenana	women's quarters in high caste Hindu (or Muslim) homes

Index of Subjects

Aaron (Pastor), 39, 41
Aboriginal religion and culture, 157
accommodate(s)/accommodation, 103, 119n5, 127, 216, 220
activist, 57, 70, 82, 108, 141, 158–59, 169
adaptation, 6n25, 7, 107n58, 123, 131, 159, 191, 201, 220
addiction, addict(s), 68, 138, 150, 155–56
Advaita, 186, 215n16, 219, 225, 235, 239
advocate, 35, 56, 82, 129, 203–4
Afghanistan, 82, 82n4
Africa, African, 4, 5, 9, 12, 21n1, 22, 29, 30, 53n2, 54, 68, 73, 78, 81, 88–90, 92, 98n13, 99–102, 110, 110nn70–71, 114, 121, 171, 180n16, 181, 182n26, 183n32, 189, 190, 193, 195, 197, 202n21, 204, 208–9, 232
African Instituted Churches, 89, 101
African worldview, 89
Alwis, Alwin R. de, 84, 152
America/American, 2, 4, 8–9, 12, 22n3, 30, 34n14, 35, 43n1, 46, 49, 52–54, 58–61, 65–68, 76, 78, 81, 88, 90–92, 95n3, 96, 99, 102, 110, 112, 140n25, 152, 158, 170–71, 181, 182n26, 183n32, 190, 197, 202n21, 209, 225, 233
ancestor(s), 3, 87, 88, 90, 97n10, 102, 164n2, 204
ancestor veneration, 87n33, 88, 102
ancient, 5, 12, 14–15, 18, 22, 24–25, 27–28, 33, 82, 96, 113, 122n19, 178, 204, 212, 227, 237–38
Andhra Pradesh, 77, 83, 95n1, 96–97, 102, 105, 107, 117, 125, 131, 133, 151, 184, 213, 233
Andrew, C. F., 204, 219
Anglican(s), 24–25, 77, 202, 213, 229
anonymous, 207
anti-Christian, 40, 61
Antioch, 2, 14, 25
apocalyptic, 191
apologetic, 119n7, 132, 191, 218, 224, 232
apostolic, 1, 12–13, 15, 35, 84, 98, 101n25, 101n32, 108, 110n70, 112–13, 184, 222n35, 224
Apostolic Christian, 12, 84, 108, 184
apostolic primitivism, 35

appropriate, 1, 37, 82, 84, 87, 152, 186, 188, 192, 218, 223
archive(s)/archival deposits, 39, 41, 108, 182
Arndt, Johann, 32
arrogance, 75–76, 121, 202
artifacts, 13
Arya Samaj, 217–18, 235
ascetic/asceticism, 84, 152, 173, 178, 239
Ashram, 85, 102, 128, 145n3, 188, 215, 216, 225, 235, 240
Asia/Asian, xi, 1n1, 4, 5, 6n27, 8, 12, 15n16, 16n19, 18–19, 21n1, 22, 23, 24n20, 25n25, 25n27, 26–30, 37n28, 40–41, 45, 47, 53n2, 54, 64n61, 66–69, 70, 73, 77–82, 84n21, 85n26, 86, 88, 90–93, 96, 98n16, 99–102, 104, 106nn52–54, 110, 113–15, 117, 121, 122n20, 124, 131, 141n26, 145n3, 158n44, 161, 163, 165–66, 171, 174, 177–83, 185, 188, 189n60, 190–91, 192, 193–95, 197, 199n5, 200, 204, 208, 210–13, 216n21, 224, 229–33
Assemblies of God, 84, 86, 103n43, 152–153, 183n29, 184
assembly, 24, 29n54, 77, 84, 87, 108, 153–54, 184
Assembly Hall Church, 87
assimilation, 227
Association for Theological Education in Nepal (ATEN), 85
assurance, 35
authenticate, 204

Avatar, 120, 217, 222, 235, 237
awakening(s), 32, 35, 50, 54, 65, 104n45, 118, 170, 172, 189n65, 195; cultural, 3–7, 15, 22–23, 28, 32–33, 43–44, 46, 48, 50–52, 54n5, 55, 56, 78, 79, 82–83, 89, 93, 98, 103, 107, 110, 118, 136n3, 141n26, 142, 144, 146–47, 149, 153, 159, 177–78, 188, 190, 193, 198–201, 212–14, 220–24, 231; evangelical, 4, 15, 24, 28, 31n1, 33–36, 39–41, 43–44, 52, 53n1, 54, 57, 67–74, 78, 80, 82n11, 83, 91–92, 97, 104n45, 106, 109–10, 111n77, 114, 121–22, 128n49, 130n62, 131, 138, 140–41, 158, 170–71, 174, 178–79, 207n55, 208–9, 222, 223n37, 225, 230, 233; social, 6, 14, 16, 23, 28, 33, 40, 43–44, 48–50, 52, 53n1, 54, 56–57, 61, 65, 67–71, 76–78, 82–83, 96, 99, 113, 118, 124, 126–27, 135–36, 138, 139nn18–19, 140, 143–44, 147, 149, 153–57, 160, 162, 169, 172, 174, 180–81, 185, 197, 199–200, 205, 209, 212–14, 216, 218, 239; spiritual, 4, 14–15, 23, 26, 27n39, 31, 40, 43, 45, 50, 54–56, 59, 63–65, 68, 71, 77, 82n9, 83–84, 90, 97, 101n27, 102–3, 107, 110n70, 112, 118n3, 119, 122, 124, 126, 130, 136, 140–41, 143, 147, 155, 159, 165, 168–72,

178–79, 180n11, 180n14, 181n18, 187, 190, 192, 203, 212, 221, 235, 237, 239
Azariah, V. S., 77–79, 193, 202, 213–14, 229
Azusa Street, 103, 104, 114, 182n26, 183

Bach, J. S., 32
"Back-to-Jerusalem" movement, 178
backward, 56, 69, 92, 119n5, 160, 208, 214, 238
"Baliraja", 57n17, 159–60
Banerjea, Krishna Mohan, 50
Bangladesh, 178, 190, 200
baptism, 63n54, 64–65, 86, 88, 92, 103, 104n44, 124–26, 159, 168–69, 172n24, 174, 236
Baptist(s), 28–29, 34–36, 44, 49, 52, 91, 101n27, 101n30, 104n37, 105, 113, 115, 158, 163, 170–71, 228
Baptist Christian Association, 158, 158n43, 158n45
Baptist Church, 104n47, 113
Baptist Missionary Society (BMS), 44, 52, 170, 228
Barnabas, 2
Basel Mission, 35
basis, 67, 118n2, 122, 149, 168, 200, 203, 205, 228
beggar(s), 137, 166, 229
believer(s), 3, 6, 26, 31, 33, 40, 68, 85, 87, 105, 126, 132, 148, 155–56, 159–60, 163, 169, 178, 184, 189
Believers' Church, 31, 40

benevolent social services, 45, 47, 155
Bengal, 35, 44, 45n6, 46, 48–49, 50–51, 82, 105, 123, 184–85, 198, 215n15, 218, 226, 229
Bengali, 6, 44, 46–48, 50, 124, 186
Berlin Mission, 35
Bernard of Clairvaux, 71, 71n19
Bethel Bible Institute, Danishpet, 230
Bhajans, 187, 221
Bhakti, 38, 54–55, 97n11, 126, 188n55, 204, 221, 236
Bhakti theology, 97n11, 114
Bharatiya Janata Party (BJP), 216
Bible Mission of Devadas, 82n13, 96, 101
Bible Society of India, 156
bible translation, 6, 8, 31, 39n39, 46, 47n12, 60, 69, 92, 158, 160, 208
Biblical-Historical Perspective, 2
Bihar, 155, 155n24, 155n26, 162
black oral roots, 104, 183
Bombay (Mumbai), 58n28, 59, 61, 66, 83, 105, 107n57, 109, 114, 138, 140n26, 144, 148, 184, 188n57, 194
bonded labour/labourers, 136–38, 155
Book of Acts, 2, 35, 98, 140n26, 168–69
Brahman/Brahmin, 13, 56–57, 62, 83, 128, 186, 213, 229, 236, 238
Brahmanic, 56, 186
Brahmo Samaj, 54, 118n2, 123, 185, 216–17, 236
bread, 160, 165–66

Bread of Life, 164–66
break-away, 83, 88, 105–6, 152
bridge, 29, 103n43, 114, 159, 183n29, 188
British, 24, 36, 43, 49, 52, 74, 75n41, 76, 77n65, 79, 188n57, 193, 241
Buddhism/Buddhist 26–28, 69, 84, 86, 128n49, 133, 152, 178, 180–81, 190–91, 195, 197–98, 200, 223n37, 225, 236, 238
Burma (Myanmar), 77, 199, 199n5, 200

care cells, 153–54
Campus Crusade for Christ (Cru), 148
caste, 2n10, 13–14, 16, 33, 39, 45, 49, 56–58, 60, 75–77, 79, 125–26, 129, 136, 138–39, 144, 151, 153, 157, 160, 201, 202, 213–14, 216, 220, 233, 236–38, 240–41; annihilation of, 76, 77n62, 79
casteism/casteist, 129
catalyst/catalytic, 44, 50, 157, 199
cathedral, 12, 26, 214
Catholic Church, 4, 8, 15, 22, 29, 73, 84, 90, 103, 110, 123–24, 132, 179, 216, 220n31, 224, 228–29
Catholicism: evangelical, 72–74, 80; folk, 102; popular, 102–3, 112; Roman, 22, 24, 38, 90, 103, 110, 179, 181, 183, 228
celibacy, 152, 178
Central America, 91
Central India, 157–58
Centre for the Study of Christianity in Asia (CSCA), 179, 180n14, 192
ceremonial bathing, 213
Ceylon, Apostle of (Sri Lanka), 84, 229
Ceylon Pentecostal Mission (CPM), 83, 84, 106, 152, 153n21, 161, 177, 178n3
Chakkarai, V., 221
Chan, Simon, 179–81
Chandran, Emil, 126, 127n41, 131
charismatic, 4, 28–29, 81, 83, 86, 101n26, 103–5, 110, 112–13, 115, 145n3, 169–71, 182n26, 183, 184, 193, 230
Charismatic Churches, 28–29, 103n42, 115, 183n28, 230
charismatic movement, renewal of, 103n43, 105, 145n3, 170, 184
Chenchiah, P., 221
Chennai (Madras), xi, 21n2, 39n42, 43n1, 52, 56n12, 58n28, 66, 81n2, 108, 109n64, 117, 140, 153, 155nn24–25, 184, 195, 209, 231
Chikaldera, 157
child labour/labourers, 136
child widows, 58, 61
children at risk, 34, 57, 65, 83, 136, 138, 149–51, 155, 160
children's homes, 155
China, 17, 26, 28, 60, 89, 92
Chinese Church, 89, 93
Chitpavan, 56, 83, 221
Cho, Paul Yongi, 153
Christ of Faith, 219
Christ-event, 205

Christhood, 205
Christian(s): Indian Christians, 5, 13–15, 18, 21n2, 113, 147n2, 182n20, 188n54, 227, 228; Malabar Christians, 15, 21; Syrian Christians, 5, 15–16, 24; Thomas Christians, 11–12, 14, 17–18, 23–24, 227 [Northists, 15; Southists, 15]
Christian action, response to human needs: creating awareness, 138; critiquing structures, 137; exposing corruption, 138; offering training, 138; providing information, 138
Christian Church, 1, 11, 32n7, 40, 88–89, 101, 187–88, 221
Christian claim, 197, 207
Christian community, 5, 11–15, 44, 111n75, 115, 122, 155, 170, 189, 204, 211–12, 227, 229
Christian Science, 91, 95
Christian foundation, 117–18, 128, 131
Christian witness, 69, 86, 91, 108, 118, 222
Christianity: ancient, 12, 15, 82, 122n19, 227; Apostolic, 12, 184; Eastern, 12, 23; folk, 179, 180n11, 181, 181n18, 191; Hellenistic Judeo-Christianity, 2; Indian, 1n1, 5–6, 8, 11, 14–15, 18, 98, 100n24, 109–10, 110n73, 113, 115n2, 146, 161, 182n22, 184–85, 187, 215, 228; Indigenous Tamil, 39; Jerusalemite, 2; Judeo-Christianity, 2, 57; Korean, 88, 191; Palestinian Judeo-Christianity, 2; Thomas, 11–12, 82; Western, 12, 98, 100, 202n21, 209
Christology/Christologies/Christological, 121–22, 130–31, 164, 185, 190, 204–5, 208n58, 210, 216–17
church/churches, 1–9, 11–12, 13n6, 14–15, 17–19, 21–28, 31, 32n7, 35, 38n35, 39–40, 49, 51, 55, 59–60, 63–65, 67–70, 72n23, 73, 74n40, 75n41, 77–80, 81n1, 83–115, 122–28, 130–33, 135, 136n2, 138, 140n24, 142–54, 156–57, 160–62, 167–72, 178–79, 181–85, 187–91, 193, 197, 199, 203, 208, 210–11, 213–16, 220–21, 223–24, 228–33
Church fathers, 122, 122n19, 127, 133
church history, 1n1, 6n26, 8, 12, 15n14, 19, 24, 29, 38n35, 51, 74n40, 85n26, 93, 99n20, 100, 108, 111, 114–15, 145n3, 161, 179, 182n24, 183, 193, 211n2, 224
Church History Association of India (CHAI), 1n1, 6n26, 8, 15n14, 19, 29, 38n35, 93, 100, 211n2, 224
Church of the East (Chaldean), 15, 15n17, 18
Church of England, 59
Church of God, 29n54, 83, 83n18, 109, 111, 111n74, 184

Churches of Indigenous Origins (CIOs), 5, 92, 146
Church of North India, 109, 148, 156, 184
Church of South India, 15, 109, 185, 229
church planting, 69, 92, 148, 160, 230
"Churchless Christianity", 126, 126n37, 132
coconut(s), 159, 160n51, 213
colonial/colonialism, 6, 12, 39, 50n23, 51–53, 74, 84, 188, 195, 200, 212, 232, 233, 241
colony, 13, 37
communal living, 152, 178
communication media, 69, 92, 160
communion, 4, 72, 86, 126, 159, 229
community action, 68
compassion ministries: EFICOR, 69, 140, 156; Tear Fund, 69, 140; World Concern, 69, 140; World Vision International, 69, 70n13, 79, 103n42, 115, 140, 141n28, 143, 183n28
computer training, 138, 151
Confession of Faith, 72
contextual theologising, 127
contextualisation, 180
conversion: movements, 28, 77–78, 99, 139, 181, 202, 213–14; spiritual change of heart, 77
convert(s), 13, 23, 34, 40, 50, 55, 63, 74, 77–78, 83, 85–86, 97n10, 111, 115, 117, 118n3, 124, 128, 133, 141, 148, 154, 157, 159, 168, 180, 186, 188–89, 191, 195, 201, 213, 217, 219–20, 222, 229, 232
copper-plates, 13
Coptic Church, 26
Cornelius, 2
Côte d'Ivoire, 189
COTR Theological Seminary, 151
Cranganore, 13
creative ministries, 69n9, 145–46, 151, 153, 160
criminal(s): activity of, 136
cross, the, 24, 122, 159, 163, 205
cross-cultural missionary effort, 155, 178
cult(s), 2n10, 89, 95, 96, 100–101, 112, 114–15, 212
cultural, 3–7, 15, 22–23, 28, 32, 37, 39, 43–44, 46, 48, 50, 51, 54n5, 55–57, 74n39, 78, 79, 82–83, 89, 98n15, 107, 110, 111, 118, 132, 136n3, 141n26, 142, 144, 146–47, 149, 153, 155, 159, 177n1, 178, 188, 190, 193, 199, 200–201, 212–13, 214–15, 220, 222, 224–25, 232
culture(s), 2–5, 7, 25, 33, 37, 39, 58n28, 61n41, 66, 78, 81, 86, 88, 92, 95n2, 96, 97, 99–100, 103, 104n44, 108n63, 109, 111n79, 114, 118n3, 122–24, 126, 129, 139n22, 140n26, 151, 156–57, 159n48, 160, 167, 178, 181–82, 184–85, 187–88, 191, 195, 197–99, 200, 203, 207–9, 220–21, 223, 227, 233, 239
custom(s), 6n25, 9, 13, 39, 49,

50n22, 52, 83, 87, 124, 132, 188, 191, 212–14, 225–26

Dalit(s), 75, 83, 99, 136, 160, 181, 186, 194, 201
Danish East India Company, 38
Danish-Halle Mission, 31–32, 39, 228
Dayananda Saraswati (Swami), 217
defenseless, 166
dehumanized, 56, 129, 155
Delhi, 1n1, 6n28, 8, 12n5, 13n6, 14n10, 15n17, 16nn19–20, 18–19, 23n13, 29n54, 30, 37nn27–28, 40–41, 50nn22–23, 51–52, 54n6, 55n11, 57nn17–18, 57n22, 58nn24–25, 64n61, 69n8, 69n10, 76n55, 79, 82n3, 82n5, 82n11, 82n15, 83n17, 92–93, 95, 100n24, 104nn45–46, 105, 113, 115, 119n7, 122n20, 124n27, 127n44, 129n55, 131–33, 136n2, 137n12, 139nn19–20, 141n26, 142n34, 143–45, 157n38, 161–62, 165n4, 171n23, 174, 178n3, 182n22, 183n30, 184, 186n44, 187n5, 190n68, 193–94, 200nn8–9, 210, 211n3, 213n6, 213n8, 215n15, 216nn20–21, 218n25, 219n28, 220n31, 223–26, 228n4, 231–33
democratic, 15, 118, 203
demography, 110
demographic shift, 110
denomination(s), 15, 83, 86–89, 91, 97–98, 105, 108n62, 109, 117, 154, 184, 229, 230
derogatory, 120
developing world, 69, 90, 140
Dey, Lal Behari, 50
dialogue, 14n10, 18, 26, 70, 73, 110, 118, 121, 128, 141, 164, 177, 186, 190n69, 191, 192, 194–95, 204, 213n6, 215–17, 218n24, 219, 223–26, 231
dignity, 3, 71, 76, 83, 97, 99, 135, 137, 143, 147, 149–50, 181–82, 199, 208
Din Bandhu Ministries, 158, 160, 236
discernment, 63, 130, 172
disciple(s), 13, 21, 99, 139, 147, 165, 168, 172, 182, 195, 203, 215, 222, 236
discipleship, 72, 82n12, 85, 122, 136n4, 140–41, 144
diversification/diversity, 2–4, 91, 100, 109–10, 130, 182, 184–85, 191
Divine Word Centre (Medak), 103
divination, 90, 97n10, 102
documentation, 17, 105–6, 108, 177, 184
Dornakal, 77–79, 202, 213, 214, 224, 229
drama, 153, 191
Dravidians, 201
dreams and visions, 90, 222

East India Company (EIC), 6, 37–38, 43
Ecclesial, 90, 179

Ecclesiology, 67n1, 105n51, 122, 124, 127
ecology/ecological, 137
economic betterment, 56
economic deprivation, 136
educate/educating/education, 4, 6, 16, 33–34, 38, 44, 46, 48, 56–57, 59, 76n54, 85, 99, 138, 147, 149–51, 155, 180, 197–99, 205n44, 208, 218, 228–30
Edwards, Jonathan, 28n49, 35–36, 170, 199n5
egalitarian/egalitarianism, 50
ekklesia, 3
Emmanuel Ministries, Kolkata, 149, 149n10, 150, 161
empowerment, 29, 56n12, 69, 91, 150–51, 160, 213
encounter, 4, 14n10, 17, 18, 58, 72, 74n40, 121–22, 126, 165, 177, 185, 190, 191, 194, 204, 213n6, 215–17, 222–26, 231
England/English, 35, 44, 48, 53, 59, 62, 155n26, 157n40, 158n43, 170, 228; English education, 180
environmental degradation, 137–38
equal rights, 56, 75
equality, 71, 76, 99, 143, 156, 181, 201, 213
eschatological, 167
essence/essential, 119–20, 124, 167, 208, 219
ethnic identity, 199
ethics, 50, 129
Europe, 5, 7, 12–13, 17, 22, 26, 32, 37–39, 43, 54, 74, 92, 106n52, 170–71, 181, 197, 201, 202n21, 216
evangelical(s), 4, 15, 24, 28, 31n1, 33–36, 39–41, 43n1, 44, 53n1, 54, 57, 68–74, 78, 82n11, 83, 91, 97, 106, 109–10, 111n77, 121–22, 128n49, 130n62, 138, 140–41, 158, 170, 171, 178–79, 193, 207n55, 208, 222, 223n37, 230
Evangelical Awakening, 104n45, 170
evangelical Catholics. *See* Catholicism, evangelical, 71–72
Evangelicalism, 31n1, 34, 35n18, 36, 71, 109, 128n49, 170, 223n37
evangelisation, 77, 135, 137, 142–43, 146, 158, 170, 179
evangelism/evangelistic outreach, 35–36, 64, 72, 87, 118, 135, 163, 166, 167, 211n1, 227, 229
Evening Bible College, 153
evil structures, 69–70, 140–41
Exodus, the, 164, 164n2, 165
exorcism, 29, 69, 86, 88, 102, 189
experience, 4n21, 27, 31, 32, 34n14, 35–36, 50n23, 55–56, 58–60, 63n55, 69, 72, 74n38, 75, 81–82, 86, 89–90, 97, 103–4, 106–7, 110n70, 122n70, 125, 128, 137, 140, 146, 155–56, 170–72, 180, 183, 186, 203, 205, 216n20, 217–19, 230
experiential religion, 31n1

exploitation, 70, 111, 136, 141, 149, 156, 199

faith, 2–6, 12, 22, 26–27, 31–34, 37, 38, 54–55, 60, 63–64, 72, 74–75, 81, 87, 89, 92, 97, 98n13, 99–100, 105, 107, 112, 118, 120–21, 124–28, 130–31, 138, 147, 152, 166, 170n18, 172–73, 177n1, 178, 179n7, 181, 184, 187, 190n66, 191–92, 203, 204n36, 205n45, 206n46, 207–8, 213–14, 217, 219–20, 222, 227
faith commitment, 203
faith mission ideal, 60
farmer(s), 137, 158–59
Fellowship of Indian Missiologists (FOIM), 69n9, 145n1
female exploitation, 136
feminist(s), 55–58, 186n45, 187
festival(s), 44, 49, 165–66, 213–14, 216
first century, 11–13, 37n28, 69, 73, 85–86, 90, 110, 178, 179, 181n19, 197, 211
First Generation Christians (FGCs), 146–47
folk religion, 97n10, 97n12, 98, 101n31, 102, 112n80
food, 16, 23, 97, 137, 149, 165–66, 213
Francis, Pope, 73–74, 84, 229
Francke, A. H., 32
Frederick IV, King, 38
Free Methodist Church, 148
Friends Missionary Prayer Band (FMPB), 155–56, 158, 230

fringe sects, 22, 91

Gandhi, M. K. (Mahatma), 75, 128, 202
Garo/Garo Hills, people of, 28
GEMS House of Prayer, 154
gender discrimination, 136
Gentiles, 2–3, 167n9
Germany, 23, 31–32, 228
Ghana, 189
Gita (Bhagavad Gita), 119n7
global: capitalism, 70; resurgence, 189; revivals, 189
globalisation, 136–39, 197
Goa, 24, 83–84, 117, 228–29
Goreh, Nehemiah, 221
gospel, 4n21, 5–6, 11, 18, 21, 27n39, 28, 29n54, 31, 33–36, 45, 69–70, 72–74, 76–78, 82, 85–86, 88, 91–92, 99, 100, 103n43, 108, 120, 123, 129, 135, 137, 139n22, 140–41, 148, 151, 154, 158–59, 164, 166–68, 172, 177, 178–80, 182, 183n29, 185, 188, 189n58, 189n61, 190, 192, 203n27, 204, 207–8, 211, 215
Gospel Echoing Missionary Society (GEMS), 154
Gossner Mission, 35
"grass-roots" churches, 90–91
Great Tradition, 91, 97n10, 98, 100, 105, 146
greed, 70, 141, 166
Greek, 2, 12, 17, 39, 127, 186
growth, 4, 25, 73, 81, 86n30, 87n31, 89n45, 90, 91n52, 99–100, 101n29, 103n43, 104n48, 106, 108, 110n71,

130, 137, 171, 178, 183n29, 183n31, 184n35, 188n57, 189–90, 230, 230n6, 230n7
Gurdwara, 107, 222
guru/s, 57, 96n5, 125–26, 191, 212, 216
Gurukul Lutheran Theological College and Research Institute, 126, 126n37

Halle University, 32, 37n27, 104n50, 228
Harijan, 75, 129
healing, 63, 69, 84, 86, 90, 102–5, 106n54, 125, 153–54, 158, 172, 189, 206
health, 125, 136, 150, 156, 166, 180, 230
Hellenized Jews, 2
helpless, 166
heresy/heretical, 91, 95, 100, 106
heritage, 5, 39n42, 54, 55, 75, 151, 170, 186–88, 221
hermeneutics, 89n43, 119
heterodoxy, 198
high caste, 16, 56, 58n27, 60, 213
high-Church spirituality, 35
Himalayas, 86n27, 230
Hindu: fundamentalism, 118; nationalism, 200–201; reform movements, 216
Hindu Catholic, 124
Hindu Mahasabha, 216
Hindu temples, 55, 213–14
Hinduised/Hinduisation, 198
Hinduism, 14, 54–55, 59, 63, 69, 74n38, 76, 78, 86, 97n10, 102, 118, 120, 124, 128n49, 129, 157, 160n52, 178, 181, 185, 187, 191, 201, 204–5, 211n1, 212–21, 223n37
Hindutva, 61, 118, 129, 136n4, 201
Hindu widows, 44, 55–56, 58
historiography/historiographer(s), 100, 111, 182
history: from below, 201
HIV/AIDS, 68, 138, 147
Hogg, A. G., 204
holiness (Biblical), 70
Holiness Movement, 105, 172, 31n1, 63, 105, 172
Holy Spirit, 29, 63–65, 72, 86, 91, 98, 104, 107, 112, 124, 130, 163, 165, 167–75, 180, 182n26
homeless, 68, 166
home schooling missionary children, 147
Hong Kong, 178
hope, 49, 67–68, 78, 83, 90n49, 99, 136n8, 137, 170n18, 182, 190, 192, 204
horoscope(s), 213
horticulture, 44–46
hostility, 27, 168, 200, 217
house church, 83, 89, 109, 178, 184
house church movement, 83, 178
human dignity, 71, 97, 137, 143, 150
humanitarian, 43, 45, 54, 190
humanization, 165
human rights, 56, 75, 112
human sinfulness, 70, 141
hunger/hungry, 77, 136–37, 165–66

Hwa Yung, Bishop, 178, 178n4, 179, 192
Hyderabad, 103, 107, 151, 152n15
hygiene, 138, 149–50, 156
hymnal/hymn book, 97

identity: Christian, 13–14, 96, 103, 135; colonial identity; confusion of identity, 74; dual identity, 6n26, 8, 78, 157, 201; new identity in Christ, 71, 142, 143, 208
incarnation, 91, 99, 107, 120, 157, 164–65, 185–86, 217, 222, 236, 249, 252
inclusivist/inclusivistic, 14, 121
inculturate/inculturation, 6n25, 7, 39, 88, 102n34, 112, 123n24, 131, 177, 189n58, 194, 199, 220
Independent Assemblies, Churches, 84, 105, 153
independent-indigenous "small churches", 96
Independent Syrian Church of Malabar, 15
India, xi, 1n1, 4n21, 5–9, 11–12, 13nn6–7, 14–19, 21, 23–24, 28, 29n54, 30–33, 37–41, 43–44, 45n8, 46–52, 53n1, 54n6, 55, 56n12, 57–59, 60n36, 61–62, 63n54, 64–66, 67n1, 69, 71, 74nn39–40, 75–79, 81, 82n10, 82n14, 83–86, 92–93, 95n1, 96n5, 97nn10–12, 98–115, 117–18, 122–24, 125n32, 126–33, 136–37, 138nn16–17, 139–40, 143–48, 151–58, 160n52, 161–62, 165n4, 170–71, 172n24, 178, 181–85, 186n42, 187, 188nn54–55, 189, 193–95, 198–200, 201n16, 201n19, 204–5, 208–9, 211, 212n4, 213, 215–16, 217n23, 218n26, 219–33, 239, 241; North East India (NEI), 5n23, 104, 117, 145n2, 198, 199; South India, 5n23, 11, 15, 18, 21, 37, 39, 81, 86n29, 97n10, 101–2, 104–6, 109, 112, 117, 124, 125n29, 133, 148, 152, 154–55, 178, 183n26, 184–85, 193, 222, 227, 229–30, 232–33
India Missions Association (IMA), 231
Indian, 1n1, 5–9, 11, 13–16, 18–19, 21, 23–25, 29, 33–34, 37, 39, 40–41, 46–48, 51–55, 56n12, 57–58, 59, 60n36, 64, 66, 69n9, 74, 75n41, 77–79, 81n2, 82, 83, 85n26, 86n29, 90n48, 92, 93, 98, 99nn19–20, 99nn22–23, 100, 101, 103n40, 104–7, 109–15, 118, 121n15, 122–23, 124n27, 125n29, 125n32, 126–29, 132–33, 136n3, 138, 140n26, 144, 145nn1–3, 146–48, 149n10, 151, 154, 158–59, 161, 171n23, 178n3, 182nn20–22, 182n24, 183n26, 183n30, 184–88, 190, 193–94, 198, 200–201, 208, 210–12, 214–17, 219–23, 225–33, 235–38; characteris-

tics, 39; architecture, 12, 23, 39, 213–214, 223; caste, 13, 16, 33, 39, 45, 49, 56–58, 60, 74–79, 125–26, 129, 136, 138–39, 144, 151, 153, 157, 160, 201n16, 202, 213–14, 216, 220, 227, 233, 236, 238, 240–41; culture, 2, 4–6, 9, 15, 25, 32–33, 37, 39, 58n28, 61n41, 66, 81, 88, 96–97, 98n15, 99–100, 103, 104n44, 108n63, 111, 114, 118n3, 123–24, 126, 129, 140n26, 151, 156–57, 159n48, 160, 167, 178, 180–82, 187–88, 191, 195, 199, 203, 209, 214–15, 220, 223, 227, 233, 239; heritage, 5, 39n42, 41, 54, 55, 75, 151, 170, 186–88, 221; music, 32, 39, 90, 145n3, 153, 223

Indian catechists, 40

Indian civilization, 98n15, 115, 200

Indian Evangelical Mission (IEM), 158, 230

Indian Evangelical Team (IET), 230

Indian Instituted Churches (IICs), 146

Indianisation, 202

Indian missionary movement, 53

Indian missionary parents, 147

Indian Missionary Society (IMS), 229

Indianness, 12, 200, 201n16, 233

Indian Pentecostal Church of God (IPC), 83, 109, 111

Indian Renaissance, 6, 8, 118, 185n39, 217n22, 226

Indian Succession Act, 201

Indian tradition, 127, 186, 217

Indigeneity, 4, 28n49, 30, 83–84, 88, 91, 103, 177, 178, 192, 199n5, 233

Indigenous, 1–8, 11, 13n6, 19, 29n54, 39, 43n1, 52, 54–55, 58, 65, 69, 79, 81, 82n5, 82nn9–10, 83–93, 95n1, 96–101, 102n37, 104, 105–11, 113–15, 126–28, 132, 145–46, 148, 152, 153, 158, 160–62, 178, 182, 184–86, 188–89, 193, 198, 201, 209, 213–15, 222–23, 228–33

Indigenous Christianity Series, 101, 101n33

Indigenous Church, 1n1, 2, 6–7, 13n6, 19, 39, 84, 99, 145n3, 178, 189

Indigenous Churches of India (Bakht Singh assemblies), 83

indigenous institutions, 128

indigenous movement, 5, 87n32, 89, 93, 99, 101n27, 109, 114, 152, 178

Indologists/Indology, 227

Indonesia(n), 101, 178–79

influence, 4, 6, 33–35, 38, 50, 52, 65, 68, 118, 128, 142, 155, 170, 172, 185, 198, 212

informants, 33

inheritance, 71, 108n60, 143, 201

Inheritors, The, 146–47, 147n6

injustice, 137, 191n73, 194

innovation/innovative, 153

"insider movements", 181

INDEX OF SUBJECTS

integral gospel, 70
integrity, 64n56, 69, 110, 137, 140
Islam, 12, 26–28, 82, 118, 128n49, 133, 157, 178, 181, 195, 200, 217, 223n37, 225
Israel, 3, 165, 203

Jainism 198, 236
James (Apostle), 1–2, 138
Japan, 26, 87, 87n32, 88, 88n35, 93, 101, 101n28, 114, 178
Java/Javanese, 188
Jehovah's Witnesses, 91, 95
Jerusalem, 1–3, 7, 28, 38, 92, 168 173, 178
Jesuit, 6n25, 7, 122, 189, 220, 228, 231
Jesus Christ, 3, 29n54, 39, 68, 72–73, 83, 95, 99, 119, 120–22, 124, 126, 130, 133, 139, 147, 158–60, 163, 166–68, 172, 182, 185–86, 192, 202n24, 205–6, 209, 222, 231; family, 89; film, 148; of history, 120, 205, 219; "I Am" sayings, 164
Jesus Sutras, 27
Jesus, Society of. *See* Jesuit
Jesuit, 6n25, 7, 122, 189, 220, 231
Jewish, 1, 3, 13, 23, 27, 125, 213
Jewish synagogue, 213
Jharkand, 155
John Paul II, Pope, 72, 72n29, 80
Jones, E. Stanley, 75, 75n44, 128, 128nn51–52, 129, 215, 215n17, 219
Judeo-Christian worldview, 57
justice, 6n27, 67, 73, 111, 137, 139, 139n20, 142, 144, 166, 191, 205, 218
Justin Martyr, 127

Kabir, 237
Kachin/Kachinness, 199, 199n5
Kancha Ilaiah, 129n55, 140, 140n23
Kanzo, Uchimura, 88
karma, 128, 204
Karnataka, 105, 117, 184
Kedgaon, 53, 55, 60–62, 63n54, 65–66, 83, 92, 104n44, 108n62, 172n24, 174, 183, 195
Kerala, 1n1, 5, 11–13, 13n8, 16, 19, 21, 23–24, 25n26, 30, 83, 105–6, 109, 111n74, 117, 152, 178, 184, 198, 213, 213n8, 226–27
Kiernander, John Zecharias, 39
kingdom/kingdom of God, 28n48, 29, 37, 70n13, 71–72, 79, 95n3, 141–43, 167, 168n10, 174, 192, 203
kinsman/kinship, 124, 157–58, 199
Kirtan, 187, 221
knowing Christ/knowing God, 206
Kolami, 158–59
Kolawar People, 158
Korea(n), 54, 60, 88, 96n5, 101, 113, 154, 178, 191, 194; contextuality of, 88; theology of, 191
Korku Church, tribe, 157
Khrist Bhaktas, 146

Krista Jyothi Ashram Kunnamkulam Diocese, 102

landless labourers, 136
landlessness, 136
language(s), 5, 14–15, 21, 26–27, 33–34, 38–39, 46–48, 86, 118, 156, 159, 162, 164, 167, 180, 192, 199, 216, 220
Larsen, L. P. (Lars Peter), 55n8
Latin America(n), 2n4, 4, 8, 12, 22n3, 30, 67–68, 78, 81, 88, 90, 91–92, 99, 102, 110, 171, 181, 190
Latino/a incarnations, 91
Latter Day Saints (Mormons), 91, 95
lay leadership training, 153
Laymen's Evangelical Fellowship, 83, 83n16
lay women and men, 40
leader(s), 55n8, 57, 58n24, 59, 64, 66, 75, 77, 84, 87, 100, 106, 107n56, 108, 112, 118, 123, 147–48, 154, 160, 169, 172, 189, 197, 202, 217, 221, 229
leadership training, 153, 158, 190, 230
learning, 25, 47, 50, 56, 156
Leonardo Da Vinci, 71
Liberia, 189
liberty, 3, 62, 156
Liebau, Heike, 33n9
literary/literature, 6, 16, 33, 38, 40, 44, 46–47, 48n18, 49–50, 52, 58n28, 61n41, 65–66, 84, 95n3, 98n15, 100, 108, 119, 129, 140n26, 157–59, 181, 187, 192n77, 193, 208–9, 215, 221, 226
Little Flock, 89
Little Tradition, 1n1, 8, 91–92, 98, 100, 105, 108, 113, 146, 161, 182n22, 200n7, 209
liturgical/liturgy, 5, 25, 84, 90, 214, 229
Living Water, 163–65, 172–73
local, 3, 5–7, 12, 27, 31, 33–35, 48, 67n2, 68nn3–5, 68n7, 69, 74n40, 80, 83, 84–88, 91–92, 97, 100, 103, 105, 107, 109–10, 147–48, 153–55, 158, 160, 178, 185, 188, 191, 198–99, 212–14, 229
local proverbs and sayings, 69, 92, 160
logos, 127, 222
Lutheran(s), 31–32, 34, 38–39, 40–41, 91, 101n25, 126, 132, 228
lyrical theology, 97

Madhya Pradesh, 155
Madras (Chennai), xi, 18, 21n2, 38n36, 39, 41, 43n1, 52, 56nn12–13, 58n28, 60n36, 65–66, 81n2, 83, 97n11, 104n48, 108, 109n64, 113–14, 117, 123n26, 126, 132–33, 135n1, 136n3, 137n14, 140, 144, 153–54, 155nn24–25, 183n30, 184, 186n41, 187n47, 187n51, 188n54, 195, 209, 217n23, 221n33, 222n34, 223, 225, 230nn6–7, 231–32

INDEX OF SUBJECTS 257

Madurai, 6, 17n22, 18, 220, 228n4, 232
Mahabharata, 47
Maharashtra/Maharashtrian, 56–57, 58n28, 61n41, 65–66, 74n38, 76, 80, 82, 140, 146–48, 158, 172, 187–88, 194, 198
Maharashtra Village Ministries (MVM), 147–48, 148n8
Malabar, 14–17, 21, 23, 37n27, 41, 227–29
Malankara (Syrian Rite) Catholic Church, 15, 229
Malayalam, 5, 24–25
Malaysia, 178–79
Maldives, 200, 200n9
malnutrition, 137, 155
Malto people, 155–56
manifestations, 54, 87, 103–4
Manipur, 117
manuscript(s), 11n1, 13, 47
Maramon Convention, 25, 229
marginalised, marginalisation, 60, 81, 91, 99, 102, 135, 137–39, 181, 186, 199
market, 5n24, 7, 67, 137, 140, 150–51
marred identity, 141
Marshman, Hannah, 48–49, 49n20, 51–52, 228
Marshman, Joshua, 118n2, 185, 217
Mar Thoma Syrian Church (Reformed), 229
Mar Thoma Syrian Evangelistic Association, 229
Mar Thoma Voluntary Evangelists Association, 229

massive poverty, 67, 137
mega-church(es), 101n26, 113, 153, 181, 184
Meghalaya, 28, 117
Mennonites, 91
Messiah/Messianic, 1–3, 13, 99, 113, 181, 182n20, 205
method(s), 123, 128, 146, 182n23, 183n29, 218, 220
Methodism, 34
Methodist Church, 148, 178
migrant workers, 179
minority/minorities, 14, 26, 28, 38, 87, 95n3, 111, 112, 114, 117, 136n4, 144
mission, 2–4, 5n24, 6–8, 16, 25, 27, 31–37, 39–40, 43n1, 44n4, 45, 48–49, 50–54, 55n8, 58–60, 62, 64–67, 68n3, 68n5, 70–71, 73–74, 80–85, 87–88, 91–93, 95n1, 96–98, 101, 104–6, 108n62, 109n67, 113–14, 117–18, 121–23, 126, 129, 130n62, 131–32, 135, 136n3, 137–39, 141–42, 144, 146, 148–49, 152–55, 157–59, 161–62, 165n4, 167, 170n18, 171–72, 174, 177–79, 181n19, 182n23, 182n26, 183, 185n36, 187n49, 189, 190n68, 193–95, 199n5, 203–5, 209, 214–16, 218–19, 220n31, 224, 228–33; famine relief, 62–63, 65, 172; rehabilitation, 63, 65, 136–37, 150, 172; rescue work, 63; revival, 63–65
missionary/missionaries, 4n21,

5n22, 6–9, 12, 24, 26–28, 31–35, 38–40, 43–56, 60, 64–66, 74–77, 78n69, 79, 83–89, 91, 96–97, 103–4, 108n63, 109nn67–68, 114, 118, 122–23, 126, 128–29, 131–32, 146–48, 153–58, 167–68, 170–71, 178, 179n7, 182n26, 183, 185nn36–37, 189, 190n67, 191, 193, 195, 197, 199, 201n19, 202n24, 209, 212, 214, 217–21, 224–25, 228–33
Missionaries of Charity, 231
missionary movement, 53, 55n8, 66, 96, 148, 170, 179n7, 195, 212n4, 217, 225, 233
Mizoram, 104n47, 113, 117
Modern Indian history, 53, 82n15, 83, 171n23, 187
modern missionary movement, 55n8, 66, 170
Modern Pentecostal movement, 103–4, 183
modernisation, 137, 151
Mogul rule, 43
money lenders, 155–56
Moravian Church/Mission, 32
Mormon(s), Mormonism (LDS), 95–96
Mother Teresa, 71–72, 231
movement(s), 5–7, 16, 23, 28, 31–36, 46, 48–50, 53–54, 55n8, 56, 58, 60, 63–64, 66, 69, 71, 75, 78–79, 82n14, 84, 86n28, 88, 90, 92, 96–99, 101–15, 118, 125, 129, 131, 139, 144, 145n3, 146, 148, 153–54, 156, 160, 170, 172, 178–79, 181–84, 189, 193, 195, 212n4, 216–18, 222, 225, 230, 233; Christian movements, 4, 85, 87, 96, 105, 110n73, 111, 179n8, 192n78, 194–95, 201; conversion movements, 28, 77–78, 99, 139, 181, 202, 213–14; independent movements, 90n46, 98, 101, 104, 111, 127, 181, 183; indigenous Christian movements, 4–5, 82n10, 83, 87, 89–90, 93, 99–100, 101n28, 114, 145n3, 152, 177, 182, 188; messianic movements, 99, 113, 181, 182n20; new Christian movements, 7, 69n9, 95, 110, 139n22, 160–61, 179–183, 182n24, 192–93; new religious movements, 95–99, 106, 114–15, 180n15, 185, 195, 218; Pentecostal-oriented movements, 181; prophetic movements, 181; Quasi-Christian movements, 181; social protest movements, 99, 181; Subaltern movements, 99, 105, 145n3, 182
Mukti Church/Mukti, 55, 63, 65, 83
music and dance, 90
Muslim, 26, 27n39, 28–29, 38, 102, 128, 131, 198, 200, 203, 214, 233
mutual enrichment, 198
mystical theology, 222
mythology, 49, 50n22, 52, 96, 107, 138, 213, 215, 226

Nagaland, 29n54, 117, 189, 199
Nagpur, 146–48
Namboodiri, 213
National Missionary Society (NMS), 229
nationalism, 1n1, 50, 88, 105, 184, 187, 198, 200, 200n8, 200n10, 201, 210, 229
nation-building, 16, 16n19, 18
native, 24, 33–35, 84, 201
Native Agency, 33
Nattu Sabai, 111n75, 115
Nazrani, 13–14
Neo-Hinduism, 215, 218
Nepal, 69, 85–86, 93, 99, 114, 178, 200, 230; Bible training institutes of, 85; Christa Shanti Sangh Ashram, 85; Gorkha Mission and, 85; Mar Thoma missionaries, 85; secret believers, 85; St. Xavier's School, 85; United Mission to Nepal, 85; Nepal Evangelist Band, 85
Nehru, Pundit Jawaharlal, 12
Nestorian Church of the East, 25
new Christian movements, 7, 69n9, 95, 110, 139n22, 145, 145n3, 160–61, 177–79, 182n24, 192–93
"New Evangelization", 73
New Life Assembly of God, Chennai, 153, 184
New Life Fellowship, Mumbai, 83, 109, 184
New Religious Movements (NRMs), 95–96, 99, 106, 114–15, 180n15, 195, 218
new small churches, 97, 100, 108
New Testament, 1–4, 38, 46–47, 71, 121–22, 127n43, 131, 143, 148, 156, 174, 217, 219, 221
New Testament Church of India, 151, 151n13
Nobili, Roberto de, 6–7, 9, 82, 122–23, 126, 131–32, 146n3, 220–21, 224–25, 228
Noll, Mark A., 4n21, 9, 34n14, 34n17, 35n19, 36, 71n18, 80, 189, 194
Nonchurch Movement, 88
Non-Baptised Believers in Christ (NBBCs), 126n37, 132
non-Christian(s), 34, 78, 102, 117, 128, 138, 190, 214, 220
non-Western majority, 68–78
non-Western world, 4, 109, 185
North America, 54n5, 59, 88, 91, 96, 170–71, 181, 202n21
North Atlantic, 137
North India Bible Institute, 86
nurturing new converts, 148

OBCs, 160, 201
Old Testament, 3, 13, 47, 71, 143, 164, 218
oppressed/oppression, 34, 70, 76, 78, 99, 130, 135, 137, 141–42, 158, 172, 181–82, 186, 214
oppressor(s), 75, 130, 156
oral/orality, 16, 23, 90, 98n15, 104, 183, 192; culture of, 100, 182; communities, 108, 182; oral theology, 105; oral traditions, 12–13, 16, 98n15, 105, 182
ordination/ordained, 24, 38–41, 84
Orientalists, 48, 212, 215; William

Jones, 215; Monier-Williams, 215; F. Max Müller, 215
Orthodox Syrian Church, 15
Outreach Training Institue, Hosur, x, 230

Pacific, 88, 92, 110, 190
Pakistan, 82, 82n3, 93, 107, 200
palm-leaf manuscripts, 13
Panikkar, Raimundo, 205, 216, 216n20, 225
Parsees, 198
Paul (Apostle), 2, 14n13, 125, 169–70
Paul, Pastor, 84, 152
Pauline Bhavan, 149
pavement club, 149
peace, 14, 137, 240
Pentecost, 72, 110n70, 139n22, 165, 167–69, 233
Pentecostal/Pentecostalism, 4, 8, 31n1, 54, 63–65, 73, 81, 83, 84, 86, 90–93, 98, 101n26, 103–15, 127, 130, 145n3, 152–54, 161–62, 169–71, 177, 178, 180–81, 182n26, 183–84, 189, 192–93, 195, 221
persecution, 23, 26–27, 74, 84, 86, 89, 99, 110n73, 115, 125, 155, 211, 221, 227, 229
Persia(n), 5, 14–15, 23, 26, 212, 227
Peter (Apostle), 1–2
Philip (Evangelist), 1, 2
Philippines, 101, 101n30, 106, 115, 178–79
Phule, Jyotiba Govind, 56–57, 159

Phule, Savitribai, 57, 57n22, 58n24, 194
pietism/pietists, vii, 31–32, 34–38, 40–41, 46, 170, 228; Lutheran, 31–32, 34, 228; Pietist Model, 6, 31
pilgrimage, 216, 230
pioneer, 39, 43, 158n43, 186, 216–17
plural/plurality, 2n5, 3, 4n19, 7–8, 16, 23, 38, 86, 117n1, 118–19, 121–22, 128, 131–33, 137, 139n22, 141n26, 164, 174, 190, 191n74, 192, 195, 197, 202–4, 206–10, 215
Plütschau, Heinrich, 31, 37–38
pneumatology/pneumatological, 130, 130n59, 130n62, 133
poetry, 50, 188, 191, 223
political, politics, 16, 22, 43–45, 50, 59–60, 70, 74–76, 77n63, 79, 96, 101n25, 122, 139, 142, 144, 158, 194, 197, 199, 203, 216
political power, 203
political process, 139
poor, 4, 6, 33, 44, 59, 67–68, 69n10, 70, 72, 79, 81, 83, 90, 99, 135–39, 141–44, 151, 153, 158, 160, 172–73, 181, 190, 231
popular Catholicism. *See* Catholicism, popular
popular Hinduism, 102
population, 2, 16, 26–27, 33, 77, 88n38, 99, 117, 136, 137, 156, 178, 188, 200–201, 216
Portuguese, 5, 13, 15, 21, 24, 74, 220, 228

post-Christian, 189
poverty, 44–45, 67, 69–70, 76, 79, 97, 102, 129, 136–38, 140–43, 151, 156, 166, 178, 191n73, 194
power for witness, 168–69, 172
prayer, prayer meetings, 1, 25, 54, 56, 64, 66, 109, 125–26, 152, 154, 158–59, 171, 173, 178, 184
praying bands, 127, 155–56, 158, 230
preaching, 6–7, 36, 45, 72, 106, 118, 138, 178, 189, 191, 207, 218, 222
pre-Christian, 28, 96, 106
preparation of the gospel, 204
Presbyterian, 88, 91
primal spirituality, 179, 180n11, 180n14, 181n18, 192
principalities and powers, 141
prosperity theology, 166, 180
prostitution, 136
protest, 96, 99, 127, 139, 181
protestant(s), 22, 31–32, 37–41, 54, 56–57, 71–73, 77–78, 79, 87–88, 90–91, 102, 111, 157–58, 181, 185, 188–89, 212n4, 216, 221, 225, 228
proto-nationalism, 50
Pune, 59, 61, 66, 69, 104, 108n62, 140, 145n3, 147n7, 171
Punjab, 105, 107, 184, 198, 221–22

Radhakrishnan, S., 119
Ram Mohan Roy, Raja, 185, 216
Ramabai Dongre Medhavi (Pandita Ramabai), 61n39, 82n15, 171n23; and conversion(s), 3, 13–14, 28–30, 32, 35, 50n23, 51, 54–55, 58, 62, 64n56, 65–66, 72, 74–75, 76n50, 76n55, 77–79, 83, 99, 122, 125n29, 128–29, 133, 135, 139–40, 141, 143–44, 157, 159, 172, 180–82, 187n50, 199, 202–4, 207–8, 213–14, 219, 221–22, 232–33; Hindu heritage of, 54–55, 188, 221; Hindu and Christian, 54, 62, 220; home for widows, 55; International Mission Project, 58–59; Keswick Holiness, 54; spiritual awakening, formation, 3, 34–35, 38, 46, 48, 54, 59–60, 63, 65, 122, 128, 130, 169–72, 229; true reformer, 55; women's equal rights advocate, 55–58, 82–83, 171, 187
Ramabai Mukti Mission, 63n54, 65–66, 92, 104n44, 108n62, 172n24, 174, 195
Ramankutty (Pastor Paul), 152
Ramanuja, 128, 238
Ramayana, 47, 238
Rastriya Swayamsevak Sangh (RSS), 216
re-conversion, 204
redemption, 70, 121–22, 141, 155, 158, 165, 203
reform, reformer(s), 25, 43, 48–50, 52, 55–57, 59, 72n23, 73, 77, 80, 118, 160, 185, 216
rehabilitation, 63, 65, 136–37, 150, 172
religion, 5, 12, 18, 28, 31n1, 33,

37, 50, 52, 55, 59, 61, 74, 75, 80, 95–96, 97n10, 97n12, 98, 101n31, 102–3, 104n43, 112–15, 118, 121, 123, 125, 128, 133, 138, 151, 156–57, 166, 180n16, 181n17, 183, 189, 194–95, 198–201, 203, 209, 211n1, 217–20, 222, 224, 233, 235–36, 238–39; folk religion, 97n10, 97n12, 98, 101n31, 102, 112n80, 113–14
religio-cultural, 199
religious, 14, 26–28, 32, 33n9, 35–36, 38, 49–51, 54–56, 61, 64, 69, 75, 78–79, 82, 88, 95–96, 99, 101n25, 103, 106, 112, 114–15, 117, 119–20, 121, 128n49, 132–33, 137, 140n25, 141n26, 142–43, 164n3, 167, 174, 177, 179–80, 181n17, 185, 190–91, 193, 195, 197–98, 200–203, 209–10, 212, 213n10, 215–16, 218–20, 223–25, 231–32, 236, 238–41; religious freedom, 69n8; religious nationalism, 200–201, 210 ; religious plurality, 117, 119, 190; religious pluralism, 121, 132, 137, 164n3, 174, 191n74, 195, 197, 202–3, 209; religious traditions, 78n71, 79, 121, 177, 190–91, 193, 213n10, 223–24, 231
renewal movements, 96, 105
research, 5, 6n25, 8–9, 33–34, 39n41, 51–52, 88n38, 101, 104n48, 106, 108–9, 113–14, 126, 128n50, 131–32, 141n26, 145–46, 179, 182, 183n31, 185n36, 190n67, 202n24, 209, 225, 230n6, 232
resident aliens, 70
resource sharing, 148
resurrection, 93, 119, 121–22, 163–64, 166, 219
"Rethinking Christianity" group, 126
rethinking mission, 137
revitalization, 48, 216
revival(s), revival movements, 25, 29n54, 36, 54, 63–65, 83, 90, 101n32, 104, 105, 113, 171–72, 182n26, 183, 189, 191, 195, 217, 222n35, 224, 230
rich, 37, 45, 70, 137, 141, 143, 153, 163, 181, 191, 198
rites of passage, 213
ritual(s), 16, 19, 23, 27, 30, 49, 56, 88, 98, 102, 124, 159, 188, 213, 214, 226, 238
Rohilkhand University, 118
Roman Catholic, 22, 24, 38, 90, 103, 110, 179, 181, 228; base ecclesial communities, 90
"round table discussions", 128

sacrament(s), 125, 126, 148
salvation, 35, 70, 74, 87, 119, 165–67, 169, 174–75, 202, 204, 206–7, 222, 238
salvation issue, 206
Sanatana Dharma, 120, 239
Sanitation, 76, 136
Sanskrit, 47, 48n16, 236; Sanskritisation, 138, 139
Sat Tal Ashram, 215

Satsang(s), 215, 232
scheduled castes, 139, 201
scheduled tribes, 201
schismatic, 100, 106
scholarly truth, 112
scholarship, 23, 31, 37, 220
school(s), 6, 28, 31, 33, 45, 48–49, 52, 56–57, 59–61, 69, 85, 92–93, 99n20, 114, 118, 141, 147–48, 150, 151n14, 154–55, 157, 160, 209, 213, 228, 230; for girls, 48
Schwartz, Christian Friedrich, 39, 39n41
scientific endeavors to uplift the poor, 43–50; agricultural society, 44–45; botanical garden, 44; crop rotation, 45; hybrid seeds, 45; irrigation, 45; livestock improvement, 45; new crops, 45; organic farming, 45; soil conservation, 45; savings bank, 44, 45; steam engine, 45
Second Vatican Council, 72
sects, 22, 38, 50, 54, 89, 91, 95, 100–101, 105, 112, 212
secular/secularism, 61–62, 140n25, 180, 203–4, 210
secular society, 204
seminary, xi, 1n1, 6, 17n22, 18, 25, 39, 69, 99n17, 117n1, 135n1, 140, 145, 147, 151, 161, 177n1, 228n4, 232–33
Sen, Amartya, 198n1
Sen, Keshub Chundra, 123
Serampore, 6, 8, 32, 34, 40, 43–52, 68, 111, 117n1, 118, 150, 170n18, 185, 193, 208–9, 214, 215n15, 217, 226, 228–29; College, 6n27, 8, 44n3, 45n8, 47–48, 50–52, 117n1, 150, 193, 208–9, 228–29; Community Development, 150; Mission, 6, 43, 43n1, 44n4, 48, 50, 52, 68, 209, 214, 228; Trio, 228
Seventh Day Adventists, 91, 96
sex trade, workers, 33, 63, 76, 103, 136, 137–38, 148, 149n9, 152, 154, 156, 177, 179, 183, 231
Shalom Mela, 148
shaman/shamanistic, 191
Sharada Sadan, 61–62
Shudras (low castes), 57
"Silk Road" merchants, mission, 27–28, 178
Singapore, 70n11, 80, 85n26, 99n20, 178–80, 181n17, 195, 233
Sinhala, 200
Sivakasi, 124, 125n29, 133
slums, 150, 153; slum dwellers, 69, 91, 149, 160
social compassion, 69, 78
social evils publicised: child sacrifice, 44; female infanticide, 44; Ghat murders, 44; hook-swinging festival, 44; leper burning, 44; slavery, 44, 71, 143; voluntary drowning, 44; widow-burning (suttee), 44
social reform movement, 48
social vision, 65, 68–69, 83
Society for the Promotion of Christian Knowledge (SPCK), 31, 35

Society for the Propagation of the Gospel (SPG), 31, 35
socio-political, 199
sojourners, 70
South Asia, xi, 5, 69, 81, 100–101, 104, 117, 158n44, 161, 182, 183, 185, 188, 192, 200, 210–13, 231
Southeast Asia, 179, 179n5, 192, 192n78, 195
Southeast Asian Christianity, 192
Southern African Missiological Society, 101
South India, 5n23, 11, 15, 18, 21, 37, 81, 97, 101–2, 104, 109, 117, 124, 148, 152, 154–55, 178, 184–85, 227, 229–30, 232–33; Mukkuvar Catholics, 102
South Korea, 88, 88n38
southward tilt, 189
speaking in tongues, 63n55, 64
Spener, Philip Jakob, 32, 38
Spirit of Jesus Church, 88
spiritual failure, 169
spiritual fervour, 65, 83
spiritual gifts, 64
spirituality of discipleship, 141
spontaneous, 90–92, 91n51, 123
Sri Lanka(n), 83–84, 93, 121, 152–53, 161–63, 166, 169–70, 177–78, 188, 190, 195, 200, 216, 218, 229, 233, 239
Staines Memorial School, 160
state religion, 200
status, 13–14, 16, 23, 71, 78, 102, 138, 143, 156–57, 213, 214
Stephen (Apostle), 2
stone inscriptions, 13

story and song, 12, 16, 97
street children, 69, 92, 149–50, 160
St. Francis of Assisi, 71, 71n20
St. Thomas Evangelical Church, 15
subaltern group(s), 142
subaltern hermeneutic, 142
Subba Rao, K., 82, 125, 125n32, 131
substance abuse, 138, 149–50
suffer/suffering, 26, 44, 69, 122, 137, 140, 165, 190, 236, 238
Sufism/Sufi orders, 26–27, 240
Sundaram, Pastor Sam, 84, 109, 184
Sundar Singh, Sadhu, 82, 221–22, 225
Sundram, Pastor G., 84
Sung, John, 179
suttee, sati, 44, 49, 49n21, 56, 239
syncretic/syncretism, 106, 106n53, 113, 180
Syriac/Syrian, 4, 5, 14–15, 16, 18, 22–26, 27n39, 211–13, 227, 229
Syrian Christians, 5, 14–16, 23–24, 212, 227

Taiwan, 86–87, 101, 101n29, 115
Tamil, 6, 8, 11, 17–18, 33, 37–40, 46, 52, 82, 111n76, 115, 126n37, 132, 138, 153, 200, 209, 220–21, 224, 228, 230, 232
Tamil Nadu, 82, 84, 104–6, 104n48, 111, 117, 125n29, 126, 133, 145n3, 152, 178, 183n31, 184, 198, 230

INDEX OF SUBJECTS

Tantric Hinduism, 69, 86
technology/technological, 16, 151, 153, 178, 180
Telugu hymnal, 97
Tentmakers, 153, 179
Teresa, Mother (Saint), viii, 71–72, 72n21, 72n28, 231
territorial, 55, 181
textbooks, 48, 97
theological liberalism, 68, 120
Thanjavur, 32, 52, 209
theocentric, 203
theology, xi, 22n8, 29–30, 32, 41, 46, 52, 63, 87, 89–90, 93, 97–98, 103n43, 105, 111n77, 114, 118, 120–22, 125n32, 126n39, 127, 128, 130–33, 141n26, 144, 150, 160n51, 166, 171–72, 174, 183, 186, 188, 190–91, 194, 203, 207n55, 209–10, 212, 215–17, 219, 221–23, 228, 232–33; biblical, 1–2, 4, 14n13, 32, 39, 53n3, 67, 69–70, 98, 100, 107, 119–22, 127, 131, 140, 145n3, 147, 152, 163, 166, 169, 172, 174, 186, 187, 205, 218; lyrical, 97, 223; narrative, 23, 90, 97–98; pentecostal, 4, 54, 63–64, 73, 81, 83–84, 86, 90–91, 93, 98, 101n26, 103–6, 109–15, 110n70, 111n74, 130, 145, 152n15, 152n18, 153–54, 161–62, 169, 171, 177–78, 180, 182–84, 193, 195, 221
Thomas/Thomas Tradition, 1, 3n16, 5, 6n25, 6n28, 7–8, 11–19, 21–24, 29, 69, 71, 81–82, 102n34, 105n51, 111, 115, 119n5, 121, 122n19, 123n24, 131–33, 140, 182n26, 185, 191, 195, 200n7, 205, 209–10, 211–13, 217n22, 221, 223, 226–28, 227n1, 231, 233
Thomas á Kempis, 71
Thomas Christians, 12–14, 15n18, 17–19, 23–24, 81–82, 212–13, 223, 228, 231
Thomas of Cana, 14–15
Tibetan Buddhism, 69, 86
Tilak, Narayan Vaman, 82n9, 187, 188n55, 221
Tirunelveli, 32–34, 34n13, 41, 104, 104n45, 111n75, 115, 229
tolerant, 14
totalitarian, 203
trade, 13, 16, 38, 45, 136, 178, 197
training, 6, 31, 65, 85, 87, 89, 99n17, 138, 146–48, 150, 151, 153–54, 190, 230
transformation, 28, 43n1, 45, 52, 53n1, 67–69, 67nn1–2, 68n7, 71, 73, 78, 80, 122, 129n55, 132, 140, 155n26, 156, 162, 174, 187, 193, 199
translatability, 4–5, 108, 182
translation/translate, 6, 8, 24–25, 31, 39, 46–47, 50n22, 52, 60, 69, 86, 92, 104n50, 107, 158, 160, 177, 190–91, 208, 215, 228, 230, 236
transmigration of souls, 128
Tranquebar/Tranquebar Mission,

6, 8, 31–32, 33n9, 34, 36–40, 37n27, 37n30, 39n39, 46, 228, 232
tribe/tribal, 3, 4n21, 28, 56, 69, 83, 92, 99, 136, 139, 148, 155–61, 167, 181, 199, 201, 209, 235; tribal dignity, 83, 199; tribal language, 199; tribal rights, 199
Trinity, 70n11, 80, 87, 118n2, 127, 127n46, 179n5, 180n11, 195, 222, 233
True Jesus Church, 86, 89
true pluralism, 206–7
true religion, 138, 219
truth, 54, 112, 121, 132, 151, 163–65, 168, 172, 187, 199, 202–4, 206–9, 207n55, 221, 232, 239
truth claims, 121, 121n16, 132, 203
types of Independent Churches, 110

underground, 84, 229
Union Biblical Seminary, Yavatmal/Pune (UBS), 69, 140, 145n3, 147, 147n7
uniqueness, 119–21, 121nn15–16, 132–33, 190, 202, 202n24, 209, 219, 222
Unitarian, 185
United States, 53, 54n7, 59–60, 59n34, 66, 91, 225
University of South Africa, 101, 110, 110n70, 112
unreached peoples, 27, 148
untouchable(s), 57, 75–76, 129, 136n7, 138, 144, 202, 236–37

untouchability, 129, 138–39, 139nn19–20, 144, 214, 219
Upadhyaya, Brahmabandhab, 124
Upanishads, 127, 215n16, 217, 225, 240
uplift of backward tribes, 56
upward mobility, 99, 139, 182
urban, 27, 90, 109, 126n37, 132, 148, 149n10, 161, 184
Uttar Pradesh, 155, 184

Vargis, P. G., 230
Varna, 129, 240
Vatican II, 179
Vaz, Joseph, 83–84, 229
Veda(s), 216–17, 216n20, 225, 235, 239–40
Vedanta/Vedantic, 119–20, 185, 215, 217–19, 240–41; Christ, 120, 218–19; mission, 215; theism, 128; Vedic religions, 212, 217
vernacular, 6, 25, 46, 48, 109, 185–86, 228; and Bible, 1n2, 2n5, 6, 8, 24–25, 31–32, 37, 39n39, 46–47, 60–61, 63, 69, 82, 85–86, 92, 96–97, 101, 105–7, 109, 119, 121, 125–26, 137n12, 140n26, 144, 148, 153, 156, 158, 160, 166n5, 167n8, 174–75, 185, 187, 191, 193–94, 203, 208, 217–18, 222, 228, 230; and education, 4n20, 6, 8, 16, 33–34, 44, 46, 48–49, 56–57, 59, 76n54, 79, 85, 99n18, 113, 138, 149–51, 155, 160, 180, 194, 197, 199, 205n44, 208–9, 228; and schools, 6, 28, 31, 33, 48–49,

56–57, 59, 69, 85, 92, 118, 148, 151, 155, 157, 160, 213, 228, 230; and textbooks, 48, 97
victim(s), 63, 70, 136, 141, 142n34, 144, 149, 155, 171
video games, 192
Vijayawada, 126
village(s), 33, 38, 49, 62, 64, 69, 92, 97, 102, 147–48, 151, 159–60, 189, 202, 213
Visakhapatnam, 151, 151n13
Vishwa Hindu Parishad (VHP), 216, 241
vision, 6n27, 7, 54, 65, 68–69, 70n13, 79, 83, 96, 103n42, 115, 125, 140, 141n26, 141n28, 143, 148, 152, 180n16, 183n28, 195
vitality, 4, 50, 110, 153, 178, 190, 202n21
Vivekananda, Swami, 58, 218, 238
vocational missionary "tentmakers", 153, 179
voice for the voiceless, 142

Wardha, 148, 159–60
Watchman Nee, 87
Wesley, John and Charles, 34–35, 170
Wesley, Samuel and Susannah, 35
Wesleyan Holiness/Theology, 31n1, 63, 170, 172
West Bengal, 105, 184
Western, 4, 12, 16, 39, 48, 54–55, 64, 74n40, 83, 88–89, 96–100, 124, 158n46, 185–88, 197, 202–3, 209, 221, 232

Westernisation, 138–39
Whitfield, George, 170
wholistic care, 146
Wilberforce, William, 44n2
Winter, Ralph, 179
witness, 2, 36, 37n27, 51, 63–64, 69, 86–88, 91, 104n47, 105, 108, 113, 118–19, 122, 133, 157, 163, 166–69, 170n18, 172, 174, 184, 186, 190n68, 212, 217, 219, 222, 231
Witness Lee, 87
women, 1, 6n27, 34, 40, 49, 55–66, 69, 72, 82–83, 85, 92, 102, 124–25, 136, 146, 151, 160, 171, 186–87, 213, 228, 241
women's amelioration, rights, 49, 56, 70, 74–75, 82, 112, 129, 141, 199
Women's Christian Temperance Union, 59
World Cassette Outreach, 148
World Christianity, 4n21, 9, 18, 34n14, 58n28, 88n34, 103, 110, 141n26, 143, 180, 183, 189, 191n72, 192n78, 194–95, 231
worldview, 57, 89, 97, 98, 203
worship, 3, 5, 14, 24, 38, 44, 50, 68n5, 72, 84–86, 107, 126–28, 151–53, 159–60, 171, 178, 189, 191, 202, 218, 222, 227, 238

Xavier, Francis, 228

Yavatmal College for Leadership Training (YCLT), 158

Youth with a Mission (YWAM), 159

Zenana, 241

Ziegenbalg, Bartholomäus, 31, 37, 38n36, 228

Zoram Baptist Mission, 158n45

Index of Authors

Abraham, Sara, 83n18, 111
Abrams, Minnie F., 60, 63–65, 63n54, 64n61, 92, 104n44, 171–72, 172n24, 174
Adeney, David H., 89n40, 92
Adeney, Frances S., 194
Adhav, S. M., 56n13, 65, 187n47
Aikman, David, 28n48, 29, 89n39, 92
Aleaz, K. P., 82n8
Alexander, Etrelda Y., 183n32
Amaladass SJ, Anand, 6n25, 7, 14n10, 18, 211n3, 213n6, 223, 231
Amaladoss, Michael, 102n36
Ambedkar, B. R., 56, 75–77, 76n55, 77n62, 79, 129
Amjad-Ali, Charles, 82n3
Anchukandam, Thomas, 6n25, 7, 123, 123n24, 131
Anderson, Allan, 92, 110, 110n70, 112, 154n23, 161, 182n26, 183n29, 193
Anderson, Gerald H., 39n38, 55n8, 66, 187n49
Andrade, Suzana, 57nn18–19, 57n21
Appasamy, A. J., 82n7, 221n33, 223
Appasamy, Grace Parimala, 145n3
Aprem, Mar, 15n17, 18
Arana-Quiroz, Pedro, 68, 68n3

Arangaden, Christopher, 6n27, 47n12, 208
Athyal, Jesudas M., xi, 5n24, 7, 16n19, 18, 40, 64n61, 82, 200n9, 232
Athyal, Saphir, 43n1, 53n1, 67n1, 85n26, 99n20, 174

Baago, Kaj, 101, 125n32, 131
Bakker, Freek L., 216n19, 223
Ball, David M., 164, 164n3, 174
Bamat, Tomás, 112
Barclay, William, 140n26
Barnat, Thomas, 102nn34–36
Barrett, David B., 4n21, 7, 89n42, 109n67, 125, 125n35, 131, 185n36
Bauswein, Jean-Jacques, 88n37
Bays, Daniel H., 54n5
Beaderstadt, Jan L., 160n51
Berg, M., 91n51, 92
Bergunder, Michael, 86n29, 104, 104n50, 112, 183n26, 183n29, 184n33, 193
Berntsen, Maxine, 74n38, 80
Beyreuther, Erich, 38n36
Bhakiaraj, Paul Joshua, 37n28, 41, 69n8, 79, 193, 200n8, 210, 216n21, 224
Blumhofer, Edith L., 54n5, 55n9, 60n37, 63n55
Boyd, Robin, 101, 188n54

Braden, Charles, 95n3, 112
Brown, Candy Gunther, 86n29
Brown, Judith M., 78n71, 79, 193, 213n10, 223–24, 231
Brown, Leslie W., 15n14, 18, 21n2, 29, 81n2, 227n1, 231
Bühlmann, W., 4n21, 7
Burgess, Stanley M., 81n1, 145n3
Burrows, William R., 7–8, 7n29, 141n26, 143

Caldera, Ravin, 161, 177n1, 233
Carey, William, 6, 8, 34–36, 35n18, 40, 43–52, 43n1, 44n2, 44n4, 45nn7–8, 46nn9–11, 47nn12–14, 48nn16–18, 68–69, 86n30, 90n49, 91n51, 92, 101n29, 115, 118, 130n62, 170, 170n18, 179n6, 193, 208–9, 228
Carpenter, Joel, 91n53, 92
Chakravarti, Uma, 66, 129n55
Chandler, Paul-Gordon, 27nn39–40, 29, 128n50, 129n54, 131
Charbonnier, Jean-Pierre, 89n39
Chatfield, Adrian, 101n25
Chatterjee, S. K., 6n27, 44n3, 47n14, 48, 48n19, 49n20, 51, 208
Chew, John, 145n3
Christian, Jayakumar, 70n13, 79, 141n28, 143
Clark, Elmer T., 95n3, 112
Clooney, Francis X., 6n25, 7, 131, 220n30, 224
Conner, John H., 88n37
Connor, Phillip, 88n38

Coote, Robert T., 55n8, 66
Copley, Antony, 50–51, 50nn23–24
Coward, Harold, 14n10, 18, 213, 218n24, 219n27, 223–26, 231
Cragg, Kenneth, 204–5, 204n36, 205n45, 208

Daniel, J. T. K., 6n27, 8, 45n8, 51, 156n33, 193, 208–9
Dassanayake, Don Alexis, 84n21
David, Mohan D., 55–56, 56n12, 74n40, 188n57
D'Costa, G., 121n15, 132–33
D'Costa, Roque, 146n5, 161
Degrijse, Omer, 4n21, 8
Dempsey, Corinne G., 93
Dempster, Murray W., 98n13, 103n41, 103n43, 104nn43–44, 113, 183n27, 183n29
Devadas, M., 82, 82n13, 96–97, 101, 105
Devadason, E. D., 140n26
Dewanji, Malay, 6n28, 8
Dharmaraj, Jacob S., 51
Dingrin, La Seng, 199n5
Dongre, Rajas Krishnarao, 66
Drewery, Mary, 51
Dupont, Jacque, 167, 167n9, 174
Dupuis, James, 122n17, 131
Duerksen, Darren Todd, 232
Durnbaugh, Donald F., 40
Dutta, Abhijit, 45, 45n6, 51

Elliston, Edgar J., 4n20, 8, 99n18, 113
Escobar, J. Samuel, 2n4, 8, 121, 121nn13–14, 122n21, 131

Faraday, Michael, 82n6
Fernando, Ajith, 169, 169n13, 171, 174, 207, 209
Fernando, Leonard, 12n5, 16n19, 18, 211n3, 223, 225, 232
Fonseca, Josué, 68n5
Frykenberg, Robert Eric, 13n7, 18, 32n7, 33nn8–9, 34n13, 34n15, 39n41, 40, 51, 54n7, 58n28, 58n30, 59n34, 61n44, 62, 62n46, 62n48, 63n50, 66, 74n39, 78, 79, 193, 201n16, 201n19, 202n22, 212n4, 213n10, 223–24, 225, 231–32
Fuchs, Stephen, 99n22, 113, 157, 157n34, 157n38, 161, 182n20
Fuller, Simon, 200n9

Gandhi, Arun, 76, 76n54, 79
Gandhi, Rajmohan, 75n44, 75n49, 76n52, 79
Ganesapandy, J., 158n44, 161
Gensichen, Hans-Werner, 39n38
George, Timothy, 51, 170n18
Ghosh, A. K., 6n27, 45, 46n10
Giles, Kevin, 127, 127n43, 131
Gispert-Sauch, G., 12n5, 18, 186nn42–43, 211n3, 223, 225, 232
Glaser, Ida, 193
Glasser, Arthur F., 167n8, 168n10, 174
Gnanasikhamani, V., 140n26
Gomes, Kshitija, 59n34
González-Balado, José Luis, 72n21
Gorospe, Adonis Abelard O., 192n77, 193
Grafé, Hugald, 6n26, 8
Greenman, Jeffrey P., 130n62

Hanciles, Jehu J., 193
Harper, Susan Billington, 77n65, 79, 193, 213n10, 224
Hawthorne, Steven C., 179n6
Hayward, Victor E. W., 90n46
Hedlund, Roger E., 5n23, 6n27, 8, 13n6, 16n19, 18–19, 37n28, 40–41, 43n1, 45n8, 51–52, 56n12, 58n28, 64n61, 66, 69nn8–9, 79, 82n3, 82n5, 82n15, 83n17, 92–93, 95n1, 98n17, 99n19, 99n23, 104n48, 113, 127n44, 131–32, 145nn2–3, 156n32, 158n47, 161, 171n23, 174, 178n3, 182n21, 182n24, 183nn30–31, 193, 200nn8–9, 208–10, 216n21, 224, 230n6, 232
Hedlund, Thea June, xi–xii, 6n27
Heim, S. Mark, 190n68, 206, 206n46, 209
Hexham, Irving, 95n2, 96n9, 113
Heyden, Ulrich van der, 101n25
Hiebert, Paul G., 4, 4n20, 8, 97n10, 99n18, 113, 216n21, 224
Hminga, C. L., 104n47, 113
Hoefer, Herbert, 126, 126n37, 126n39, 127n41, 131–32
Hollenweger, Walter J., 4n21, 8, 92, 104n49, 113, 154n23, 161, 182n26, 183, 183n32
Horner, Norman A., 55n8, 66
Hrangkhuma, F., 230n6, 232
Hudson, D. Dennis, 40n44, 218n26, 224
Hughes, Dewi, 141n27, 143
Hunt, Robert A., 188, 189n58, 194

Irwin, Dale T., 179, 179n8, 194

Jacob, Plamthodathil S., 82n9, 141n26
James, Jonathan D., 232
Jayapathy, Francis, 102n35
Jayaprakash, L. Joshi, 230n7, 232
Jenkins, Philip, 21n1, 22, 22n5, 22n9, 25, 25n29, 26, 27n42, 28n47, 29, 180, 189, 194, 232
Jeyakumar, D. Arthur, 16, 17n22, 18, 228n4, 232
Jeyaraj, Daniel, 6n26, 8, 36–37, 37nn27–28, 37n30, 39n39, 39n42, 40n43, 41, 145n3, 146n3, 232
Johnson, B. W., 174
Johnson, Cydric B., 140n26
Johnson, Harmon A., 91n52
Johnson, Rajkumar Boaz, 56n12, 58n28, 66, 82n15, 171n23, 183n30, 186n45, 187, 187n48
Johnson, Todd M., 109n67, 185n36
Jones, A. H. M., 96n4, 113

Kadankavil, Thomas, 200n7, 209
Kalantzis, George, 130n62
Kalapati, Joshua, xi, 16n19, 18, 40, 64n61, 82n3, 117n1, 119, 119n7, 120, 120n8, 122, 128, 132, 200n9, 219n28, 224, 232
Kalliath, Antony, 190n69
Kalu, Ogbu U., 40, 182n26
Kärkkäinen, Veli-Matti, 22n8, 30, 130n62, 182n26
Karotemprel, Sebastian, 4n21, 8
Kealotswe, Obed Ndeya, 101n25

Khatry, Ramesh, 69n8, 85n26, 99n20
Kim, Mantae, 188nn56–57
Kim, Sebastian C. H., 56n12, 58n28, 64, 64n56, 66, 69n10, 75n41, 79, 82n15, 136n2, 141n26, 143–44, 171n23, 183n30, 191, 191nn72–73, 194–95, 232
Kirwan, Michael, 194
Klaus, Byron D., 98n13, 103n41, 103n43, 104n44, 113, 183n27, 183n29
Knitter, Paul, 209
Koder, S. S., 13n8
Kosambi, Meera, 55n11, 58, 58n29, 66, 225
Koshy, T. E., 82n14, 101n32, 107n55, 113, 222n35, 224
Kotian, Noel, 157n40, 161
Kumaradoss, Y. Vincent, 233
Küng, Hans, 3, 3n16, 8
Kuriakose, M. K., 228n4, 233

LaSor, William Sanford, 1, 1n2, 8
Latourette, Kenneth Scott, 53n2, 53n4, 55n10, 123, 123n25, 132
Legrand, Lucien, 2, 2n5, 3n14, 4n19, 8
Lewis, Donald, 41, 194
Lewis, Gordon, 95n3
Lindberg, Carter, 32nn2–3, 32nn5–6, 41
Lipner, Julius, 186nn42–43, 212n5, 224
Lynch, Owen M., 139, 139n19, 144

INDEX OF AUTHORS

Ma, Julie, 106n53
MacNicol, Nicol, 54n6, 66, 185n38
Maliekal, John, 138, 139n18, 144
Maliekal, Jose D., 195
Mallampalli, Chandra, 201, 201n16, 233
Malony, H. Newton, 140n26
Mani, Braj Ranjan, 57n22, 58n24, 129, 129n55, 132, 194
Mangalwadi, Ruth, 6n27, 52
Mangalwadi, Vishal, 52, 54n6
Manoharan, S., 156n27, 162
Marak, Krickwin C., 69n10, 79, 136n2, 140n24, 141nn26–27, 143–44
Marshman, John Clark, 44, 44n4, 52
Martin, Paul C., 83n19, 152n15, 153, 161, 178n3
Martin, Walter, 95n3
Massey, Ashish Kumar, 6n27
Massey, James, 194
Mathew, C. V., 43n1, 53n1, 68n1, 132, 174, 218n25, 224
Mattam, Joseph, 141n26
Matthias, Markus, 32n6
McClung, L. Grant, 103n43, 114, 183n29
McConnell, Douglas, 130n62
McGee, Gary B., 53n3, 103n43, 182n26, 183n29
McGrath, Alister, 41
McPhee, Arthur, 194
Merugumalla, Sudheer, 145n3
Michael, George, 46, 46n9
Michael, S. M., 132, 140n26, 220, 220n31, 224

Mihindukulasuriya, Prabo, 161, 177n1, 233
Minderhoud, Jan, 85n26, 99n20, 114
Minz, Nirmal, 199n7, 209
Mitchell, Robert C., 90n46
Moffett, Samuel H., 15n16, 19, 24n20, 25n25, 25n27, 30, 41, 98n16, 114
Moffitt, Bob, 68n7, 80
Monterroso, Victor M., 91n52
Moreau, A. Scott, 53n3
Muck, Terry, 194
Mukhopadhayay, Indira, 48nn16–17
Mullins, Mark R., 87n32, 88nn34–36, 93, 101n28, 114
Mundadan, A. M., 15nn14–15, 19, 93, 103n40, 114, 211n2, 224
Myklebust, Olav Guttorm, 205, 205n44, 209

Nag, Kalidas, 47n13, 48n18
Naik, Samanta, 145n3
Nallappan, Francis, 136n4, 144
Neill, Stephen, 11, 12n3, 19
Neufeldt, Ronald, 218n24, 225
Newbigin, Lesslie, 139n22, 202–3, 202n24, 203n27, 204n34, 208–9
Niles, D. T., 166n6
Ninan, A. George, 136, 136n2, 136n5, 137, 137n9, 137n13, 144
Nirmal, Chiranjivi J., 136n3, 144
Noll, Mark A., 4n21, 9, 34n14, 34n17, 35n19, 71n18, 80, 189, 189n60, 189n62, 194
Nongsiej, T., 104n46

Nuñez C., Emilio Antonio, 90n49
Nystrom, Carolyn, 189n60

Oddie, Geoffrey A., 52, 212n4, 225
Oden, Thomas C., 119n5, 122n19, 132, 202n21, 209
Omvedt, Gail, 58n24, 129n55
O'Mahony, Anthony, 194
O'Neill, Tom, 136n7, 144
Oommen, T. K., 200n8, 200n10, 210
Oosthuizen, G. C., 90nn47–48
Orr, J. Edwin, 104n45
Ositelu II, Gabriel, 4n21, 9, 89n45, 110n71, 114
Oussoren, Aalbertinus Herman, 45n7

Pachuau, Lalsangkima, 190nn68–69
Packer, J. I., 170, 170nn17,19, 171, 173–74, 173n25
Packiamuthu, David and Sarojini, 34n13, 41
Padilla, C. René, 67n2, 68, 68nn3–6, 80
Pannenberg, Wolfhart, 121, 121n16, 132
Patterson, Josephine F., 66
Paul, Whitson, 83n16
Payne, Ernest A., 51–52
Perry, Cindy L., 85n26, 86n27, 93, 99n20, 114
Peskett, Howard, 165, 165n4, 174
Petersen, Douglas, 98n13, 103n41, 103n43, 104nn43–44, 113, 183n27, 183n29
Petersen, William, 95n3, 114

Phillips, James M., 55n8, 66
Phule, Jotirao, 194
Pobee, John, 4n21, 9, 89n45, 110n71, 114
Poewe, Karla, 95n2, 96n9, 113
Pomerville, Paul A., 98n14, 114
Poobalan, Ivor, 161, 177n1, 233
Poon, Michael Nai-Chiu, 179, 179n5, 179nn9–10, 180n14, 192n78, 195
Poplin, Mary, 203, 203n33, 210
Potts, E. Daniel, 52
Prakash, P. Surya, 82n10
Premanendham, M., 82n14
Pretiz, P., 91n51, 92
Pye, Michael, 87n33

Raj, Muthusami, 155n26, 162
Raj, P. Peter, 82n5
Raj, Selva J., 93
Rajamani, R. R., 107n57, 114
Rajamanickam, S., 6n25, 9, 132–33, 220n32, 225
Rajendran, K., 233
Rajkumar, Evangeline, 6n27
Ramabai, Sarasvati Dongre Medhavi (Pandita), 195
Ramachandra, Vinoth, 70, 70n11, 80, 121, 121n14, 132, 165, 165n4, 174, 233
Ramm, Bernard, 168, 168n11, 174
Ray, N. R., 6n27, 46n11
Read, William R., 91n52
Redfield, Robert, 98n15, 114
Richard, H. L., 82nn11–12, 101, 125, 125n30, 125nn32–33, 126n36, 133, 188n55
Richard, Jessica, 16n19, 18, 40, 64n61, 82n3, 200n9, 232

Richardson, Cyril C., 122n19, 133
Robeck, Cecil M., Jr., 182n26
Robert, Dana, 109, 109n68, 114, 185n37, 195, 232
Robinson, Bob, 215n18, 225
Rooney, J., 93
Roxborogh, W. John, 111n77, 114, 192, 192n78
Roy, Arundhati, 76, 76nn55–56, 79
Roy, Binoy Bhusan, 6n27, 45, 45n8, 49, 49n21

Saldanha, Julian, 141n26
Saliba, John A., 96n6, 114
Salve, Gouri, 136n8, 144
Samartha, Stanley, 121, 208, 208n58, 210
Samuel, Edwin, 108n61
Sanneh, Lamin, 5, 5n22, 9, 93, 108n63, 114, 182, 182n26, 189, 189n61, 189n64, 195, 233
Sardar, Pamela, 57n22, 58n24, 194
Sardar, Sunil, 158, 158n47, 159n48, 160nn51–53
Sarkar, R. L., 137n12, 144
Satyavrata, Ivan, 104nn44–45
Sauliére, Augustine, 6n25, 9, 133, 220, 220n32, 225
Scherer, James A., 38n37, 39n40
Scott, David C., 123n26, 133, 186n41, 217n23, 225
Seitz, Jonathan A., 28n49, 30, 199n5, 233
Sen, Amartya, 198, 198n1, 210
Shah, A. B., 58n28, 61n41, 66
Sharma, Bal Krishna, 86n28

Sharpe, Eric J., 55n8, 187n49, 187n53
Shaw, Mark, 189, 189n65, 195
Shaw, R. Daniel, 97n10, 113
Shenk, Wilbert R., xi, 91n53, 92, 96, 96n7, 114
Singer, Milton, 98n15, 115
Singh, Bakht, 82, 82n14, 83, 101, 101n32, 105–8, 113, 222, 222n35, 224
Singh, K. S., 156n27, 162
Singh, Sundar, 82, 82n10, 221–22, 221n33, 222n34, 223, 225
Smith, A. Christopher, 52
Snaitang, O. L., 5n23, 29n54, 104n46, 115, 146n2, 162
Solomon Raj, P., 82n13, 96n1, 97n12, 101, 101n31, 112, 112n80, 114, 145n3, 233
Somaratna, G. P. V., 84nn22–23, 93, 152, 152n18, 161–62, 177–78, 177n1, 178n2, 188, 188n57, 195, 233
Spencer, Leon P., 190n67
Spittler, Russell P., 103n41, 183n27
Srinivas, M. N., 138, 138n16, 144
Stackhouse, Max L., 190nn68–69
Staffner, Hans, 124, 124n28, 133
Stanley, Brian, 52
Stark, Rodney, 95, 95n2, 182n23
Stewart, Wilma S., 47n13, 48n18, 52
Stein, K. James, 32n3
Sugden, Chris, 101n27, 115
Sundara Rao, R. R., 97n11, 114
Sunquist, Scott, 139n22, 145n3, 179, 179n8, 194

Swanson, Allen J., 86n30, 87n31, 101n29, 115
Synan, Vinson, 103nn42–43, 115, 182n26, 183n28

Tang, Edmond, 193
Tathagatananda, Swami, 215n16, 225
Taylor, John V., 180, 180n16, 195
Taylor, William David, 90n49, 119n4, 121n13, 131, 133
Tennent, Timothy C., 52, 93, 124n27, 127nn45–47, 128, 128n49, 133, 181n19, 186n44, 195, 223nn36–37, 225
Tenney, Merril C., 174
Tesch, Karla, 68n7, 80
Thangaraj, M. Thomas, 111, 111n75, 115, 191, 191n74, 195
Thatamanil, John J., 5n24, 7
Thomas, Jacob, 69, 69n10, 140, 140n24
Thomas, M. M., 6n27, 121, 121n15, 133, 185, 185n39, 205, 210, 217n22, 221, 226
Thomas, P. B., 105n51
Thomas, Pradip Ninan, 233
Thompson, David M., 191n72
Thonippara, Francis, 13n6, 14n12, 19
Tiénou, Tite, 97n10, 113
Tippett, A. R., 141n26
Tiwari, Ravi, 117n1, 118n3, 122, 128, 133, 145n3
Todhunter, Andrew, 11n2, 12n4, 19
Tong, C. K., 181n17
Torrey, R. A., 168n12, 174
Tuggy, A. Leonard, 101n30, 115, 158n46
Turner, Harold W., 89n44, 106, 106n52, 115, 180, 180n15, 195

Uday Kumar, Jyothi, 146n3

Van Baalen, J. K., 95n3
Van Engen, Charles, 4n20, 8, 99n18, 113
Varadarajan, A., 139, 139n20, 144
Vischer, Lukas, 88n37
Viswanathan, Gauri, 58n25, 66, 141n26, 144, 187
Visvanathan, Susan, 16, 16n20, 19, 23n13, 24n23, 25n26, 30, 213n8, 226
Voth, Esteban, 67, 67n2

Wacker, Grant, 54n5, 182n26
Walvoord, John F., 174
Walls, Andrew F., 91, 91n53, 141n26, 143, 179, 179n7, 195, 233
Ward, William, 48–49, 50n22, 52, 214, 215n15, 226, 228
Ward, W. R., 41
Warrington, Keith, 106n54, 115
Webster, John C. B., 219n27, 226
Wiegle, George, 72–74, 72nn22–23, 72n29, 73n33, 74n37, 80
Wiest, Jean-Paul, 102nn34–36, 112
Wilfred, Felix, 111, 111n76, 115, 137, 137n14, 144, 195

Williams, Raymond Brady, 218n26, 224, 226
Wingate, Andrew, 125n29, 133
Wolf, Thom, 57nn17–19, 57n21
Wong, James, 233
Woodberry, J. Dudley, 4n20, 8, 82n4, 99n18, 113, 233
Wright, Christopher J. H. (Chris), 119, 119n4, 133, 166, 166n5, 167n7, 175
Wu, David, 145n3, 189

Wuthnow, Robert, 189, 190n66

Yamamori, Tetsunao, 67n2, 68nn3–5, 80
Yong, Amos, 130, 130n59, 130n62, 133, 139n22, 233
Young, Richard Fox, 28n49, 30, 195, 199n5, 201n16, 233
Young-gi, Hong, 101n26, 113

Zelliot, Eleanor, 80, 74n38

Index of Biblical References

OLD TESTAMENT
Genesis
11:1–9......168

Exodus
3:6......164n2
3:13–15......164

Deuteronomy
14:1–2......71n15, 142n38
15:15......71n16, 142n39

Isaiah
12:3......165
40–55......164
61:1......172
61:2......172

Joel
2:28–29......167

NEW TESTAMENT
Matthew
24:14......167

Luke
4:18–19......172
24:49......168

John
1:4–9......166

3:8......170
4:10......164
4:39–41......165
4:42......165
4:46......164
5:36......168
6:1–15......165
6:4......165
6:35......164–65
6:51......164–65
7:37......164
7:38......165, 170
7:39......165
8:12......164, 166
8:58......164
10:7......164
10:11......164
10:14......164
10:30......164
10:31–33......164
11:25......164
13–16......167
14:6......164
14:26......167
15:1......164
15:5......164
15:46......167
16:7......167
16:13......167
16:14......167
20:21......167

Acts
1:4–5......168
1:8......168
1:12–14......1, 2n3
2......167
2:5......167–68
2:6–8......167
2:16......167
2:39......168
6:3......169
8:5–25......2n10
8:14–17......168
9:1......2n11
10:1–48......2n12
11:19–26......2n8, 14n13
13:1......14n13
13:14......14n13
14:19......14n13
14:26......14n13
15:1–35......3n13
18:22......14n13
19:6......168

Romans
15:18......168

1 Corinthians
12:3......130

Galatians
2:11......14n13
5:22–23......169
5:25......170

Ephesians
5:18......169

2 Timothy
3:11......14n14

James
1:27......138n15
2:14–26......138n15

1 Peter
1:9–10......3n15
2:9–10......71n17, 143n40
2:11......70

1 John
4:2–3......130

Revelation
3:14–22......170
22:17......165